DISCARD

Drug Abuse in East Asia

Drug Abuse in East Asia

C. P. SPENCER
Visiting Research Fellow

V. NAVARATNAM
Associate Professor/Director

Prepared for
The National Drug Dependence Research Centre
University of Science Malaysia
Penang

KUALA LUMPUR
OXFORD UNIVERSITY PRESS
OXFORD NEW YORK MELBOURNE
1981

Oxford University Press

OXFORD LONDON GLASGOW
NEW YORK TORONTO MELBOURNE WELLINGTON
KUALA LUMPUR SINGAPORE HONG KONG TOKYO
DELHI BOMBAY CALCUTTA MADRAS KARACHI
NAIROBI DAR ES SALAAM CAPE TOWN

ISBN 0 19 580476 7 (*boards*)
ISBN 0 19 580482 1 (*limp*)

Printed in Singapore by Koon Wah Printing (Pte) Ltd.
Published by Oxford University Press, 3, Jalan 13/3,
Petaling Jaya, Selangor, Malaysia

Contents

Introduction

DRUG abuse is a matter of considerable public concern in all the countries of East Asia at the present time: people are keenly aware that there have been recent changes in the pattern of illicit drug taking, and know that youth has become increasingly involved. What is the extent of the problem? Who exactly are involved? These and many other questions are often asked by an anxious public, but the answers are not easy to give. Why do people start using drugs? What can be, and is being, done? And in particular what kinds of campaigns against drug abuse are being mounted in schools and in the media? How effective are they? What is being done for those who are already dependent upon drugs? Are they being treated as sick or as criminals? What policies are being pursued to control supplies of drugs, and those who traffic in them? What is being done about the problem at international level? How did the present state of affairs come about? And, most difficult of all, what of the future?

In this book, we shall attempt to side-step this last question; but we will, in one form or another, try to throw some light on the other issues for each country in South-East Asia, South Asia, and East Asia. (For convenience we will be referring, with apologies, to the whole of this region as 'East Asia'.) The light thrown may fall unevenly: some countries and some issues will receive more attention, not necessarily because they are intrinsically more important, but because more has been published about them.

When starting to review and research the drug dependency situation in Malaysia some five years ago, the authors, both new to the field, sought a central source of information on the drug problem in the country, or in the region, but found none. Searching the literature, we found that there was indeed considerable research activity in several countries in the region; but for these research workers, as for us, the central point of reference in the drug dependence literature was, of necessity, the Western (and predominantly American) literature. This is an excellent source for many purposes: thus, for example, the published research on psychopharmacology—the action of drugs on brain and behaviour—comes very largely from American laboratories, but is clearly applicable to all countries, and can be quoted without hesitation in the Asian context (providing of course that the drugs are taken in the same way, in the same quantities and quality, and by individuals with equivalent drug histories).

As a source of observations and hypotheses about the social and psychological aspects of drug abuse, this Western literature is almost overwhelming: it is a very active research field indeed, and reflects the degree of public, professional, and governmental concern and debate. Many of the hypotheses offered have looked sufficiently general for the researchers in East Asia to adopt them as the basis for their own studies; and in many instances they have done this so convincingly that their reports have been accepted for inclusion in the same international journals whence the hypotheses had been drawn in the first place.

In these research reports emanating from East Asia, there tend to be a few opening sentences which say something to the effect that 'drug use has a long history in our country'; but once this introduction is out of the way there is generally very little acknowledgement that the cultural tradition of drug use in the country could considerably affect the present pattern, or the reasons why individuals use drugs, or how society chooses to respond to the problem.

Thus, one might find a paper describing cannabis use (in the form of bhang or *charas*) in a South Asian student population, which quickly moves to compare incidence rates with published American studies which the author sees as comparable. Now, indeed, there is a considerable literature (mainly American) on the social correlates and personal motivations of cannabis users. Much of this relates to the use of marijuana by young, often middle-class and college educated, Americans: and the authors tend to use personality tests, to interview subjects about their social relationships, to administer attitude inventories—in short, to apply the whole armoury of social science. A picture emerges which—although the authors, standing in the middle of the culture themselves, seldom bring it out clearly enough—relates the 1970s epidemic of marijuana smoking to aspects of the contemporary American scene.

Now, even given the much-talked-of 'shrinking of the world' by the media, the worlds of the American and the East Asian still retain many important differences. Cultural differences do not disappear simply at the adoption of the international youth uniform of jeans and tee-shirt: strength of family loyalties, self images, ideal social roles, perceived opportunities, religious and ethical beliefs may all vary sufficiently to make adolescents East and West importantly different. Thus, although contemporary Asian youth has clearly changed considerably in its outlook when compared with the parental generation, the convergence upon the 'international' has not gone to the point where researchers can justifiably assume that Asian youth and their behaviour can be assimilated with the American adolescents who are described in the majority of the published drug literature. Nor can one lightly dismiss the very different role—and thus reputation—cannabis has had in the different cultures.

Most East Asian research workers are up to date with the American—European literature; but few cross-reference their work with that of other regional workers. We argue that the research teams in the various countries in the region could gain considerable insights into the problems, as experienced in their own country, by examining what is going on in neighbouring countries. Of course, the same cautions about the cavalier transfer of observations across cultural barriers must be observed within the region as, we have argued, must be made in comparing Asia with America. However, many features *are* common in the regional experience of drugs: for example, many countries share the same sources of illicit drugs; in many, the Overseas Chinese have played a significant part in the early history of opium smoking; and the pattern of youthful use of synthetic drugs has many common elements throughout the region.

There are also important differences among the countries of the region, for example, in the contemporary responses made by society to the drug problem. Comparison of these varying approaches and of their effects could well be made, with the region acting as its own 'laboratory', in which different combinations of factors (or strategies) are being employed to test for their effects in meeting the problem. Yet the comparison is not being made, or at least the data from the 'laboratory' and its 'experiments' are not systematically reported and compared in a form that the general or indeed professional reader can have access to.

Many official governmental and international agency reports are indeed published but, although not confidential, are not readily available. Since 1973 the Colombo Plan has made a major contribution to intra-regional discussions on the drug abuse problem, by organizing conferences and workshops in member countries, at which many local workers present papers and also hear contributions of visiting speakers from other countries in the region and beyond. There have been several other international conferences organized in the region by UNESCO, UNFDAC, ICAA, WHO, and the Commonwealth Regional Working Group on Illicit Drugs. These have generally been around special themes; they have brought workers together to discuss problems of mutual interest; and they have often published their proceedings. However, such reports have had only limited circulation. Indeed, those research papers published by regional workers in the international scientific and medical journals tend to be available only to those with access to major university and hospital libraries (and the time to search), and only if they knew of the existence of these papers: but there is no up-to-date regional checklist or bibliography.

Given, then, our initial feeling that little research was being done in the region, because it was not immediately obvious, and our subsequent discovery that there was in fact much research but that it was being reported in relatively obscure places, we felt that it might be worthwhile to share this discovery with others who may be generally or professionally interested. Hence came the idea for this book, which attempts to be a compendium of what has been reported in East Asia—from the Indian subcontinent, through South-East Asia, to Hong Kong, Japan, and China. It is an incomplete record (during the writing of this introduction several further articles have come to our attention) and one which is necessarily *not* culturally attuned to all the variations in the region, our base of thought being our particular research area, Malaysia.

What this book aims to do is to bring together much of the regional literature on drug abuse: it is now *our* turn to be parochial, and references to and comparisons with the familiar American–European literature have been kept to a minimum in order to concentrate on the problem of drug abuse in East Asia. The book is explicitly limited to this: it does not include sections describing the pharmacological and behavioural properties of drug substances, nor does it indicate how clinicians or parents could recognize whether a patient or child of theirs was using drugs. Many excellent guides exist which cover exactly this ground: they range from detailed medical textbooks to easily approached pamphlets published by local voluntary organizations and aimed at the general public. There will therefore be an assumption throughout the book that the names of the commonly abused drug substances, and their actions upon body and mind, will be relatively familiar: the presentation, however, will not be technical.

Similarly, the book contains no section devoted to reviewing the methods currently used by the medical and social work professions in the treatment of drug dependence. The medical procedures for detoxification, and the various approaches to rehabilitation and after-care will not receive detailed discussion: again, they are described by many writers. One exception will be made: the various forms of treatment which are specific to the region—and are thus not easily accessible in the international literature—are described in somewhat greater detail.

The book, then, does not seek to be a primer on illicit drugs and society's response to them. Rather, it aims to describe the genesis of today's drug abuse problem in East Asia, to discuss the patterns of abuse which prevail in the region, to give a profile of the adult and of the adolescent drug user, and to illustrate the kinds of preventative education, treatment and rehabilitation, and legal and enforcement responses made to the contemporary drug problem in the various countries in the region. We hope, in other words, to have addressed ourselves to those questions of public concern noted at the outset.

Chapter I starts with an historical account—necessarily brief and probably idiosyncratic—of the origins of drug use and of trafficking in the region; it mentions some of the early attempts to control the problem; and it devotes some space to the situation in East Asia fifty years ago (when a major international inquiry into opium smoking, then the major problem, was undertaken by the League of Nations). It concludes with the recent rapid social, economic, political, and legal changes which have led to today's pattern.

The details of this most recent period are given in Chapter II, which describes, country by country, the contemporary pattern of drug abuse in the region. Which are the principal drugs of abuse? What estimates have been made of the numbers involved? What is the relative involvement of old and young, and of particular communities or localities or ethnic groups? Are any trends discernible?

The country-by-country approach is taken in each of the six central chapters of the book, allowing the reader whose interest is mainly in one particular country to read the relevant sections in each chapter, while the reader wanting to take the subject topic by topic may read the six topic sections, introducing those chapters and covering all countries in the region.

Thus, Chapter III discusses, for each country, the social background and circumstances of the adult drug user, his reported motivations for starting and for continuing with drugs, his experiences with other people and with work as a result of his drug use, and his reports of any attempts to stop drug use. Chapter IV gives a similar profile for the adolescent drug user, and rounds off the first part of the book, which is a description and an attempt at an explanation of the patterns of drug use in the region.

The next three chapters could be described as an account of society's response to the drug abuse problem, with the concluding chapter rehearsing some of the points implicit in these chapters, and in particular examining the variety of approaches to the problem which have been taken.

Logically—although generally not historically—prior to other responses by society is its approach to the problem of drug abuse by preventative education and by public information campaigns. Chapter V describes the various philosophies held by the countries in the region, and the resultant programmes of action which have been taken. (The reader will note that some countries are not represented in this chapter.) One issue raised is that of the evaluation of the effectiveness of such campaigns: do they really have much impact upon the audiences, given all the factors working against them? Indeed, what dangers are there in taking detailed and interesting information about drugs to audiences which may well have been uninterested or simply (and ignorantly) scared?

How has society treated those individuals who *have* abused drugs, and, in particular, those who have become dependent upon them? Chapter VI describes the treatment and rehabilitation available in each country, and the differing philosophies underlying them. There is also information, for some countries, of the traditional local treatments which have been used, and Chapter VIII, concluding the book, has more to say about these.

Chapter VII briefly reviews the legal position of drug substances in each country, without setting out the exact letter of the law (the authors are most definitely not comparative international lawyers) and considers what impact the laws relating to the individual have had on the pattern of drug abuse in the various countries. This chapter also described some of the anti-drug measures taken to control the flow of drugs unto and through each country—the work of customs and excise, police, and narcotics bureaux. Here, most definitely, the whole story is *not* told: whereas the statistics of seizures and arrests are generally published, the 'inside stories' and suspicions about who is involved in the big-time drugs trafficking are seldom committed to paper. This book does not pretend to go beyond its (published) sources, especially in so perilous an area!

The final chapter, rather than trying to summarize the diversity of information presented in earlier sections, develops a theme about the variety of approaches to the problem of drug abuse which have been taken in the region: what place has such diversity in our study of the problem, and how can traditional and modern approaches work side by side?

We hope in this book to provide some information not readily available to a wider audience, and to give the reader a chance to follow up his interests via the bibliography at the end. We have undoubtedly left out much that we should have included, but we hope we have not misrepresented those whom we cite. As already mentioned, the authors are amateurs where it comes to matters of law: as will become evident to the reader, the same is true of our expertise in history, economics, politics, sociology, education, medicine, and social work; and we therefore crave the indulgence of professionals in these fields. However, it is only from a multidisciplinary approach to the problem of drug abuse that we can hope to offer descriptions and explanations, and thence be able to provide an appropriate and culturally sensitive response to one of the major social problems of the day.

The History of Drug Production and Use in East Asia

THE use of dependence-producing drugs is by no means purely a modern problem in East Asia, nor is public concern about their abuse: there exist many accounts of social and legislative action to control drug use in the past five hundred years, and the use of drugs in the region dates back until at least Neolithic times. The focus of the present book is on contemporary patterns of drug abuse in the region, but as a background this first chapter will briefly review historical and geographical aspects of drug abuse: the origins of drug use in the region, traditional uses, supply centres, and trade patterns; political and criminal involvement, and control policies; and the evolution of the contemporary patterns of supply and usage. Documentation is, as the reader can imagine, very variable: for some periods and some areas we have very little recorded information, whereas for others the amount of evidence is overwhelming. In general, as one would expect, the most recent period is much better documented than all others; but the situation fifty years ago, when the League of Nations commissioned a survey of opium smoking in the region, is recorded in some considerable detail.

Most of the history of drug use in the region relates to two principal plants: cannabis, and the opium poppy. The earliest archaeological evidence for the growth of cannabis as a fibre plant in North-East Asia dates back to about six thousand years BC; and the Chinese character for hemp is derived from the plant's fibre-producing property. It was listed as one of the five major 'grains'; and its medicinal properties were recognized in ancient times. The classical Chinese herbals describe the stupefying and hallucinogenic effects of cannabis; but the later pharmacopoeias indicate that the plant was by then rarely used. Li Hui Lin (in *Cannabis and Culture*, edited by V. Rubin, Mouton, The Hague, 1975) describes how the drug was associated with Shamanism, which was widespread in the northern area of China, and how the Shamans, as they migrated nomadically, carried the plant with them to West Asia and India, where its use flourished while it declined in China.

The discontinuation of cannabis use in China was clearly not the result of any aversion to the taking of drugs to alter states of consciousness: mineral drugs, wine, and tobacco have been employed at various stages of Chinese history for just such a purpose. Rather, suggests Li, the effects of cannabis were inconsistent with the developing philosophy and traditions of Chinese life, whereas opium (first introduced from West Asia in about the eighth century) was much more fitted to this way of life. This imported euphorica, opium, was adopted, and the indigenous phantastica, cannabis, was discontinued long before nineteenth-century foreign pressure spread opium use widely through China. Li sees the effects of cannabis—a hallucinogen causing mental exhilaration, excitation, and the distortion of subjective time and space—as being inconsistent in every respect with the Chinese way of life, in contrast to the action of opium—a sedative of mental activity.

The religious and mystical use of cannabis in its various forms continues to this day in the Indian subcontinent. Aldrich has described the early tantric cannabis use in India (*Journal of Psychedelic Drugs*, 1977, 9:227–33). This arose about the seventh century AD, in an explosive mingling of the doctrines of Sivaite Hinduism and Tibetan Buddhism. The Mahanirvana Tantra, a dialogue between Siva and Kali, was composed during the eleventh century, and is still consulted with more modern manuals. The ceremonial use of cannabis, with the conscious employment of poisonous or dangerous substances, and drug- and sex-yoga together, became a fully developed system for achieving *Mahanirvana*.

Whereas such ritual and medical uses of a drug are described and recorded, we understandably lack early accounts of social drug use; but there is reason to believe that the kinds of 'traditional' patterns observable at the present time in many parts of the region have a lengthy history. There was little tradition in most parts of the region for recording the details of everyday life, and one is dependent on the occasional relatively recent account given by an outsider or traveller.

One such was Engelbert Kaempfer (1651–1716), a German physician, who was the leading scholar-explorer of Asia in the seventeenth century. He left a meticulous chronicle of his travels to Persia, Arabia, India, Ceylon, Java, Siam, and Japan, in his *Amoenitatum Exoticarum* (Lemgo, Meyeri, 1712, extracts from which have been translated by J. Z. Bowers and R. W. Carrubba, *Journal of the History of Medicine and Allied Sciences*, 1978, 33:318–43). Kaempfer found various drugs 'employed to exhilarate, intoxicate, or brutalize the spirits'. The most common of these, after tobacco, was *pinang*, or betel, an expectorant consisting of the leaf and fruit of the betel palm (*Areca catechu*) and lime derived from the burning of sea shells. Rolled and chewed in the mouth, it 'gently soothes and exhilarates the spirits by intoxicating the brain'; and the traveller records widespread addiction to the drug, especially in South India, in all classes of society, although for his part he was 'never able to chew any preparation of betel without experiencing intense anxiety, cold sweats and vertigo similar to the effects of tobacco'.

Opium was in common use from Persia to India and beyond, and was responsible, in Kaempfer's opinion, for the cases of amok found in Java 'and the further Orient'. Opium was either eaten or inhaled in a mixture with tobacco; and there was much trade by the Dutch through the East Indies of this *afiuun*. Some of the uses of the drug were religious (Kaempfer witnessed a festival in Malabar where the vestal virgin went into drug induced trances), but many individuals used opium (and other drugs such as *datura* and other locally growing plants) for social purposes. Many extravagant claims were made to the traveller about the power and effects of the various substances, most of which he dismissed, although he personally could attest to the intoxicating powers of at least one drug administered to him and his companions by one of his Indian hosts.

Opium had been introduced into India, the East Indies, and China by Arab traders in the eighth century AD; and its cultivation had been a considerable industry in Asia Minor for some time before this. It seems that opium use took a firm hold in India earlier than it did in China, but the extent of the habit must be inferred from the mentions of drug use made by travellers in their letters and chronicles. The opium trade from India to Java, Formosa, and China from the seventeenth century onwards is much better documented, and represents one of the least creditable phases in what was to become the most despicable international traffic after the slave trade.

From the establishment of the Mogul Empire in the sixteenth century, poppy cultivation and the sale of opium became the monopoly of the Muslim rulers of India; but it was the Arab, Portuguese, Dutch, and British traders who carried the drug to the rest of the region. The Dutch East India Company became a major force in the eastern trade during the seventeenth century, taking opium and tobacco to Java and China (H. B. Morse, *International Relations of the Chinese Empire*, Longmans Green and Co., London, 1910). The Chinese settlers of Formosa (ruled by the Dutch from 1624 to 1662) rapidly adopted the practice of smoking the opium and tobacco mixture, and from Formosa the habit spread to the mainland of China. As methods for refining opium were improved, tobacco was omitted from the mixture, and only the prepared opium was smoked. By 1660 opium smoking became recognized as a problem, and the first anti-opium edict was issued by the Emperor Yung Chang in 1720. Even though the sale of opium was expressly forbidden, the import of opium to meet the growing demand rose from 200 chests a year, in the year of the edict, to 1,000 chests by 1773, brought by the Portuguese to Canton. An average chest of opium weighed between 120 and 160 pounds. In 1773 the British East India Company first began to send opium to China, and rapidly became the major supplier: by 1790 the Company was supplying over 4,000 chests a year (A. Fields and P. A. Tararin, *Br. J. Addiction*, 1970, 64:371–82; R. J. Gregory, *Drug Forum*, 1977–8, 6:235–47). It should be noted that, except for one small venture in the 1780s, the Company never itself *shipped* the opium: consignments were sent in private ships, and opium was never part of an Indiaman's regular cargo.

Further imperial edicts were issued in 1796 and 1800, making opium smoking punishable by death, and prohibiting the import of the drug. Yet by 1800 the East India Company was able to import nearly 17,000 chests with the connivance of corrupt Chinese officials, who levied private 'taxes' and took bribes as they facilitated the drug's conveyance to local dealers (Gregory, op. cit.). (M. Collis, in *Foreign Mud*, Faber, London, 1946, gives lower figures for the number of chests imported; but both Collis and Gregory agree on the rapid increase in numbers during the early nineteenth century.) As the volume of opium imported rose, the form in which it was consumed shifted from *madak*, with a low morphia content, to *chandu*, which had a high content. 'The great object of the Bengal opium agencies is to furnish an article suitable to the peculiar tastes of the population of China', wrote D. Butler, a former opium examiner on the preparation of opium for the China market (*Journal of the Asiatic Society of Bengal*, 1836, 5:171–9). In supplying opium in cake form to China, the merchants were able to offer the drug in a sufficiently moist state to be soluble for the preparation of *chandu*. Opium smoking spread north and west within China, and involved both rich and poor—including even the officers of the Imperial Palace guard.

The East India Company lost its monopoly of the China trade in 1834; and the events which followed, leading up to the Opium War of 1840–2, have been well documented by many historians (two of the most accessible accounts are: M. Collis, *Foreign Mud*, Faber, London, 1946; and P. W. Fay, *The Opium War*, University of North Carolina Press, 1975). In 1839 the Manchu government appointed the zealous Viceroy of Hupei and Hunan provinces, Lin Tse Hsu, to be Imperial Commissioner, with full powers to investigate and suppress the opium traffic. Initially, Lin asked the country traders not to supply opium, provided prescriptions for the cure of addicts, and set penalties for trading in and smoking opium. Later he used stronger measures against the traders. They were forced to surrender over 20,000 chests of opium, and these were then publicly destroyed. Military skirmishes ensued; the British were victorious; and by the 1842 Treaty of Nanking they obtained the island of Hong Kong, and free trade rights at five mainland ports. A huge increase in the opium trade then followed, with the Manchu government too weak to be able to take effective action, and many foreign powers obtained privileges and concessions to trade. By the 1880s the annual import of opium was 100,000 chests, that is, over 5,000 tons. Cultivation of the opium poppy within China then began to overtake the imports, and by 1906 the annual Chinese manufacture of opium was estimated to be over 35,000 tons (Fields and Tararin, op. cit.).

Contemporary European accounts give some idea of the role opium played in the Chinese way of life during the nineteenth century. Thus Dudgeon (cited in Gregory, op. cit.), who was resident in Peking in the 1860s, described the abuse of opium as an evil throughout China: when medical cures were of no avail, people resorted to opium to stop pain and provide relief (although, given the cost of the drug, it was not easily available to the poorest in society). The second group of users were leisured classes (and the relatively unemployed) whose use of the drug was purely recreational. Families and friends of the addicted individuals sometimes resorted to desperate measures to check the habit.

During the twentieth century, the opiate trade in China came to be controlled by criminal syndicates made up of individuals from certain of the Triad secret societies. The relationships between the various syndicates were and remain extremely complex, but accounts of their operation within China, throughout the East Asian region, and even in America and Europe have been attempted by some writers, e.g., R. Solomon, *J. Psychedelic Drugs*, 1978,

10:43–9; J. Marshall, *Bull. Concerned Asian Scholars*, 1976, 8:19–48; A. W. McCoy, *The Politics of Heroin in Southeast Asia*, Harper and Row, New York, 1972; and L. P. Adams, in McCoy, op. cit.

The public measures taken to reduce, and then to eliminate, opium use in China during the twentieth century—from the earliest international discussion in 1905 to the country-wide social revolution after 1949—will be discussed in later chapters. The Chinese opium problem during the eighteenth and nineteenth centuries was the most dramatic in the region in its development; by many accounts, the mid-twentieth century has witnessed in China the most dramatic solution to the problem.

Migration of Chinese from the southern coastal provinces rose throughout the nineteenth century, and continued into the twentieth; and the vast majority settled in Burma, Thailand, Indo-China, Malaysia, Indonesia, and the Philippines. With them travelled the opium smoking habit; and in most of these countries opium smoking was not generally considered a major social issue, and the governments of these states generated considerable tax revenue from the trade. In addition to these migrants, another wave of people from China—hill tribes people from the southern provinces—were to be of major significance for the pattern of drug production in the region, as they settled in the mountainous areas of northern Burma, Thailand, and Laos. Poppy cultivation and opium consumption had been common among many of these tribes people when in China; and, as will be described, they became, in response to economic and political pressures, the region's major cultivators during the twentieth century, in what has come to be called the Golden Triangle. China itself, meanwhile, continued to exert a direct influence upon the region: by 1931 China produced seven-eighths of the world's narcotics, trading through Hong Kong, Macao, and Shanghai (Marshall, op. cit.). The economics of the south-western provinces depended heavily upon opium: Yunnan and Kweichow as producers, Kwangsi and Kwangtung as shippers and consumers. The Japanese-controlled areas of the north—Tientsin and Manchuria—also produced large quantities of opium at low prices.

In the rest of the region, the changing pattern of drug use can be seen as one part of the general history of commercial and social development of the region: traditional patterns of agriculture, mining, and commerce gave way to more highly organized and commercialized ones, as the countries in the region became colonies or protectorates of the European powers during the eighteenth and nineteenth centuries. This was the period when Asia's great urban centres grew up—Singapore, Jakarta, Bangkok, Rangoon, Saigon,

Hong Kong, and Shanghai—and major population movements took place, both to populate these major trading centres and to work in the plantations and mines in the hinterland. Thus, for example, in the Malay Peninsula, the indigenous Malay and long-settled Chinese populations were augmented by South Indians, brought in as indentured labourers on the rubber plantations, by Sikhs and other North Indians, as members of the defence forces and the public services, by Achinese, Javanese, and Bugis, as agricultural settlers, and by Chinese, as labourers and craftsmen in tin mining, estates, and later in a great diversity of occupations, including the retail trade. (For a detailed study of such immigration in one state's development during the late nineteenth century, see Lim Teck Ghee, *Origins of a Colonial Economy: Land and Agriculture in Perak, 1874–1897*, Universiti Sains Malaysia Press, Penang, 1976.)

In terms of sheer numbers, the Chinese migrations were by far the most important. By 1910 there were 120,000 Chinese in Saigon and the Mekong Delta, 200,000 in Bangkok, and over 60,000 in the Rangoon area (V. Purcell, *The Chinese in Southeast Asia*, Oxford University Press, London, 1951). And in terms of changing the pattern of drug consumption in the region, this community was clearly the most significant. To meet the demand for opium among these immigrant workers, to attempt to control and regulate the supply of the drug, to tax the opium trade as a major source of colonial revenue (one takes one's choice of motivation according to which commentator one reads), each nation and colony from Burma to North Borneo had established a state-regulated opium monopoly by the end of the nineteenth century. The mechanisms, controls, and regulations varied from country to country: in some, the system of licensing smokers was strictly applied; in others, strong attempts were made to limit the habit to the Chinese community. But in general, the government opium den in South-East Asia supplied a mainly Chinese population of smokers, with, in many countries, a growing indigenous group—Thai, Malay, Vietnamese, Burmese. Initially, all the opium was imported from India, but, as production in China became increasingly plentiful, Yunnan province began exporting opium overland, to be sold illicitly to addicts in Burma, Thailand, and Tonkin (the region which is now the north of Vietnam), at a price which undercut the government monopolies in those countries. Yunnanese merchants were also responsible for marketing the small-scale opium poppy crop of the Chinese ethnic minority hill tribes, as they migrated and settled in the mountains south of the Chinese border. During the nineteenth and early twentieth centuries, Meo and Yao tribesmen migrated into Indo-China and Thailand, to escape Chinese persecution, while

Lisu, Kachin, Lahu, and other tribes settled on the Burmese border. Travellers in these regions in the late nineteenth century noted how extensively many of the tribes had deployed their poppy farming skills (see McCoy, op. cit.), but production was limited by very active campaigns by the governments of those countries to stop local cultivation, because the governmental opium revenues were raised on the legal importation, manufacture, and distribution of monopoly opium. Hence, up until the 1940s, the hill tribes' cultivation of the opium poppy did not contribute much to the pattern of consumption, away from the area immediately surrounding the growing area.

In each of the countries of the region, the governments managed the opium trade in somewhat different ways, but most came to run and profit from government monopolies of the trade. Thus, we find in Thailand an initial strong reaction to combat the opium problem among the Chinese community: King Rama II banned the sale and consumption of the drug; and subsequent edicts introduced the death penalty for major trafficking. Under commercial and political pressure, however, King Mongkut established a royal opium franchise in 1852; and the Thai government came to rely heavily on the revenue from the franchise, which was leased to Chinese merchants. In Burma, the British imported large quantities of opium from India, and marketed it through a government monopoly established shortly after their arrival in Lower Burma in 1852; but they began restricting its use, with some success, after the 1878 Opium Act had been passed in Britain. The Shan states, to the north, however, were beginning to produce appreciable quantities of the drug; and the control of cultivation in the states and smuggling out into Lower Burma was made extremely difficult by the rugged terrain and the fierce independence of the local population. The various Indo-Chinese states attempted, during the early part of the nineteenth century, to check the new habit of opium smoking for both moral and economic reasons. The proximity of China, and the ease of smuggling over the borders, rendered these checks ineffective; and the occasion of the French invasion of the Vietnam coast in 1858 led the Vietnamese emperor to establish an opium monopoly, in order to raise revenue for defence. The French, too, raised considerable revenue in each of the territories they colonized, by establishing autonomous opium monopolies: in Cambodia in 1863; Central Vietnam, 1883; Tonkin, 1884; and Laos, 1893. Much of the development of French Indo-China was based on the huge revenues thus collected (McCoy, op. cit.).

The opium smokers of the region were, as already mentioned, predominantly found in the Chinese community, although in nearly all countries in the region increasing numbers of the indigenous population also became regular smokers. This was least true of Japan, where even the Japanese who were in closest contact with opium-using Chinese communities were reported to show no inclination to adopt the habit. Why should the Chinese abroad have been so susceptible to the drug? An answer to this question was offered by the League of Nations Commission of Enquiry into the Control of Opium Smoking in the Far East (Geneva, 1930).

It was argued that, whether born in China or overseas, the Chinese, more than any other people in the region, were familiar with the opium smoking habit from an early age because of its prevalence in their community. This early familiarity made the overseas Chinese, in middle and old age, more susceptible to take up the habit, particularly if he was by then earning more than a subsistence wage, and was away from the restraining influences of immediate and extended family. (Many of the earlier Chinese immigrants remained unmarried.)

The 1930 report of the League of Nations Commission is an extensive, painstaking, and informed document which, as it describes the general pattern of opium abuse, and then gives detailed accounts for each country in the region, provides a picture of drug abuse in the region fifty years ago which had never been attempted before, or achieved since.

Estimating absolute numbers of drug users in the population was and remains a difficult art; nonetheless, the Commission provided estimates for each territory which bear out the reported Chinese predominance in opium smoking. The report tabulates total population; total Chinese population; proportion of the Chinese population who are male; the number of legal smokers; the estimated number of illicit smokers; and statistics of seizures of the drug, for Burma, the Straits Settlements, the Federated and Unfederated Malay States, Brunei, Sarawak, North Borneo, the Netherlands East Indies, Thailand, French Indo-China, Kwang-Chow-Wan, Hong Kong, Macao, Formosa, and Kwangtung. Registration of smokers was more strictly enforced in some territories than others, and thus we can have greater confidence in some of the country statistics than others. Nevertheless, the estimates indicate a considerably higher rate of involvement among the Chinese male population of each country than among males of the indigenous communities.

The Commission found that, in all countries, the smoking of opium was held in considerable contempt by the majority of the population (and the local term for opium smoker had, in several instances, generalized into a broader term of disparagement).

There was, however, a widespread regard for opium as a medicine, 'reaching sometimes to a superstitious belief in its value', as well as some opinion in favour of its use in moderation as an aid to work and relaxation. Indeed, amongst the circumstances the Commissioners believed led to the smoking of opium, the users' faith in its medicinal role ranked high: 'It is a recognized fact that opium has the effect of dulling pain, although it has no curative value' as believed by many of its users. But first among the circumstances cited are the 'social and hygienic conditions' under which many of the labourers of the Far East lived. Isolated in the tin mines and plantations, housed in primitive conditions, and subjected to considerable physical hardships, many workers 'strove for some form of diversion which permitted them to forget at least for some moments the hardship of life'. Curiosity about the effects of the drug, especially when many around one were regular users, was a final reason why individuals took up opium smoking.

The Commission took many opinions on the effects of opium on smokers, and found a wide range—from those who maintained that under some circumstances opium could benefit the smoker, to those who saw the smoker as becoming a useless member of society. The Commissioners were *not* impressed by the reasoning of those who argued that opium was less harmful to the Chinese than to the other races; but nonetheless they found in operation laws and regulations which were much more protective of the local races than they were of the Chinese in Burma, British Malaya, Thailand, and the Netherlands East Indies. The report lists the physical and mental weakening that was usually consequent upon regular opium use.

Fifty years later, it is difficult to realize all the factors acting upon the control (and lack of control) of opium smoking. One such factor is vividly described in a section of the 1930 report: the constantly repeated fears about the effects that restricting opium smoking would have on the labour situation. The Chinese were perhaps the key element in the economic development of South-East Asia, having by 1930 diversified into all branches of trade and industry. 'This importance . . . was often emphasized before the Commission by officials, industrialists, and other employers of labour, who stated that too strict control of opium smoking, or total prohibition, would endanger the supply of labour'. The Commission was not at all convinced by this argument, and felt that even total prohibition would not seriously affect the settlement of immigrants from China.

Several factors, the Commission felt, prevented the further spread of the opium smoking habit. Whereas all religions were strongly opposed to opium smoking, and some countries had anti-opium societies backed by religious organizations, the report suggested that education and an improved standard of living would be the most effective forces working against the spread of the smoking habit. Fifty years later, the same hopes are still being widely expressed. Indeed, there is a very familiar quality to the discussion by the Commissioners on the likely effects of education and propaganda about opium: then, just as now, opinions were divided as to whether such education served to prevent drug use or to awaken interest in the habit. Again, one finds, foreshadowed in the 1930 report's section on the treatment of opium addiction, a theme which is constantly repeated in the contemporary literature on treatment and rehabilitation: it is technically not too difficult to withdraw and detoxify the addict, and the subsequent rehabilitation may be successfully conducted, especially with occasional users. However, the long-term prospects are not good for those (the majority) of ex-addicts who return to their former milieu after treatment, coming back into contact as they do with their former acquaintances who are still regular drug users.

The Commission was sympathetic and aware of the role opium smoking played in the community:

The public opium-smoking establishments never correspond to the sumptuously fascinating divans of romantic imagination, just as they differ materially from the idea of the 'opium den' as a breeding place for crime and immorality. They are the only available resting places of the poor and, though they are not attractive, they are scarcely, even at their worst, more repulsive than the localities where the common classes of the Western peoples consume beer or stronger alcoholic beverages.

Government control of these social resources would serve to control the spread of the opium smoking habit; but, as the Commission saw, the only really effective way of controlling or eliminating opium taking is to limit poppy cultivation to the amount required for the production of opiates for medicine. Of all the producing countries, only India, in 1930, was effectively controlling production; and thus consumer states were recommended to fall back on the suppression of trafficking across their borders. Countries adjoining China were recognized as having particular difficulties in stopping such traffic, and the Chinese production of opium was seen by the Commission as the most unsettling factor in the region, the government in Nanking being unable to regulate affairs in more than a very few of China's eighteen provinces. The neighbouring countries—Burma, Thailand, and Indo-China—had in their turn underpopulated and inaccessible borders with China, making the checking of opium imports exceedingly difficult.

The governments of each country were, in 1930, under considerable international pressure to control opium smoking, and, to quote, 'the enquiry brought the Commission to the conclusion that all governments concerned were endeavouring to fulfil their obligations'. Some countries faced a more formidable problem than others, but the Commission felt that control would be possible if its recommendations for a complete government monopoly system were carried out in each country. Total prohibition was in force only in the Philippines; and it was concluded that total prohibition of all opium smoking did not lead to total suppression of the habit—where a demand existed, smuggling would always supply it:

It seems better that the opium smoking habit should be suppressed gradually by legalizing smoking by confirmed addicts, and by supplying such smokers with Government opium. This method only offers the possibility of limiting individual consumption and preventing the spread of the habit to more individuals. Whether the system be prohibition or Government control, limitation and, as far as possible, eradication of the illicit traffic is indispensable to success.

For this purpose, the League of Nations Commission recommended that each government should reorganize and better equip its preventative forces: 'fast motor launches' and special 'flying squadrons' would be needed to take prompt and effective anti-trafficking action. Each country should establish a single central intelligence bureau, and these should keep in constant touch with each other to exchange information on illegal traffic.

Most agencies had tackled the opium problem as an internal matter: the Commission recognized the international nature of the trafficking agencies, and therefore recognized that the response to the problem would have to be concerted international action. Sadly, as the history of the drug trade in the fifty years since the Commission reported has shown, such action was not taken with sufficient co-operation, vigour, or even conviction on the part of the governments of the region. The period has seen the rapid development of the Golden Triangle between Burma, Thailand, and Laos as the major opium producing area, overtaking Yunnan, and now itself perhaps being overtaken by the North-West Frontier Province of Pakistan. It has seen well-intentioned international pressures upon individual governments to introduce strong anti-opium measures, leading to the replacement of opium by the more dangerous opiates, heroin and morphine, almost throughout the region. It has witnessed, most recently, the growing involvement of the region's youth with a whole range of hard and soft drugs. And throughout the period, there has been more than a little evidence that the political will to act effectively to curb trafficking has not been present among many governments and agencies, because these very agencies and political figures have themselves become part of the drug trafficking process.

The most detailed documentation as to how widespread this corruption has been is given by A. W. McCoy in his study, *The Politics of Heroin in Southeast Asia* (Harper and Row, 1972). Even if one acknowledges that the book was written by an American at the height of America's self-criticism of her involvement in Vietnam, Laos, and Cambodia, and that he is incensed by the West's cynical involvement in the heroin trafficking in the region, the plethora of well-documented stories of official—Asian and American—corruption and double-dealing during the 1950s, 1960s, and 1970s makes a convincing and saddening story. Whilst national and international anti-narcotics agencies were at work tackling the later stages of the drug trafficking problem, local and foreign governments, and high-placed individuals were, in many countries, involved with organized crime at every stage of the trafficking. When the League of Nations Commission presented its report, opium—then the major drug of abuse—had not been prohibited in any country other than the Philippines. Since World War II, narcotics have been outlawed in practically every area of the region; but this has not improved matters. Indeed, rather the opposite. The revenue raised from government monopolies was at least ploughed back to some extent into projects which benefited the community; now, the corresponding profits go to private traffickers, and the only redistribution of these monies that occurs is in the criminal corruption of local police, customs, military, and narcotics bureau officials. As governments have further removed themselves from legal involvement in the controlled provision of drugs, so the way has been opened not only for criminal elements to run the trade, but also, as an appalling side effect, for the corruption of some of society's guardians.

The late 1940s marked an increasing international pressure on countries in the region to tighten their drug-control laws; and a succession of Conventions, Agreements, and Protocols were promulgated by the United Nations Commission on Narcotic Drugs. In 1953 the major opium producing countries in South Asia, the Middle East, and Europe signed the United Nations Protocol, thereby agreeing not to sell opium on the international market for legalized smoking or eating. It was also the time when the most momentous political change in the region occurred: the establishment of the Chinese People's Republic in 1949. China had been a major supplier of opium to the region; and when the new Communist government introduced an opium eradication programme, the supplies of opium to neighbouring countries dwindled rapidly. McCoy (op. cit.) gives an account of how a crash programme of opium production was started in the Golden Triangle, mainly under the protection of the expelled Kuomintang forces in the area, and financed by Chinese syndicates based in Bangkok. United Nation and United States statistics indicate how effective this 'initiative' was: between 1945 and 1962 Burma's annual production of opium increased from an estimated 40 tons (mostly consumed locally) to 400 tons; Thailand's from 7 tons to over 100 tons; and that of Laos from an estimated 30 tons to between 100 and 150 tons. By the end of the 1950s the Golden Triangle had become the source of more than half the world's illicit opium supply.

It is McCoy's contention—and his argument is heavily documented from both official sources and from interviews with many of the main actors—that a key factor in this explosive rise in production was the American Central Intelligence Agency's (CIA) backing of the Kuomintang armies operating in Thailand as one element in their anti-Communist campaign. The CIA were equally implicated in the growth of the narcotics traffic in Vietnam and Laos. Combined intelligence and illicit drug traffic operations recur again and again in the detailed accounts McCoy gives, often drawn from the very United States intelligence advisers and case officers who took part in the operations.

As McCoy indicates, 'Almost without exception it was governmental bodies—and not criminals—whose decisions have made the major changes in the international narcotics trade'. Thus, it had been the French colonial government which had given the first impetus to the Meo tribe to increase opium production in 1940; it had been the new Chinese government which had sealed the border and phased out opium poppy cultivation. Later, after Iran had become the region's major supplier during the early 1950s, it was the Iranian government which, in 1955, announced the complete abolition of opium growing in Iran.

And in the 1950s the Thai, Lao, Vietnamese, and American governments made critical decisions that resulted in the expansion of South-East Asia's opium production to feed the habits of the region's growing addict population and transform the Golden Triangle into the largest single opium-producing area in the world. (McCoy, op. cit., p. 89.)

The present authors are in no position to evaluate McCoy's account of the development of the narcotics trade, with all the bizarre involvements of major figures that he relates. P. D. Scott (*Bulletin of Concerned Asian Scholars*, 1973, 5:49—56), in reviewing McCoy's study, argues that he does not go far enough in pressing his charges against the United States government. Nor is it possible for the

present book to attempt an equivalent exposé for the years since
The Politics of Heroin in Southeast Asia was published. Undoubtedly there remains in many countries some corruption of local
officials who, instead of suppressing illicit trafficking, protect it
and profit by it. Occasional court cases, following dismissal of an
official discovered to have been involved in trafficking, indicate to
the general public something of what must have occurred; but one
is unable thence to judge whether this had been an isolated involvement or not. Certainly, in most countries in the region, anti-
narcotics campaigns are currently pursued with a vigour not
witnessed in the past. It also remains true that, whilst anti-narcotics
bureaux and other agencies are often effective in actions against
pushers and minor traffickers, few of the major drugs syndicate
bosses tend to be apprehended.

During the late 1960s and early 1970s, in virtually every country in the region, drug abuse and addiction increased alarmingly,
especially amongst young people. Serious public concern—often
leading to the setting up of voluntary bodies—was manifest. New
synthetic chemical drugs joined opium-based drugs, cannabis, and
other 'traditional' drug substances as causes of drug dependence;
and consequently, new routes of trafficking were established to
supply this demand. Initially, diversion of legally produced pharmaceuticals could supply the barbiturates, amphetamines, and
other drugs which were being used by the young for non-medical
purposes; but, as the demand continued to grow, illicit local factories and illegal imports from factories abroad began providing
the drugs.

As concern increased, so the philosophy of control changed, at
markedly different speeds in the various countries of the region, as
later chapters of the book will indicate. Increasingly, it has come
to be recognized that it would never be possible to stamp out drug
dependence and trafficking by measures against dependants and
traffickers alone. Selective punishment needed to be accompanied
by measures to reduce the demand for drugs, to rehabilitate dependent individuals once detoxified, and to stop the flow of drugs at
source. Preventative education programmes had been one of the
major recommendations for controlling drug abuse made by the
1930 League of Nations Commission; and yet it was not until the
1960s and 1970s, when the youthful population was seen to be at
risk, that such programmes were introduced on any scale in the
region.

The international agencies and the governments of drug producing countries have also relatively recently changed their approach
to the elimination of illicit drug production. Punitive measures for

stopping the flow of drugs, especially opium, from their rural sources would, by themselves, be ineffective unless the inhabitants of those rural areas were also offered alternative sources of income. Most such communities are relatively isolated, by geography and by culture, from the mainstream of economic and social life in their country: and it is now recognized that drug control via crop substitution involves a whole programme of rural development. Thus, for example, when the history of the *general* economic development of the North-West Frontier Province of Pakistan during the latter part of the twentieth century is written, one may expect the United Nations Fund for Drug Abuse Control to be mentioned as a seminal influence.

Ironically, poppies are in many ways an ideal crop for regions such as the North-West Frontier Province. They grow well in the rural mountainous regions of Pakistan, where there is little or no irrigation or other infrastructure. The entire plant is used, including the dried stalks which are used as animal fodder. Poppies grow equally well with chemical or animal fertilizer, and are labour intensive in a labour surplus economy. This is important in a region where there has been a substantial population increase without a corresponding increase in the amount of land being cultivated. Crop substitution programmes must therefore aim to replace one well-suited crop with perhaps a whole range of less ideal crops.

The present pattern of opium production and illicit trade can, in outline, be fairly briefly described. Almost all the opium produced in South-East Asia is grown in the mountainous areas of northern Burma, Thailand, and Laos; and the illicit opium of South Asia is grown in the Pakistan–Afghanistan border region. Both areas are remote from the centres of government in their countries, and are difficult to police and control, both because of the terrain and because of the fierce independence of the producing peoples. Crop substitution programmes have made a start in both regions, but many economic and criminal pressures operate to maintain opium as a major cash crop. In areas where transport is poor, and the marketing infrastructure for other cash crops virtually absent, opium is a product whose high value on the international market makes the risks inherent in its trading worthwhile to the chain of middlemen.

In the Golden Triangle area, the patterns of opium collection and marketing were relatively simple until the mid-1960s (R. Solomon, *J. Psychedelic Drugs*, 1978, 10:89–98, 193–206). Local merchants, generally expatriate Chinese, came up into the producing areas to purchase the new crop, and in turn sold the opium to Chinese opium syndicates or to local distributors. Thus,

in Burma, the majority of the crop was transported by local insurgent groups into northern Thailand and Laos, with only a small
proportion of the crop being sent south for consumption in Rangoon. At this time, the laboratories in the Golden Triangle produced opium for smoking, and morphine base: any heroin required
in the region was prepared in laboratories in Hong Kong and Bangkok. The first local laboratory capable of producing smoking and
injectable heroin was established in late 1962 in the Golden Triangle; and several further small laboratories were established in
subsequent years. It was the proximity of the American military
in Vietnam which, according to Solomon, produced a sufficiently
large and lucrative market for heroin: by 1971, there were approximately thirty refineries in the tri-border region, many of which
were producing injectable heroin. Kuomintang forces protected
laboratories in Burma and Thailand; local police and military officials were also implicated; and in Laos protection was provided by
the commander of the Laotian Army (McCoy, op. cit.) before the
change of regime in 1976.

During the 1950s and 1960s Bangkok became the region's (and
probably the world's) largest opiate refining and distribution centre, while Hong Kong was not only one of the largest consuming
centres but also a key producer of injectable heroin for the international market, being supplied with raw opium and morphine
base from Bangkok. As enforcement activities increased in Thailand
during the 1970s, the Thai laboratories were moved to more inaccessible regions, or over the border into Burma. By moving the
laboratories closer to the producing areas, the distributors reduced
their risk of arrest, cut transportation costs (including protection
money to all those through whose areas the drugs are moved), and
thus substantially increased their profits.

It was well recognized during the early 1970s that much of Hong
Kong's imported opiates came via Thai trawlers, which fished up
towards the China coast: indeed, the names of the twelve main
ships, and those of the leading personalities who protected the
trade, were known to the United States Congressmen who were
campaigning to end international complicity in the trafficking. It
was political pressure by the United States, and a change of government in Thailand, which brought an end to the trawler trade to
Hong Kong. The establishment of Communist governments in
Laos, Vietnam, and Kampuchea ended the eastward flow of opiates
across South-East Asia—a trade which had involved virtually every
group involved in the Indo-China War. Smuggling of South-East
Asian opiates to Europe and America continues, however, having
had to find and develop new routes. During the Indo-China War,

small-scale smuggling had been common among addicts in the American military. More significantly, the most important of the known American trafficking syndicates operating from South-East Asia were composed of servicemen or ex-servicemen, based either in Vietnam or in Thailand (Solomon, *J. Psychedelic Drugs*, 1978, 10:201–2), as subsequently Europe-based American servicemen have been shown to be central to West Germany's heroin trafficking problem.

Since 1972, Chiu Chau and other Chinese syndicates have been responsible for the bulk of South-East Asian smoking heroin appearing in Europe. Solomon (op. cit.) indicates that almost all of these opiates pass through the Thai distribution system, usually using couriers on commercial airflights to Europe from the region. (As enforcement pressures build up on one route, the trade switches for a while to another: thus, at one period, many of the seizures in Europe had originated from Malaysia and Singapore.) Some heroin is then onward smuggled from Europe to North America: in particular, Vancouver's Chinese syndicates are known to have extremely strong ties with the Chinese syndicates of Amsterdam and Hong Kong (Solomon, op. cit.); and thus both westward and eastward routes are used to bring the drug to Canada. The amount of South-East Asian heroin on the American market varies according to the availability of the Mexican-produced drug: were the latter to become scarce, the 'trade links' between the United States of America and South-East Asia would undoubtedly be further strengthened.

Much international enforcement activity is directed at the traffic of opiates out from the region to other parts of the world; but there is also a substantial traffic within the region itself, some of which is secondary to the interregional traffic, and some of which is conducted purely for the local market. Details of such traffic, and of the enforcement response each country in the region has taken, will be described in the chapter on the legal and enforcement aspects of the drug problem.

Forecasting the future is a perilous and foolhardy pursuit: consider how surprised (and disheartened) one of the 1930 League of Nations Commissioners would have been to learn of the state of the drug problem in East Asia fifty years later. And yet, would he have believed how completely China could have ceased to be the major supplier to the region midway through the period? Various factors may affect the situation, such as a sudden world demand for one of the substitute cash crops, injecting new impetus into the replacement programme, or a change in youth fashions in behaviour, switching the young trend-leaders from drugs to alcohol. Political changes have had profound effects on the drug traffic in

the past, and will continue to do so. As the Philippines have discovered under martial law, even the removal of a few key traffickers
can profoundly affect drug availability; similarly, the involvement
of just a few key politicians or enforcement officers in the protection of the traffic can enormously increase the flow of drugs to or
through a country. One can but hope that the positive factors will
be dominant. Certainly, as the subsequent chapters on preventative education, treatment and rehabilitation, and enforcement
activities will show in some detail, there are many major programmes under way in the countries in the region, as varied in their
approaches as are the circumstances which obtain locally. Although
there is a general similarity in the pattern of drug abuse now found
in each country, and in the profile and motivations of adult and
adolescent drug dependants, there are also sufficiently important
points of difference for them to be considered separately, and to
be responded to by local and international agencies in appropriate
ways. The current conditions and cultural traditions of urban Hong
Kong and rural Sumatra are sufficiently dissimilar from each other
to make any blanket prescription for, say, programmes in preventative education worse than useless. Equally, as the international
agencies have now come to recognize, what was true of the American drug problem is not necessarily true of the drug problem any-
where in Asia: and thus 'international approaches' (which tended
to be American approaches) needed to be tested and modified,
and blended with local traditional approaches, for the particular
context in Asia.

Contemporary Patterns of Drug Abuse in East Asia

THE first chapter surveyed the history and development of the current drug abuse situation in East Asia; and the present chapter brings the account up to date, taking the region country by country. What have become the predominant patterns of abuse? How many individuals are involved, and how considerable is their use? How far is the younger generation involved? Do different communities, or different areas of the country, show characteristic patterns of drug use? We shall attempt in this chapter to give a brief account of the general pattern obtaining in each country, in so far as it is known, and then, in the two chapters following, give a more detailed description of the adult and the adolescent drug users respectively.

The reader will recognize that information about the extent of an illegal behaviour is likely to be considerably less precise than it would be about a non-criminal and socially acceptable activity, where a conventional survey of a random representative sample would give one, with some confidence, a good estimate for the country as a whole. Which drugs are predominant can be assessed by seizure records and from general narcotics bureau information, as well as from the accounts given by known drug users. But the extent of the drug use habit is altogether more difficult to assess. Unless—as only one survey to be reported in this chapter was able to do—one can conduct a random, representative survey of the general population, and assure them of the anonymity and confidentiality of their admission of any drug experiences, then the estimate of drug use in the country must be extrapolated from populations of known drug users. Such identified populations might be those who come to hospital drug clinics, or are arrested by the police on drugs charges. As yet in the region, only Malaysia has a comprehensive monitoring scheme to identify patterns of known users on a national scale, although other countries, notably Hong Kong, Singapore, and Indonesia, have also embarked on national data collecting projects. Extrapolation from known users to the general population involves, as the reader will appreciate, making assumptions which may not be warranted. Those who come to the attention of the various agencies are indeed almost certainly unrepresentative of the total drug user population in some respects: they are generally regular users, whose habit has lasted for some years already before they seek help from a hospital or are detected by the police. Thus, such known user samples do not help one to estimate the numbers of casual or experimental users of drugs, and often represent an earlier 'generation' of drug users in that their period of initiation was under drug supply circumstances which no longer exist. However, such samples may well provide an excellent guide to the geographical and social distribution of the various drug using practices throughout a country. And indeed, in some countries in the region, there have been some fairly detailed studies of the over- and under-representation of different ethnic groups amongst the known drug using population; the emergence and stabilization of a youthful drug user population; and the spread of narcotics abuse from urban centres to the countryside. Most countries have, however, only preliminary data to back up general official statements of recent trends.

Each country is presented separately, as each has had a somewhat different experience of the drug problem. There are, however, several common features found in many of the countries: a move away from opium to heroin and morphine at some time during the past thirty years; a subsequent diversification of drug substances being abused; a rapidly increasing population of youthful drug users during the late 1960s and the 1970s; and, where there had been distinctive ethnic patterns of consumption, a tendency for these to converge on the new poly-drug pattern. The reader, as he reads the separate country accounts might like to consider first why these similar changes in pattern came about. He can then contemplate the exceptions: for example, the continued presence of opium rather than heroin in South Asia; the unique series of stimulants abuse and quiet phases in Japan; the long tradition of firm control over trafficking and use in the Philippines, which has apparently rid itself of heroin; and the claim by China to have eliminated drug abuse altogether.

MALAYSIA

From antiquity, there has been some use of opium and cannabis in the area which is now Malaysia. Opium has always been an imported drug, and its use has been most closely, though not exclusively, connected with the Chinese community; whereas cannabis, which can be grown in the country, has traditionally been associated with the Malay and Indian communities. At some periods during history, control over the use of drugs was exercised more by social than by legal means. Thus, writing in 1826, James Low argued in support of the then method of limiting opium use via licensed opium premises:

Where the propensity to the vices of smoking or eating opium can only with safety be openly indulged in, the dread loss of reputation will deter numbers from risking its loss. But where a prohibition exists, and these practices may be privately enjoyed, at a slight risk of detection, that salutory dread is removed, and the temptation becomes irresistible. No *respectable* Chinese or Malay is ever seen in an opium-house, and as the holders of the licenses and their people are very alert, it is believed that the use of the drug is much less general than it otherwise would be. (*The British Settlement of Penang*, 1826; republished in 1972 by Oxford University Press, Kuala Lumpur.)

Each community has had its forms of drug use *and* its social conventions to limit and specify the occasions and users of the drug substances, and in this way was able for a time to contain the problem. According to many accounts, the Chinese labourers in Malaya, as in other parts of South-East Asia, used opium as a panacea against tropical diseases, and as a means of relief from the pains and the loneliness of work in tin mines and rubber estates. (It may also have satisfied a vanity, remembering that opium use had been a rich man's vice back in China.)

At times when there was registration of opium smokers, there were fairly careful records kept, and estimates can be given much more confidently for opium than for cannabis use. Thus, for example, in 1929 there were 52,313 registered opium smokers in the Federated Malay States, all of whom were Chinese. (Thus, approximately one in ten of the Chinese population of the Federated Malay States were registered at that date.) In addition, fifty-one Indians and eight Malays were allowed to smoke opium under special permits. In the Straits Settlements the estimated number of opium smokers in 1929 was 73,000, again almost exclusively Chinese. (The adult male Chinese population at the time was 350,000.) And in the Unfederated Malay States, while the majority of opium smokers were again Chinese, the habit was not so exclusively confined to this community. A report on opium use in Perlis

and Kedah shows considerable Malay involvement. In the Unfederated Malay States there were complete records only for Johore
State at the time of the survey quoted: *Report of the Commission
of Enquiry into the Control of Opium Smoking in the Far East*,
League of Nations, Geneva, 1930. By 1936, registered smokers
numbered about 28,000 in the Straits Settlements, and over 32,000
in Malay States, with probably a large number of users who obtained their drug illicitly.

Cannabis, *ganja* in Malaysia, grows naturally in the country,
and has been used by the Malays for various medicinal purposes,
such as the relief of asthma (Tan and Haq, *Med. J. Malaysia*, 1974,
29:126—30). Reports also indicate its use for such purposes as
maintaining the fisherman who was working overnight, and the
agricultural worker during times of heavy activity.

The registration of opium users and the control of sale of the
drug was introduced at various times in the various states during
the two decades before World War II. During the Japanese occupation there was no restriction in imports, but at the end of the war
there was a total ban imposed on the import of opium into the
country. However, as Tan and Haq remark, 'legislation did not
necessarily make the substance significantly less available'. The
stringent controls on movement of all goods during the Emergency,
however, did mean that the traffic in opium had to use routes such
as the jungle courier paths from Thailand.

By the late 1960s, in common with most of the other countries
in the region, the traditional patterns of drug abuse had been over-
laid by a new one: younger drug users, who were using a wider
range of drugs, including synthetic drugs diverted from the pharmaceutical trade. The figures for drug seizures in the early 1970s
clearly indicate the emergence of the new pattern: raw opium
seized remained at about 5,000 pounds per year, and morphine,
too, remained relatively steady at around 150 pounds per year.
Heroin, in contrast, leapt from a mere 8 ounces to more than 130
pounds in the first nine months of 1975. In 1970 about 2,300 tablets of psychotropic drugs were seized; by 1975 some thirty times
that amount was seized.

Seizure figures, together with the growing numbers of drug
dependants seeking treatment, and the increase in arrests for drug
offences, gave some clear indication that the new problem was of
some magnitude. There were several studies undertaken of known
populations of users, for example, those who were attending hospitals or clinics for drug problems (Deva, *Med. J. Malaysia*, 1977,
31:183—7; Tan, *Med. J. Malaysia*, 1973, 28:23—8; Tan and Haq,
Med. J. Malaysia, 1974, 29:126—30). Parameshvara Deva reported

on the changing pattern of opiate dependence in the country, and based his sample on the male opiate addicts admitted to the University Hospital in Kuala Lumpur between 1970 and 1976 (*Med. J. Malaysia*, 1978, 32:249—54). Out of a sample of 209 patients, the Chinese formed the single largest ethnic group at 43 per cent; the Indians accounted for 28 per cent of the sample (with, interestingly, over half this number being Sikhs); and the Malays formed the remaining 27 per cent of the sample. The Malays were entirely absent from the figures in the early 1970s, but by 1976 they had taken over as the largest single group. Thus, seen through the eyes of one major hospital, there have been rapid changes in the pattern of opiate addiction in Malaysia during the 1970s, with changing ethnic balances and an increasingly youthful group of users.

Another hospital survey which was published in the same year sampled the whole range of drug dependants volunteering for treatment in the General Hospital, Penang (Navaratnam and Spencer, *Bull. Narc.*, 1978, 30:1—7). The sample base for this survey was larger during the peak year, 1975, when the hospital had approximately 1,700 visits from drug dependants seeking treatment. In Penang, as more recently in Kuala Lumpur, the youthful character of the drug-using group coming for treatment was evident: in Penang the 21- to 25-year age-group represented 38 per cent of the sample; and of that nearly 50 per cent had commenced their habit before the age of 20. Virtually all patients were male, and all were either heroin or morphine users, with some using *ganja* (cannabis) and opium in addition.

It is apparent that those drug dependants who attend hospital clinics or receive in-patient treatment may well provide indications of change in the drug use pattern in society as a whole, but that they cannot be taken as representative of it. Many factors influence the individual's translation from drug user at large to hospital patient, and they include: the individual's ability to tolerate drug substances; his financial ability to continue with the habit (the largest single reason for seeking treatment was indeed the financial burden); pressure from friends, family, or the law to seek treatment; and belief in hospital as opposed to traditional medicine as the appropriate source of help, once the individual has decided to seek treatment of some kind.

Clearly, another agency, such as the police, sees a somewhat different segment of the total drug using population; and indeed this was brought out when comparing the hospital surveys with another study by Navaratnam and Spencer, which surveyed drug offenders before the courts and in prison in Penang and Selangor States (*The*

Drug User and the Law, Centre for Policy Research, Universiti Sains Malaysia, 1977).

In the period surveyed, 1970 to 1975, there was a six-fold increase in the number of convictions in the two states. Out of a total of 3,339, only five individuals were charged with an offence other than the possession of drugs. In no year does the ethnic breakdown of the offenders match the overall ethnic background of the state: some communities are overrepresented and some are underrepresented. Thus, in Selangor (including Kuala Lumpur) Malays moved from 20 per cent to 41 per cent of offenders between 1970 and 1975 (as against 35 per cent of the total population in the state), with corresponding drops in proportion (although not of absolute numbers) among the Chinese and Indian communities. In Penang the increase among Malays was also recorded, from 18 per cent to 22 per cent, but this community was still underrepresented (the state population comprising 31 per cent Malays). The vast Indian overrepresentation in 1970 (there were more than three times the expected number of Indians in the sample of offenders that year) dropped to an overrepresentation rate of just under double the expected number in 1975.

Such differences between the communities as they emerge in the court statistics cannot, however, be let pass without comment. Clearly there have been changes in the pattern of communal involvement with drugs, *but* the courts and prisons are perhaps even less representative of wider society than are the hospitals. Ethnicity in part reflects social class, and social class in turn influences the individual drug user's chances of detection by enforcement agencies. Thus, if police activities are concentrated in some areas at a particular time, the resultant arrests and convictions will reflect the social characteristics of these particular districts.

The single most important age-group appearing in the courts was, and has remained, the over-35 age-group. But, whereas in 1970, 50 per cent of drug offenders were these older individuals, their relative importance had diminished, such that by 1975 less than 25 per cent of the total were over 35. In terms of absolute numbers, this represents a very steady number of older individuals coming before the courts during the study period; and the dramatic increase in convictions for drug offences is entirely accounted for by the youthful segment of the population.

To gain an overall picture of the drug abuse problem in Malaysia, the National Centre for Research on Drug Dependence, at Universiti Sains Malaysia, has adopted two strategies: first, of general population surveys, and second, a national monitoring scheme.

As has been stressed above, known drug user populations, seen by a particular agency, represent a predictably skewed segment of the total drug using population. Yet drug abuse, being an illegal activity, is not one which individuals in the community readily admit to in opinion-poll type surveys. Thus, the strategy adopted by Spencer and Navaratnam was to sample one in ten of the secondary school population in three states—Penang, Selangor, and Kelantan (*Studies of the Misuse of Drugs Among Secondary School Children in the States of Penang, Selangor, and Kelantan*, Universiti Sains Malaysia, 1976, 1978 (two monographs); and Spencer and Navaratnam, *Drug and Alcohol Dependence*, 1980, a, b, c, 1981). Further surveys of non-student youth are to be undertaken to complement the school surveys (WHO Meeting of Collaborating Investigators, Research and Reporting Project on the Epidemiology of Drug Dependence, Penang, 1979).

Such surveys are representative of the *total* youthful population (in and out of school); and, where anonymity can be guaranteed to respondents, then cross checking indicates that a high level of honesty characterizes the self report data on the extent and nature of drug experience among youth.

The second strategy adopted by the National Centre has been the development of the National Data Bank on Drug Dependence for Malaysia (Navaratnam and Lee, *Proceedings, Colombo Plan Workshop*, Penang, 1978). Currently, data are provided by the Ministry of Welfare Services, the police, the customs, the narcotics bureau and the Ministry of Health; and it is anticipated that the private medical practitioners will also be linked to the system. Thus, a standardized inventory, covering such items as personal and drug history, income and drug expenditure, reasons for starting drugs, and agencies seen, is administered to all drug dependants seen by any one of these agencies, and the results forwarded to the National Centre for coding, compilation, and analysis. In the Canadian national monitoring system, which preceded the Malaysian (Rootman and Yard, 'Trends in Reported Illegal Narcotic Use in Canada', 1956–1975, *Bull. Narc.*, 1978, 30:13—22), there has been a problem of over-reporting, because drug users may see a number of different agencies, using a variety of aliases. In Malaysia the existence of an identity card system eliminates such a problem, as computer search can trace all cases of multiple reporting.

The accumulation of data over time (the system has been running as a fully integrated system since 1977), and assembled from a range of agencies, is clearly important for policy making, and enables planners and administrators to make well-informed decisions. There has been active debate about whether such data can be a basis for epidemiological studies, with some writers taking the view that the number and nature of cases in contact with the reporting agencies is an indication of the total number of cases in the community, and that changes in the former indicate changes in the latter. However, it may be argued that the very reasons why a segment of a population comes to the attention of the agencies guarantees that this segment is not representative of the whole. Thus, those drug users who seek professional help include those with unusually high motivation to stop, or who have reached a crisis point in their habit. The type of experimenting drug user which (as will be described below) characterizes the school drug using minority is unlikely to be seen and thus reported by an agency, and thus will not appear among the monitoring survey statistics. Nonetheless, the monitoring system *does* counterbalance the various systematic reporting biases of the various agencies, and, if used realistically, can provide as accurate an overview of patterns and trends in a country as is possible, short of continued national anonymous surveys.

The results of the surveys of Malaysian schoolchildren will be described below in the section on the adolescent drug abuser in Malaysia. The overall incidence and pattern of drug abuse was as follows. Out of a total sample of 20,894 schoolchildren aged 13 to 19, just under 11 per cent had had any drug experience. This percentage was fairly constant across the fairly urban state, Penang, the urban and rural state, Selangor, and the largely rural state, Kelantan, and *in each state* the highest rate of drug experience occurred in the first and sixth forms, with the children in forms three and four reporting a lower rate. Again, consistent across the three states, the drugs most frequently reported as having been ever experienced varied between the lower forms (whose drugs of preference are sedatives, tranquillizers, and amphetamines, but who seldom mentioned *ganja*) and the upper forms (for whom *ganja* was the main drug of abuse, followed by sedatives, tranquillizers, and amphetamines). In neither group, nor in any area, were opiates a drug of first experience.

The use of a single drug was the most common pattern amongst all age-groups, with, typically, only a few experimental sessions before the complete abandonment of the substance (generally, *ganja* among the older sample, and sedatives among the younger). However, a quarter of those who had ever used drugs reported that they had experienced four or more drugs, and were likely to have progressed rapidly to heroin. This progression may be facilitated by the ready availability of heroin in all areas, and the local tradition of smoking or inhaling, rather than injecting opiates. (Clearly,

Western models of migration patterns between drugs are inappropriate in countries where both the local market situation and the cultural tradition are so different.) Even among the individuals who reported experience of heroin, morphine, or opium, often rather glibly assumed to be hardened drug users, the experimental pattern, rather than the regular dependent use pattern, describes the majority of this relatively small number. Curiosity is high: regular use, if it does occur, seems to develop only after school. (The projected surveys of non-student youth, referred to above, will begin to show whether those who drop out from secondary school report higher incidence of regular use of opiates and other drugs.)

To summarize: there is evidence for a country-wide interest and experimentation with drugs amongst a small minority of those who are in secondary school. The youngest pupils, if they try drugs, are likely to have access to sedatives and other pharmaceuticals; the older pupils are more likely to try *ganja*; and approximately a quarter of those who start experimenting will continue to try at least four different kinds of drugs, often including opiates. The problem of predicting *which* experimenters will move on to regular use of drugs has exercised many investigators before, and factors which might be involved include personal history, patterns of drug experimentation, personality, social acquaintance network, and changing market and legal factors. Disentangling the possible predictors may be either difficult or impossible, but we propose, in our future studies, to join in the investigation.

THAILAND

Drug dependence in Thailand has a long history: the repeated references to it in the historical records of the country have been likened to an old acquaintance who keeps on coming back to visit (Poshyachinda, *Workshop on Reduction of Demand for Illicit Drugs in South-East Asia*, Penang, 1978). The old familiar problem always involves one or more of the three main drug substances: opium, cannabis, or *kratom* (*mitragyna*).

Cannabis (*gunja* in Thailand), being easily cultivated throughout the country, was widely used; cannabis smoking, unless carried to the extreme, was well tolerated by the general public, who took an amused attitude towards its use. The fact that *gunja* had hallucinogenic properties was well known, and in no way inhibited its use in Thai cooking. *Kratom* use was common amongst those with access to the tree, particularly market gardeners, peasants, and labourers (Suwanlert, *Bull. Narc.*, 1975, 28:21–7). It has been used for its narcotic properties, as a traditional substitute in the treatment of opium addiction, as a treatment for diarrhoea in Thai folk medicine, and as an ingredient in cooking.

Opium had been smuggled into Thailand during the early nineteenth century to meet the demand from the urban Chinese population of Bangkok, but despite this ready market for illicit opium there was actually very little poppy cultivation within the country's borders until the late 1940s. The earliest of the hill tribes people to settle in northern Thailand produced only sufficient opium for their own needs, plus some surplus, which was consumed by Thai and Chinese addicts in the immediate area (McCoy: *The Politics of Heroin in Southeast Asia*, Harper and Row, 1972). During World War II, when the country was cut off from its major suppliers of opium, Iran and Turkey, there was a considerable increase in opium smuggling from the Shan States in Burma (occupied by Thailand in alliance with the Japanese empire), and from Yunnan province in China. The continued availability of substantial amounts of inexpensive opium for addicts in Thailand meant that the country came through the war years with her enormous addict population intact, and with her dependence on imported opium as great as ever.

After World War II, large numbers of hill tribes people began settling in northern Thailand: Meo and Yao from Laos, and Akha, Lisu, and Lahu from China via northern Burma. All these groups brought with them the skills for cultivating the opium poppy, and found land in the mountains of northern Thailand suited to it.

For about one hundred years opium smoking was regulated by a system of registering addicts, and allowing smoking only in authorized opium dens. The illegal trafficking of opium was, however, only somewhat reduced by this, because the government's revenue raised from the sale of opium kept prices high. Thus, the quoted figure of registered addicts in the country in 1958–70,985–clearly does not represent the total opium using population (Suwanwela, *Drug Dependence in Thailand—a Review*, Chulalongkorn University, Bangkok, 1976).

Under pressure from the United Nations and other agencies to control opium production and use, the Thai government passed legislation in December 1958 to end the legalized opium trade and non-medical consumption. Opium dens were ordered to be closed before the end of June 1959, and a treatment centre was set up for the detoxification of opium addicts (Suwanwela, op. cit.).

Government physicians, now obliged under the new law to treat narcotics addicts, reported that initially all the patients whom they saw were addicted only to opium. By early 1960, however, the physicians were reporting that large numbers of heroin addicts were being seen; and the trend towards heroin rather than opium use has continued. Thus, by 1971, the National Hospital for Addiction reported that 85 per cent of its admissions were of patients addicted to heroin or morphine or both; 14 per cent to opium, and 1 per cent to other drugs. The heroin-morphine addicts were mostly ethnic Thai city dwellers, while the opium addicts were almost exclusively tribal people from the north (Westermeyer, *Arch. Gen. Psychiatry*, 1976, 33:1135–9).

Westermeyer has made the case, comparing the very similar experiences of Hong Kong in the 1940s, Thailand in the 1950s and 1960s, and Laos during the 1970s, that the anti-opium laws have actually caused the rapid switch from an almost exclusively opium using pattern of narcotics addiction to one dominated by the less easily detected heroin and morphine.

Not only did the available drugs change, but the number of addicts increased considerably during this period. Estimates of the numbers abusing drugs in the urban communities come from police arrest figures, treatment facilities, and some limited community surveys (Suwanlert, op. cit.).

Police statistics indicate that heroin abuse has become a feature of most urban centres in Thailand. The onset of what was to become an epidemic can be seen in the year of first use which addicts later reported when they came to the attention of the police or hospitals. A small proportion of addicts started their habit in the 1950s; the incidence started to rise in 1964 and 1965; and it escalated rapidly from 1967, with some decline in the numbers reporting that their first use had been in 1975 and 1976. A marijuana epidemic occurred about a year or two ahead of the heroin epidemic. Some confidence in the dating of the epidemic can be had from the fact that data collected from three separate institutions show very similar curves.

A survey of 2,000 households selected by stratified sampling from the total population of Bangkok was carried out by Punnahitanond (cited in Suwanwela, op. cit., p. 3). He found that 24 per cent of the 21- to 25-year-old age-group reported to have tried one or more illicit drugs; 16 per cent of adults above 25 years of age reported that they had had the experience, as had 11 per cent of those below 20 years of age.

If one excludes alcohol and tobacco, marijuana was the most common drug used for the first time (at least amongst those who were convicted or given hospital treatment, as reported in two surveys quoted by Suwanwela, op. cit., p. 3): 70 per cent of male convicts and 47 per cent of patients used marijuana as their first drug, while only 17 per cent of convicts and 27 per cent of patients started directly with heroin. For the large majority of these individuals, heroin became, either quickly or eventually, the main drug of abuse, with, in more than a fifth of all cases, other drugs being used as well: these included opium, morphine, tranquillizers, sedatives, and stimulants. By the time they came to be hospitalized, intravenous injection of heroin had become the usual method of administration for 77 per cent of the patients, 1 per cent using intramuscular injection, and 22 per cent who are smokers.

More than half of those coming to the attention of hospitals and the police report that they had first experienced illicit drugs before the age of 21 (Suwanwela, op. cit.).

The pattern of a drug abuse found among the hill tribes people of northern Thailand remains much closer to the traditional opium using pattern than does the contemporary pattern in urban areas (Suwanwela, 1976, op. cit.; and Suwanwela, *et al., The Hill tribes of Thailand: Their Opium Use and Addiction*, Bangkok, Chulalongkorn University, 1977).

The hill tribes people have changed little in their social customs and way of living. Opium plays its part in medical care and as a source of pleasure (as well as a major source of income). Information about the extent and nature of addiction among the hill tribes is difficult to obtain, and estimates have ranged from 3.6 per cent (a 1967 United Nations Survey Team estimate for several groups) to the Department of Public Welfare's estimates of 10 per cent addiction among the Meo, 12 per cent among the Lahu, and 16 per cent among the Yao. However, such figures may be misleading, as Suwanwela (1976, op. cit.) suggests: the range between villages within any one tribe may be extremely great, and some villages may have more addicts than they have households, and are thereby disintegrating. Age of first use of those seeking treatment was most commonly between 16 to 25, although the decision to seek help might not be taken for many years. For the majority, the opium was smoked often mixed with salicylate to enhance its potency.

SINGAPORE

As in many other countries in the region, the oldest pattern of drug usage in Singapore is that of opium smoking; and Leong (*Addictive. Diseases*, 1977, 3:93—8) estimates that just after World War II, the average opium addict was a Chinese male, aged 49, who had smoked opium for about 18 years. He was likely to be a labourer or semi-skilled worker, who smoked 3.2 packets of prepared opium (about 2.4 grams) each day, and whose habit accounted for three-eighths of his daily income. There had been, at the last count of the registered opium addicts in 1941, 16,552 addicts on the registers. After 1946, when the sale and smoking of opium was made illegal, there are thus no year-by-year figures, and estimates have been made on the basis of those charged or treated. Leong estimates a current figure of between 7,000 and 8,000.

During more recent years some younger opium addicts were introduced to morphine, and Leong estimates an average daily injection of 1.4 grams of morphine, at approximately the same daily cost as that of the average opium smoker, but with much more powerful effect.

The use of cannabis (in the form of *ganja*) was also present, especially amongst the Indian, Pakistani, and other non-Chinese communities. Although the practice was illegal, it attracted little attention until it was taken up by the young of all communities in the late 1960s and early 1970s.

In this period the main drugs of experimentation by youth were cannabis and a range of pills—especially methaqualone (Mandrax, MX pills). Leong reports that, at a hospital drug dependence clinic, he was seeing many young persons from middle-class backgrounds, aged between 12 and 23, and with more males than females in the patient population.

Then, between 1972 and 1973, morphine and (for the first time ever in Singapore) heroin began to replace soft drugs, such as MX pills and *ganja*, in popular consumption. Leong estimates that at the time of writing, 1976, there were 2,000 heroin addicts, many of whom would be young men, 16 to 25 years, who smoked heroin-tipped ('spiked') cigarettes. An addict could be smoking 25 such cigarettes a day, and could thus be spending S$60 to S$90 a day. Thus, to summarize Leong's estimates at 1976:

Opium smokers	7,000–8,000
Morphine addicts	3,000–4,000
Older cannabis 'chronic' users	500
Younger MX and cannabis users	5,000–7,000
Heroin users	2,000
Total	17,500–21,000

The total Singapore population at the time was 2.25 million, thus giving an estimated 0.78 to 0.96 per cent figure for drug abuse.

After Leong's paper had been written, but before it was published, the population of heroin abusers grew by geometrical progression (Ng, *Colombo Plan Workshop*, Penang, 1978); and by 1977 it was estimated that there were as many as 13,000 heroin addicts and abusers in Singapore.

As a result of the major 'Operation Ferret' initiative launched in 1978, numbers were first contained and then reduced: the Singapore Central Narcotics Board estimate for the end of 1978 was 8,500 heroin users, of whom 4,600 were under detention. The aim of the Operation was to arrest heroin users rapidly enough, and to detain them for rehabilitation more quickly than there were new heroin users being created. At the beginning of Operation Ferret the ratio of new heroin abusers to old abusers was 2.2:1; by the end of 1978 this ratio was reduced to 0.22:1.

The Central Narcotics Bureau *Report to the Commonwealth Regional Working Group on Illicit Drugs* (Kuala Lumpur, June 1979) indicated that heroin abusers, unable to obtain the substance, were resorting to substitutes like opium pellets, cannabis, alcohol, and depressant drugs, such as Rohypnol and barbiturates. If heroin were again to become freely available, then, in the opinion of the Central Narcotics Bureau, these ex-heroin addicts would return to heroin abuse.

The pattern of drug abuse in Singapore, and in particular the details of this pattern since 1972, show the extent to which description and explanation of the contemporary drug picture must be tied in with an account of legal and enforcement policies operative at the time, as well as of the factors such as personal motivations, cultural traditions, and so on which are usually given. Thus, for example, in the case of the ex-heroin addicts, the switch they made to Rohypnol was swifty followed by the classification of the substance as a controlled drug under the Misuse of Drugs Act. With enforcement action directed towards Rohypnol, the ex-heroin addicts then shifted towards the use of barbiturates in August 1978. In turn, there was an official alert on the dangers of barbiturate abuse, and the Singapore Medical Association warned its members of the dangers of creating a barbiturate problem through liberal prescription.

INDONESIA

The traditional patterns of drug use in Indonesia reflected the regional and ethnic variety of the country: cannabis was very common in Acheh and northern Sumatra, where people used the plant to flavour their food; erythroxylon coca was grown in East Java 'for export purposes' (Soegomo, in *Drug Abuse in Indonesia*,

1975); and there was opium use amongst the Chinese community in several areas. West Java, east Java, Bali, and perhaps other areas of Indonesia now also produce considerable quantities of cannabis, and coca growing has also extended to these areas.

From the late 1960s onwards, it became apparent that drug abuse, especially among young individuals, was on the rise (Setyonegoro, *ICAA Conference*, Hong Kong, 1971), and the increasing number of voluntary self-referrals to mental hospitals, and to the very few specialist sanitoria, indicated that the situation was changing. At the time of the 1971 conference paper, however, Setyonegoro could only speculate on the overall picture, there being no major research projects then in operation.

Reviewing that period after seven years, Widjono (*Colombo Plan Workshop*, Penang, 1978) records that, in addition to the traditional drugs, the prevalent drugs were morphine, barbiturates, and sedatives, generally in poly-drug use with each other, occasionally in combination with hallucinogens and amphetamines, but with no case of cocaine or solvent abuse.

The problem quickly came to public notice; much media coverage was given to the new drug problem in Indonesia; but, as Salan recalls, there were no reliable data, and the rough estimates for one year were multiplied each succeeding year. It so happened that a national monitoring scheme for mental hospital cases was being inaugurated during the early 1970s, and was extendable to include the drug abuse patients who were beginning to be referred to hospitals and clinics. Analysis of the data thus collected from hospitals throughout Indonesia reveals a rise of epidemic proportions up until 1973, with a falling away then of numbers to the end of the survey period, 1977 (Salan, *Colombo Plan Workshop*, Penang, 1978). It should be noted the total sample was 777 over the five years of the survey, which gives a relatively small number of cases reported for any one year upon which to base any detailed analysis. Salan neither claims (nor yet disclaims) that the 35 reporting institutions are representative of the Indonesian hospitalized drug abuser population, but makes clear that the hospitalized drug abuser population only gives clues about the non-hospitalized.

The survey showed that 57.9 per cent of the patients were 11 to 20 years old; and that 36.3 per cent were 21 to 30 years old if one takes the 1972 to 1977 period as a whole, with, in the first two years, an even greater proportion of the patients being 20 or under. The large majority of patients were male (89.5 per cent): the reason for this will be discussed below, when the reasons for individuals becoming involved in drug abuse are discussed. Most of the drug abusers (90 per cent) were brought up in urban areas, particularly Jakarta and Surabaya, although there was some indication from police reports that more recently drug abuse was also to be found in suburban areas.

Most patients in the sample were multiple drug users, with more emphasis upon hypnotic and sedative drugs than upon morphine and heroin; but detailed information on individual or national changes in drug use patterns is not recoverable from the rather broad diagnostic categories of the questionnaire employed in the monitoring scheme (Salan, op. cit., p. 59).

The picture of drug abuse in Indonesia that is gained from the medical statistics is somewhat at variance with the picture painted by Army General Yoga Soegomo, the Chairman of BAKOLAK INPRES 6/71, the Co-ordinating Body for the Implementation of Presidential Instructions (Soegomo, in *Drug Abuse in Indonesia*, 1975). BAKOLAK INPRES 6/71, to quote its Chairman, exists to 'co-ordinate efforts and actions to break up any kind of obstacles, challenges, threats, or disturbances which could jeopardize the social order and security, and the course of the national development plan and implementation'. It sees illegal trafficking as a product of the nuclear stalemate of the Cold War, in which foreign powers, seeking to gain non-nuclear weapon advantages over each other, use narcotic drugs as a subversive device to create nation-wide mental breakdown. Thus, the BAKOLAK INPRES 6/71 picture of drug abuse in Indonesia is of a 'devastating effect of illicit drug abuse and trafficking, which has evidently created a huge problem for the state and nation, demanding continuous efforts and a considerable amount of money which could otherwise be appropriated for other productive purposes'. General Soegomo does not present any statistics.

THE PHILIPPINES

The Philippines have always had a relatively low incidence of drug abuse, which is attributable to the drug control policies during the Spanish and American periods of the country's history; and the country continues to operate control measures with sufficient effect to have a major impact on the present-day pattern of drug abuse.

Opium use in the Philippines had started in the seventeenth century, reputedly to 'steady the nerves of the soldier', and by the nineteenth century the Muslims of Jolo and Sulu had acquired the use of opium smoking from, it is presumed, the Chinese, who were the only group which the authorities would tolerate using opium.

Filipinos, by and large, did not in fact have much opportunity to abuse opium, for the Chinese were residentially segregated from the native population in enclosed camps called *parian*. By 1903 there were 190 opium establishments, exclusively for Chinese use, and one in twenty persons in Manila was estimated to be addicted to opium. When, subsequently, a system of licensing individual addicts was introduced, and all were encouraged to seek treatment, facilities were totally inadequate for the estimated 20,000 addicts (Zarco and Manuel, *Colombo Plan Workshop*, Laguna, 1974).

The American civil government of the Philippines, in taking over from Spain in the early twentieth century, ordered a systematic survey of the drug problem and, taking the view that drug use was a potential social danger to the Filipinos, banned the non-medical use of opium in 1908. (This was, incidentally, seven years before opiates were banned in the United States mainland.) The American campaign continued until the Japanese occupation in 1942, at which point all supplies of illicit opium were cut off from the country, and by the 1950s the number of opium addicts was probably the lowest in Asia: from a population of 20 million, only 50 to 60 persons were arrested annually for drug offences. Almost all opium use during this period was among the Chinese.

By 1963, however, a new trend had appeared: there was a waning of opium addiction among the Chinese, and a concurrent increase among the Filipinos such that the latter community contributed 63 per cent of the total arrests for drug offences. At the same time, morphine was gaining in popularity. By the 1970s addiction among the Chinese community was definitely decreasing, while the Filipino involvement continued to increase. In the Philippines, as elsewhere in the region, the new drug users were typically from much lower age-groups, and a whole range of drugs was being used by people from all strata of society.

One of the drugs characteristic of this latest phase is cannabis: it is not native to the Philippines but was first grown in the mid-1950s by American residents. Marijuana smoking spread from local taverns to the schools and colleges; and today cannabis is grown widely throughout the country (Zarco and Almonte, *Addictive Diseases*, 1977, 3:119–28).

Heroin abuse is reported to have declined in Greater Manila from 1972, as a result of some or all of the following events in that year: the Dangerous Drugs Board came into being as a powerful arm of government; United States anti-narcotics activities in the region were stepped up; and martial law was declared, following which some prominent traffickers and manufacturers of heroin were arrested (Zarco and Almante, op. cit., pp. 121–2). At the time of writing, the last recorded case of heroin addiction was in February 1974. Only sporadic abuse of opiates has since been reported.

However, there is continued poly-drug use among some parts of the youth population, with pharmaceutical products and marijuana predominant. Zarco and Almonte (op. cit.) list a startling range of proprietary and other drugs which had been revealed in their surveys of college students or prisoners, and of rehabilitation centre clients. Marijuana was found to be the most abused substance for all groups, but thereafter students and delinquents showed different preferences. Most of the first ten ranked drugs reported by the student users were pharmaceutical products, whereas heroin and opium were in respectively third and ninth place in the delinquents' list.

Zarco reported in 1972 on student patterns of marijuana use (Zarco and associates, Narcotics Foundation of the Philippines, 1972 (a)). Regular use of marijuana was a characteristic of the first two years of the four-year college programme studies; but, although many individuals in the final two years had had some earlier experiments with the drug, none reported current use. Amphetamines were reported used by 8 per cent of students (compared with 30 per cent who had ever used marijuana): characteristically, this drug was used as an occasional study aid before examinations rather than on a regular basis. Mandrax had been used by 4 per cent of the sample, as had L.S.D.

In general, non-marijuana users were not users of any other drugs (apart from amphetamine and benzedrine, whose users were quite likely to have no experience of any other drug).

Street-corner abuse of illicit drugs by non-student youth involved, as mentioned above, a different range of drugs. In their second survey, Zarco and associates (Narcotics Foundation of the Philippines, 1972 (b)) report that the use of drugs by individuals who were subsequently imprisoned was characterized by a lack of restraint: the users of each drug reported using it on average at least twice a week. Indeed, for such poly-drug users, the initial period of experimentation had been followed by a rapid progression from drug to drug once the individual had joined the active drug-using groups.

These pioneering studies by Zarco *et al.* were supplemented by a nation-wide survey of 13- to 23-year-olds by Cudal and associates (*A. Study of Youth and Use of Drugs in the Philippines*, UNESCO, mimeograph, 1976). In the ten areas of study within the three main geographic areas of the country—Luzon, the Visayas, and Mindanao—a simple, self-administered questionnaire was given to the young people, including questions about their personal experiences, if any, with the use of drugs.

Twenty-one per cent acknowledged having used drugs without a doctor's prescription, but, when questioned further, the vast majority of these indicated that the drug that they had mentioned was a proprietary pain reliever, taken for a headache or fever. Less than 3 per cent of the total sample claimed to have taken any prohibited or regulated drug. Marijuana was mentioned by four times as many individuals as mentioned hallucinogens or Mandrax as their drug of first use.

Thus, from official figures and the surveys quoted above, it would seem that the Philippines have a drug abuse profile unique in the region: although, as in other countries, the main problem group is found amongst urban youth, the main difference lies in the drugs most abused—marijuana and non-controlled pharmaceutical drugs, with opiate abuse reported to be almost absent in the country. The most common single pattern is marijuana with cough syrup.

LAOS

Almost all detailed information available about patterns of drug abuse in Laos predates the full coming to power of the present Communist regime, which has made considerable claims about limiting the extent of drug abuse in the country. So far, only journalistic accounts, rather than statistical surveys, have been published, documenting this programme.

Westermeyer, the main research worker in the area prior to 1976, has contrasted patterns of consumption in Vientiane and other towns with that in the producing areas; and, within the towns, between those whose drug use is home based and those who are opium den based (Westermeyer, *Arch. Gen. Psychiatry*, 1974, 31: 237—40). Those who only frequented opium dens tended to be lower class people who were single or divorced, or who were for one reason or another unintegrated into the community. In contrast, those in Westermeyer's sample who smoked opium only at home were all married, with families, jobs, and homes of their own, and some were of superior social status. Those who used both den and home to smoke opium tended to be intermediate in status.

Opium had been the major drug of cultivation and consumption in Laos since at least the time of the first contacts with France, and had remained of considerable economic importance up to recent years. In the earliest of Westermeyer's studies (*Am. J. Psychiatry*, 1971, 127:1019—23), only opium users were encountered among the several scores of addicts whom he interviewed in northern Laos; and until early 1972 none of the users he met or heard of used other drugs. However, by March 1972, heroin had become readily available in Vientiane, and within the first eleven months of the setting up of the new National Detoxification Centre, 17 per cent of the 439 addicts admitted were users of heroin or morphine (*Arch. Gen. Psychiatry*, 1976, 33:1135—9).

In the first year's treatment programme of the centre, 52 per cent of the sample were ethnic Lao—approximately their percentage in the total population. Meo and Yao were overrepresented, and the non-producing hill tribes were underrepresented. Virtually all of the heroin using minority were town dwellers. Westermeyer and Soudalay (*Proceedings of 1975 ICCA Bangkok Conference*) observed that this addiction to opium among young urban males progressed more rapidly, and exacted a higher personal cost than did the former pattern of opium use. (Opium smoking, the traditional pattern of use, continued to be the most common, and was sometimes so episodic that, within their sample, the authors describe one man who had been an occasional user for a full 38 years before becoming addicted.) In most instances the Lao user retains his place in the community, in sharp contrast with many other cultures, and, because he smokes his drug substance, he avoids the disabling consequences of intravenous administration.

We lack large-scale survey data for Laos, but Westermeyer (*Am. J. Psychiatry*, 1974, 131:165—70) suggests that in some respects opium addiction in Laos resembles alcohol addiction in the United States, with users throughout the social scale: 'Although some highly visible addicts in Laos could be categorized as lower class, most Laotian addicts were self-sufficient productive members of their society.' However, in Laos at this time, criminality was not associated with addiction; opium use was widespread in rural areas; and female addicts were much less rare than in other parts of the world. Whereas in other countries (e.g., the United States and Korea), narcotic addition had become an epidemic, Westermeyer characterizes pre-1972 opium use as endemic in Laos. Even the succession of violent disruptions to the area (the Japanese occupation, Viet Minh violence, the Vietnamese invasion, and the American War) had not succeeded in changing the pattern of opium use.

By 1977, however, Westermeyer was writing about a *heroin* epidemic in Asia (*Am. J. Drug and Alcohol Abuse*) and particularly in Laos. With yearly visits to Laos during the period 1971—5, he and his co-author, Bourne, had the opportunity to observe the sudden appearance and rapid spread of heroin addiction, to the point at which, they estimated, there were 1,000 to 1,500 heroin addicts in a country of 3 million people. By the end of this period, these included a number of Caucasian world travellers, but the switch to heroin, and the steep rise in numbers, predated the period when Laotian borders were open to such travellers.

The traditional opium production, the involvement in clandestine export to the West, and the recently superimposed heroin epidemic were all dramatically affected by the Communist government achieving full power. One estimate (*Far Eastern Economic Review*, 30 April 1976, p. 26) suggests that opium production had been cut back from as much as 100 tons a year at its peak to between 10 and 20 tons, 'sufficient only for the domestic market', and that 'heroin addiction is limited to a tiny handful (who) wander the streets of Vientiane, begging'.

HONG KONG

Hong Kong has had a serious narcotics problem almost throughout its history. The colony played an important historical role in the development of opium abuse in China, having been ceded to Britain in 1841, after the Opium Wars; and served as a centre for the opium trade with China for a long period thereafter. There were periodic efforts at restriction from the 1880s onwards, and in 1914 the government attempted to reduce the morphine content of the opium in use, by establishing an opium monopoly and producing the drug itself. The use of opiates continued unabated, such that, when the League of Nations Commission of Enquiry visited Hong Kong in 1930, it estimated that 10 per cent of the *male* Chinese population was addicted to opium smoking. (League of Nations Commission of Enquiry, *Report to Council*, 1930.)

It was not until 1959 that intensive efforts were carried out to enforce the law against consumption (Singer, *Br. J. Addict.*, 1974, 69:257–68), and yet the most reliable estimates of prevalence in the 1960s and early 1970s gave figures of between 6 to 10 per cent of the male adult population as being addicted to narcotics (Action Committee against Narcotics, *Hong Kong Progress Report*, 1966 and 1973) but only 3 per cent of females are addicts.

Prior to 1945, narcotic addicts had overwhelmingly used opium. Fort (*Bull. Narc.*, 1965, 17:1–19) was the first writer to record the prevalence of heroin addicts over opium addicts during the early 1960s. Clinical studies cited by Westermeyer (*Arch. Gen. Psychiatry*, 1976, 33:1135–9) also show that only opium addiction occurred before World War II, and that heroin addiction was an entirely post-war phenomenon. Two further trends emerged in his year-by-year analysis of the clinical records: a trend for more new addicts to initially use heroin, and for the existing opium addicts to switch to heroin. By 1962, 83.1 per cent of all addicts were heroin users, and the 1972 figure was 90.4 per cent. Thus, as Westermeyer argues, the trend towards heroin use began in the late 1940s, shortly after the Hong Kong authorities began to enforce the narcotic laws with some vigour, and within the decade the majority of addicts, old and new, were users of heroin. A further effect of enforcement upon patterns of usage is related to the practice of self-administration. As drug prices increase, there is a greater incentive to switch from heroin smoking to injecting the substance. Injection of heroin, either under the skin or into a vein, ensures that none of the substance escapes, and thus saves money whilst heightening the experience. Fewer than 0.5 per cent of addicts in Hong Kong began by using heroin by injection, but a significant minority have adopted this method by the time the hospital clinics see them as patients (the 1972 figure was 16 per cent).

By mid-1979, Ley (*Commonwealth Working Group*, Kuala Lumpur, 1979), estimated that the number of addicts in Hong Kong totalled between 35,000 and 40,000 in a population of 4.6 million, of whom 85 per cent were users of Heroin (No. 3); 13 per cent opium users; and 2 per cent users of amphetamines, synthetics (especially MX pills), and cannabis. The average age of the heroin users is strikingly lower than that of the opium users: 25 to 28 for heroin users, as against an average of between 40 and 50 for opium users. He described the typical users of the last group of synthetics etc. as 'Europeans and night people'. During 1979, the trafficked price of heroin doubled within three months, with ever greater pressure for addicts to switch from inhalation to injection. According to Ley, the average addict need only use one packet of heroin per day to produce three injections per day, as compared with two packets for inhalation.

As the reader will have noted in Ley's figures of average ages, Hong Kong, although it still has a very serious narcotics problem, has at least contained drug abuse among young people. The anti-narcotics programmes have been accompanied by a steady decline in the number of young people involved in drug abuse, at least as far as the records of the three main treatment centres show: thus, for example, in 1969, 25.4 per cent of one of the centres were under 21; by 1976 this had dropped to 8.6 per cent (*Hong Kong Narcotics Report*, 1976).

There are only approximate estimates of the total numbers of drug addicts in the Hong Kong population as a whole, although there have been various surveys. (Thus, for example, in 1974, a survey of the 15- to 19-year-old age-group was undertaken by the Central Registry of Drug Addicts, which showed that only 0.28 per cent of the age-group were addicted to drugs.) However, the Central Registry of Drug Addicts was reported, in 1978, to be about to set up a systematic data collection system (Wu, *Colombo Plan Workshop*, 1978) to answer questions about the numbers of new addicts becoming known to agencies, their background, and their geographical distribution.

The typical profile of a drug addict in Hong Kong which the Central Registry of Drug Addicts records so far show (*Hong Kong Narcotics Report*, 1976) is of an adult male over 21, who has had no more than five years' primary education, and now works as an unskilled labourer or factory process worker. He is likely to be single, or, if married, is now separated from his family and lives in overcrowded accommodation.

As already indicated, he is most likely to be a heroin rather than an opium user, and to take his drug by 'chasing the dragon' (inhaling heroin fumes by heating through tin-foil paper). Sixty per cent of cases seen by the voluntary organization, SARDA (the Society for the Aid and Rehabilitation of Drug Addicts), use this method of consumption, with 12 per cent smoking spiked cigarettes, and 20 per cent injecting intravenously (Ch'ien, *Addictive Diseases*, 1977, 3:99—104). Given that inhalation or smoking are the most common methods, the average Hong Kong addict has much less chance of accidentally dying as a direct result of his habit than has the average Western heroin addict, whose 'mainlining' method puts him at risk either from infection from dirty needles, or through overdosing.

If an 'average addict' was born in Hong Kong, then it is most likely that he began cigarette smoking in his early teens, and was gradually induced by drug-using friends to add heroin to the tip of his cigarette for greater stimulation. Physical dependence on heroin is rapid, and after a year or two he switched to 'chasing the dragon' to increase the effect, and now spends about HK$40 a day on heroin (Ch'ien, op. cit.).

The Central Registry of Drug Addicts' narcotics register system (Wu, op. cit.), when operational, is designed to identify trends in the nature of addiction and in the addict population over time; to describe and contrast the characteristics of addicts reported from specific sources; and to provide a data bank so that the addict's various contacts with the different agencies can be mapped. Such information, it was hoped, would provide a better basis for policy making than would an attempt to estimate the total addicted population.

CHINA

Just over a hundred years ago, in 1880, when the opium trade with China was at its height, as many as 4 per cent of the total population of three hundred million were addicted to the drug; and, whatever contemporary or retrospective accounts (e.g., Singer, *Br. J. Addiction*, 1974, 69:257–68) may say about the importance of ritual (including that of smoking opium) in the fabric of Chinese culture, the evidence of over one hundred medical missionaries at the time was that opium caused nothing but social problems, economic hardships, and a great drain on the country's resources (C. L. Park, 'Opinions of over 100 Physicians on the Use of Opium in China', Shanghai, 1899; cited in Gregory, *Drug Forum*, 1977–8, 6:235–47). In 1906 the Chinese government issued an edict to reduce the amount of land devoted to opium production, and to enforce registration of opium smokers and of opium shops. The 1911 revolution only temporarily shelved the progress of the campaign against opium; and, to quote Gregory (op. cit.), by 1917, China was free of opium for all practical purposes.

The political turmoils of the following years meant, however, that opium growing and trading became important sources of revenue for provincial leaders and, later, for Chiang Kai Shek's military campaigns, and Japan began smuggling in large amounts of opium during this period. By the 1930s it was estimated that one-tenth of the population of China, more than 40 million persons, were opium smokers (Fields and Tararin, *Br. J. Addiction*, 1970, 64:371–82). Clearly, such estimates have wide margins of error, but nonetheless they can indicate the extent of the problem. The Japanese occupation encouraged rather than interfered with the habit; and Fields and Tararin present an eye-witness account of opium addiction in Yunnan during this period, indicating the pervasiveness of the habit at all social levels. They also report that in Shanghai in 1945–6, after eight years of Japanese occupation, there was provision for every class of opium smoker: from lavishly furnished divans for the rich to crowded, filthy opium dens for the coolies.

Within six months of assuming power in 1949, the Communist government prohibited the private production, importation, and sale of opium and other narcotics. Illicit cultivation was, according to Solomon (*J. Psychedelic Drugs*, 1978, 10:43–9) almost entirely eliminated, and there was a strict limitation of licit cultivation.

The anti-opium campaign was closely linked with land reform, the first mass reform of the Revolution, and distribution of the land from landlords to the peasants was followed by their switching from the cash crop, opium, to food crops (Lowinger, *Am. J.*

Chinese Medicine, 1973, 1:275–82).

In terms of a rhetoric which is now familiarly identified with China, the anti-opium campaign spelled out that the import of opium into China was the imperialists' way of destroying the Chinese nation, and any previous anti-opium campaigns by earlier regimes were reinterpreted as a further spreading of the habit in collusion with the imperialists (Lowinger, op. cit.). Published estimates of the numbers involved in opium use after the Revolution are perhaps even less reliable than those before, but American monitoring services (cited in Lowinger) indicated rapidly diminishing numbers; travellers during the 1960s and 1970s reported that they saw no evidence of any addiction; and, most significantly, the proportion of refugees to Hong Kong who had been opium users in China dropped appreciably between 1949 and 1953. Interviews with refugees since then indicate that narcotic addiction is no longer a feature of Chinese life (Lowinger, op. cit.; Gregory, *Drug Forum*, 1977–8, 6:299–314).

There is, as the reader might expect, a polarization of literature about the Chinese response to the drug problem: as with everything else to do with contemporary China, there are those writers for whom China has discovered the solution that all the world should follow, and on the other hand there are strongly anti-Communist writers who claim that one cannot believe the propaganda which emanates from a still largely closed society. Neither group of writers can back their claims with the kind of statistics available for most other countries, and thus one must rely upon the more anecdotal or indirect sources of information mentioned above. However, as Gregory (*Drug Forum*, 1977–8, 6:299–314) indicates when summarizing the strongly anti-Communist writers' account of present-day drug abuse in China, the few verifiable facts in their articles appear to be inaccurate, and the tenor of their abuse is such as to leave one dubious of the rest of their argument.

One source of intelligence which might be seen as a credible witness to China's control of the opium problem is the United States Government Bureau of Narcotics. Hardly likely to take a starry-eyed view of China's progress, the Bureau reports during the 1960s indicated that there was no opium exported from China; and their report in 1971 on opium production indicated that, at 100 tons a year, it exactly matched China's estimated medical needs (Lowinger, op. cit.).

JAPAN

With a strong historical sense, writers on the recent pattern of drug abuse in Japan have divided up the post-war period into a series of clearly differentiated phases, with calm periods and drug abuse epidemics. Thus, Kumagai (*Med. J. Malaysia*, 1974, 29:136—44) talks of four periods: the calm period prior to 1945; the period 1946 to 1954, was the stimulants period; 1955 to 1962 was when heroin use was rampant; and the period of narcotic control from 1963. The same terminology is used by Ishii and Motohashi (*Addictive Diseases*, 1977, 105—14), who, writing later than Kumagai, saw that there was another stimulants phase, from 1970 onward, to be added to the chronicle, and that this rather different pattern of stimulants use has continued (*Far Eastern Economic Review*, 1 September 1978, pp. 20—1).

The Calm Period (prior to 1945)

According to the official account (*Drug Abuse and Counter-Measures in Japan*, Tokyo, Ministry of Health and Welfare, 1975), there were, before 1945, no substantial problems concerning narcotics or any other drugs within the country (although Japan's record abroad should be noted: see the sections describing drug abuse in China prior to 1949). There had been a narcotic treatment centre in Tokyo, catering for voluntary patients who, it is reported, were mainly foreign residents who were addicted to opium.

The Stimulants Period (mid-1946 to mid-1954)

Commercial advertising of stimulant drugs after World War II, using slogans such as 'Shake off sleepiness—become energetic', boosted the sales of such drugs to people needing to work long hours whilst they were in an impoverished condition. The dependence on stimulants was first evident amongst urban workers and students, but soon the drugs were being abused in farming and fishing villages. Abuse became prevalent throughout the country, and the government applied control measures to limit stimulants to strictly medical purposes.

The demand for stimulants was so great that clandestine laboratories found many customers, and there were considerable numbers of new addicts each year. To cope with the epidemic, the Stimulants Control Law was passed in 1951, and further amendments in 1954 and 1955 reinforced the penalties and regulations relating to stimulants. At the same time, by an amendment of the Mental Health Law, compulsory hospitalization of stimulant addicts was introduced.

These legal changes were backed up by a country-wide campaign to familiarize the general public with the medical dangers of stimulant abuse, and the combination produced a dramatic fall in the numbers of people involved with stimulants, if one can take the only firm statistics—those relating to arrests for drug offences—as a general guide. In 1955, 55,664 people were committed for trial on stimulants offences; by 1958, the corresponding figure was 271, and it remained at a low level for the next decade.

In the opinion of Shimomura (*Drug Enforcement*, 1975–6, 3:39–40), Japan was next 'threatened by a rise in the abuse of narcotics, especially heroin, but succeeded in suppressing it at this time'. Other commentators are less bland about what they term the heroin period (see Iishii and Motohashi; Kumagai, op. cit.).

The Heroin Period (mid-1955 to 1962)

Narcotics had in fact been abused since World War II in Japan, but came to be a major social problem as stimulant abuse declined. An estimated 40,000 heroin addicts (at the 1961 peak of the epidemic) were supplied their drug by illicit traffickers controlled by gangster bands. Many of those involved were young people in their twenties and thirties, and two rather different kinds of explanations for their drug use emerge from impressionistic studies done at the time. Some were indeed slum dwellers, unemployed, casually employed, or prostitutes. Many individuals gave as their reasons for use, however, not reasons of social or personal problem solving, but of curiosity, temptation, the influence of friends, and moving on from stimulants: reasons which do not necessarily link with social deprivation.

The Narcotics Control Period: The Period of Declining Drug Abuse (from 1963)

A fundamental amendment to the Narcotic Control Law stiffened the penalties for offenders (life sentences were introduced), and introduced compulsory hospitalization for narcotics addicts. Again a nation-wide campaign was mounted, this time to inform people specifically about the effects of heroin abuse; and again the combination of legal action, compulsory hospitalization for addicts, and preventative education and information campaigns brought the numbers of heroin addicts right down to the point where the various writers could document only tens rather than tens of thousands of addicts at the time of writing. (Most of these few live in Okinawa prefecture.) There was briefly a period when medicinal narcotic drugs were being diverted onto the illicit market, but stronger regulation of prescriptions, and general availability of the drugs eliminated that problem. Marijuana was also abused, but the use seemed to be experimental or recreational, and few writers make much of it.

The Stimulants Revival Period (from 1970)

In 1969 there had been only 704 offences involving the use of stimulants; by 1973 the corresponding figure was 8,510, and a second wave of stimulants abuse was well under way throughout the country. If the first stimulants period was attributed to the aimlessness and purposelessness of the Japanese people after the war, this second stimulants period has been characterized as being much more 'epicurean': the reasons users nowadays tend to cite include curiosity, to improve their sexual performance, and to feel good. In contrast to the first epidemic, when the illicit traffic was supplied by drugs diverted from internal production centres, this second epidemic has been fuelled by drugs smuggled in from South Korea, Taiwan, and from Europe via the Philippines (*Far Eastern Economic Review*, 1 September 1978, pp. 20—1). International co-operation to halt this traffic at source has been limited in its success, in part because Japan has in the past done little to help other countries in drugs control. Thus, for example, despite international requests, Japan has not controlled the export of acetic anhydride, and has become the major supplier to the world's heroin manufacturing.

Illicit trafficking of stimulants within Japan has been mainly in the hands of bands of gangsters, and the problem of enforcement, difficult in any country, is made more so in a country where the roots of the drug traffic lie deep in organized crime.

INDIA

Prior to the 1960s the problem of drug abuse in India was mainly confined to the older generation, whose main drugs were opium and cannabis. As in many other countries, the variety of drugs used increased during the late 1960s and early 1970s, as a much younger age group (many of whom were students) started to use cannabis, hypnotics, and sedatives (secobarbital and methaqualone), stimulants, and hallucinogens (L.S.D.). There were also reports of pethedine and morphine abuse, but this was almost confined to medical and para-medical personnel. Studies showed that, although the numbers of young people using drugs had increased rapidly, the number of hard core addicts was not significant (United Nations Commission on Narcotic Drugs, *Report on 27th Session*, 1977). An additional group of opiate users, not generally included in the official reports, are those who use the opium poppy heads, a practice apparently widespread among the youth of (at least) Jullundar, and now, as the inhabitants of the town migrated, also throughout the industrial midlands of England (Smith and Burnside, *Br. Medical J.*, 19 February 1972, pp. 480–1). Heroin has not posed any problem in India so far, and there are no known users of this drug (*Commonwealth Regional Working Group on Illicit Drugs,* Kuala Lumpur, 1979).

There are, as yet, no reliable data for the entire country on the numbers of patients in treatment who are drug abusers, let alone for the numbers of those using drugs in the general population. Wig and Varma (*Addictive Diseases*, 1977, 3:79–86) attempted to gain data on the patient population: their data cover 13 psychiatric centres in general hospitals around the country (out of a total of perhaps 60 to 70); but only one mental hospital responded to their survey. Opium users seem to be definitely older (over 40 years) than those abusing other drugs (20 to 40 years old). Males were found to be in the large majority, except in the case of Mandrax, where female abusers are almost as frequently noted as males.

In the experience of these hospitals, there were more abusers of alcohol coming for treatment than abusers of all other drugs combined. Alcohol abuse is reportedly fairly widespread, but most of those who seek treatment do so in the west and south of India; and the other drugs also show some regional patterns. Patients with opium abuse problems were reported mainly by hospitals in their northern Indian sample, whereas those abusing cannabis are mainly reported from the south and east (Wig and Varma, op. cit.). Within each region of the country, drug abuse is noticeably higher in cities and industrialized areas (Chopra, *Int. J. of Addictions*, 1972, 7:57–63).

Two surveys, one of an urban and one of a rural area, enable one to make some assessment of relative rates, although, given their approaches, they cannot be taken as strictly comparable. The urban study was conducted as a house-to-house survey of the Agra region, by Dubé and Handa (*Br. J. Psychiatry*, 1971, 118:345–6); and the rural study took five communities in the Hoogly district of West Bengal (Elnagar, Maitra and Rao, *Br. J. Psychiatry*, 1971, 118:499–503). In the rural communities, 1,383 adults were surveyed, of whom 15 were alcohol and 3 opium 'addicts', whose only withdrawal symptoms were reported to be weakness and lack of energy to work. In Agra, 16,725 adults were surveyed, of whom 227 were regular alcohol users, 75 used either bhang or *ganja*, and 80 were poly-drug users. The percentages involved are small, and thus the comparison of urban and rural rates in these studies must be made with caution.

Dubé and Handa report that the prevalence of mental illness in their sample showed some differences between users and non-users of drugs: whereas the general level of mental morbidity in the non-using population was 3.6 per cent, it was 6.8 per cent among the drug users; with the use of more than one intoxicant being highest amongst the mentally ill, followed by bhang; alcohol was the least common pattern among this subgroup.

Several recent surveys have estimated the prevalence of drug abuse among younger age-groups in India; and here self-reported drug use is strikingly higher than in the adult urban and rural populations of the earlier studies. Thus, for example, Dubé *et al.* (*Acta Psych. Scand.*, 1978, 57:336—56) report a 50 per cent overall prevalence rate of drug use amongst the 1,192 post-graduate students of their (largely urban) university sample. They found that 61 per cent of males, but only 19 per cent of females, had drug experience, with medical students having significantly higher rates than non-medical. Male students preferred to use alcohol and bhang, while females preferred meprobromate and alcohol. If, as is conventional in drug-dependency research outside India, one considers alcohol use separately from the use of other drugs, then the rate of drug usage reported by the student sample drops considerably. Again, in Varma and Dang's study (*Indian J. Psychiatr.*, 1978, 20: 318—23) of 570 schoolchildren and students aged between 10 and 24 years old (a very wide age range indeed), alcohol was the main drug of preference (21.6 per cent had experienced it), with tobacco the next most frequently experienced (12.1 per cent), although only just over 4 per cent were still currently using tobacco, and a similar percentage currently used alcohol. There was a negligible current use of any other drugs, although a few students admitted to some brief experience with amphetamines, cannabis, sedatives, or tranquillizers. This low level of continued usage is borne out by five further student surveys briefly reported in this paper.

Surveys conducted on the pattern of drug abuse in India are variable in quality, and there are some differences in reported prevalence rates, which are probably attributable to sampling or definitional defects. To sum up, one can follow Wig and Varma (*Addictive Diseases*, 1977, 3:79—86) in ·combining survey and impressionistic data to estimate that in India:

Opium is regularly used by 2 to 3 per cent of adult males in the rural north; some use of codeine; but heroin use is very uncommon.

Morphine and pethedine: 0.25 per cent of the population, mainly medical and para-medical personnel.

Barbiturates: increasingly used as a cheap substitute for alcohol; but severe dependence is relatively rare.

Amphetamines: the single largest drug problem among students, who use these drugs to help them in their studies.

Mandrax: increasingly used among urban youth.

Cannabis: bhang drinking is a well established social (and often religious) custom in many parts of east India (5 to 10 per cent in many religious cities). *Ganja* smoking is widespread in Uttar Pradesh and Bihar among cultivators and unskilled workers. *Charas* smokers are somewhat more likely to seek treatment. (Cannabis use in ceremonies of the Hindu god, Siva, is described by Hasan, 'Social Aspects of the Use of Cannabis in India', in *Cannabis and Culture*, V. Rubin (ed.), Mouton, 1975; the drug, in its various forms, is offered to the god on Shivaratri day as being 'foods of the god'. Because of this religious association, these drugs were not traditionally proscribed, although alcohol is abhorred. In particular, Bhagats, devotees, and holy men are free to use cannabis, although they are forbidden to take alcohol, and their use tends to be moderate and sociable. See also Fisher, 'Cannabis in Nepal', in Rubin, op. cit.).

PAKISTAN

Pakistan's drug problem varies widely from area to area, as far as it is possible to say for a country where there are only localized surveys of drug abuse. All sources of information, however, indicate that the pattern and extent of drug abuse is as diverse as the country itself. There is some evidence that some rural areas are virtually free of drug abuse, whilst in other localities (both urban and rural), there appears to be a very high prevalence. Kuria, in Buner, and Gilgit, amongst the rural areas, and Lyari and Karachi among the urban areas, have particularly high rates: 50 to 75 per cent of the male population of these areas have been estimated to be drug users (*World Health Organization Project Report*, 1978). The most common type of abuse, taking the country as a whole, is the smoking of cannabis resin prepared as *charas*. The second-rating substance is opium, either eaten or, in some areas, smoked. Poly-drug use is reportedly on the increase in the urban areas, and involves locally manufactured (illicit) morphine, barbiturates, Mandrax and other synthetic sedatives and tranquillizers, and to some extent, alcohol (McGlothin, Mubbashar, Shafique, and Hughes, *Opium Use in Pakistan*, WHO, 1976).

At the time of the first Colombo Plan Workshop on the Prevention and Control of Drug Abuse (Rawalpindi, 1975), there was very little systematic evidence on the extent of the drug problem in Pakistan; since then, the Pakistan Narcotics Control Board has published a series of studies on the North-West Frontier Province and other regions; a number of studies have been conducted on hospitalized drug-dependent populations; and, more recently, under the auspices of WHO and UNDND, there have been some small-scale epidemiological surveys. Thus, for example, Ijaz Haider, of the Government Mental Hospital in Lahore, has published an analysis of the drugs of preference amongst dependent patients at the hospital. (Whilst total admissions to the hospital remained relatively stable over the eight-year study period, 1968–75, the percentage who were addicts rose from 2.6 per cent to 18.9 per cent.) Here, as nationally, *charas* was the commonest drug reported, typically being used by an individual in his twenties, with opiates (including injected pethedine and morphine) as the next most frequently abused group, followed by amphetamines and barbiturates (Ijaz Haider, *Colombo Plan Workshop*, Rawalpindi, 1975).

The most recent centre-by-centre survey of drug abuse patterns in Pakistan has been conducted by the UNFDAC with the Pakistan Narcotics Control Board (various mimeographed reports, unpublished, 1977–80). To summarize: in Hyderabad the majority of patients were *charas* smokers, with a further quarter who were opium users, and a few who were Mandrax, pethedine, or amphetamine users. Rawalpindi has a majority of patients who are poly-drug users, and this pattern is also common in Peshawar, where, closer to the production areas, opium abuse is more common than *charas*. Quetta, in Baluchistan, also has a large proportion of its drug-dependent patients who are opium users.

Note that, in each area, the surveys report the pattern of abuse amongst those who eventually find their way to hospitals or clinics, and this may well be a very selective group from amongst the drug-abusing population in a particular area. (As Ijaz Haider, op. cit., states, typically patients are only brought to hospital when they become a problem to the community, when their behaviour, for example, becomes disturbing, or when they become unable to do their work; and thus many *charas* smokers may well remain outside this method of sampling for a long period.) Yet such surveys may well be of value in comparing the effects upon the patterns of abuse, and the policies of the various States and Provinces on the control and licensing of drugs. Lahore, for example, introduced a registration and rationing scheme for opium addicts early in 1979; Baluchistan had by then already been operating a similar scheme for two years. Some provinces have strictly regulated, and others even banned, the licit use of pethedine, morphine, and codeine in order to prevent the diversion of these drugs into the illicit market. (Illicit trading of these drugs, however, continues.)

A major source of other pharmaceuticals which can be abused is the multitude of chemist's shops, medical halls, and pharmacies, ranging in size from simple bazaar shops to large stores in the larger cities. Although medical prescriptions are officially required to purchase such items as hypnotics, sedatives, stimulants, syrups, and tinctures, it is clear that the system is lax, and that prescribing practice allows a considerable amount of drugs to be diverted. (Mandrax, in particular, is reported as one of the most worrying cases of overprescription in many areas.) One of the effects of this situation is that the non-medical use of psychotropic drugs is no longer confined to the affluent but is rapidly penetrating all other strata of society.

The Pakistan Narcotics Control Board has sponsored a series of social surveys on the subject of drug dependence in North-West Frontier Province (*A Survey of Opium Smoking in North-West Frontier Province*, 1975; *Socio-economic survey of Buner (Swat)*, 1975; and *The New Hazard: A Study of Abuse of Psychotropic Substances in the NWFP*, Islamabad, 1977). Thus, from being one of the least known and least well documented areas of the country, North-West Frontier Province and in particular the Buner district of Swat, have become well studied to the point that we now have a comprehensive picture of the abuse of opium and psychotropic drugs in both rural and urban North-West Frontier Province. Opium and cannabis have been shown to be the two major (and traditional) drugs of abuse, but the abuse of psychotropic substances has been growing rapidly.

Buner is a relatively isolated and poor agricultural area: although there are many physical resources, the average per capita income is less than one-third of the average for Pakistan as a whole (even when one includes in the calculation the value of agricultural produce consumed domestically). Despite such low income levels, the populace is given to spending lavishly on ceremonies, and, under the heavy loan burdens incurred, the incentive to grow the most profitable cash crop—opium—is obvious. Yet, in spite of extensive cultivation of the poppy, the percentage of addiction among the population is negligible. In fact, only in one village, Kuria, is there addiction to opium, and throughout the area there is widespread condemnation of opium use, which the survey team thought augured well for any anti-narcotics campaign in the area. Nevertheless, although addiction was localized, it was felt that the situation was sufficiently threatening to warrant urgent action; and, indeed, since the survey was done, crop substitution projects and a treatment and rehabilitation centre have been started in Buner. (See the section on treatment and rehabilitation in Pakistan.)

The Pakistan Narcotics Control Board study of the abuse of psychotropic substances in Peshawar identified 1,007 individuals who were dependent upon opiates, barbiturates, stimulants, hallucinogens, or tranquillizers (Pakistan Narcotics Control Board, *The New Hazard*, Islamabad, 1977), of whom over 90 per cent use either Seconal or Mandrax or both. Abuse of cheap drugs was overwhelmingly evident, with the typical drug of initiation being *charas*, opium, or liquor; and migration to Seconal or Mandrax might come only after some considerable single drug use. Nearly one-quarter were now using a combination of drugs with different effects—mind-deadening Seconal with mind-altering *charas*, for example.

The majority (76 per cent) of drug abusers in the survey were over 21 years of age (including 24 per cent who were in their thirties); and the majority, although regular users of drugs, take a small dosage. Few students at the local university (1.44 per cent of the total student population) were users of psychotropic drugs. A further 4.8 per cent are *charas* users.

One of the least documented aspects of past and present opium consumption in Pakistan is the amount which is dispensed by the Hakims, the 68,000 registered local practitioners of traditional medicine. McGlothin *et al.* (op. cit.) concluded that the Hakims were probably *not* a significant source of addiction: very few respondents in the various surveys mention becoming addicted through a Hakim's treatment, although many traced their dependence back to self-medication.

Opium has been sold through opium vends (licensed shops) for nearly a century. When Pakistan signed the Single Convention on Narcotics, the government attempted to minimize the production and sale of opium via a multi-agency control programme. The pilot opium rationing schemes were developed in Sialkot and Jhelum; and in February 1979 the government introduced the Prohibition (Enforcement of Hadd) Order, 1979, which put a complete ban upon the sale, consumption, etc., of all intoxicants including opium. The promulgation of this law, without any alternative intervention measures, is likely to produce profound changes in the pattern of drug abuse in the country. The immediate consequence was that, in the first 4 to 6 weeks of the law's existence, large numbers of drug abusers came forward for treatment, but the numbers were too great for the system to cope with, and the illegal market, it was presumed, would expand to cater for their needs. Noteworthy were the differences in response to the law between the urban and the rural producing areas. The urban hospitals experienced a great surge in numbers after the promulgation, whereas the Peshawar hospital in the North-West Frontier Province showed no such trend.

In the longer term, drug abuse in Pakistan may follow the trend documented by Westermeyer (*Archiv. Gen. Psychiatry*, 1976, 33:1135—9) in Hong Kong in the 1950s, Thailand in the 1960s, and Laos in the 1970s. In the 1980s, Pakistan may well find that the enactment of anti-opium laws has opened the way for a criminalized traffic in heroin, as has happened in those other countries where the legal position of opium was changed.

The opium vend system of licensing opium use had been inherited by Pakistan at Independence, having been the practice throughout the whole of undivided India. Private individuals were licensed as vendors, the licensing going to the highest bidders in annual auctions. Competition for the licences drove the auction prices so high that the licensed vendors came to use the vend as a sale point for illicitly obtained opium, in addition to the legal, excise opium.

The effect of the system in the urban and other non-producing areas was to concentrate the sale of intoxicants at the vends, and because individuals became regular customers, it was possible to identify and know the addict population. The existence of a commercial system meant that illicit trafficking was virtually eliminated from these areas.

Some of the advantages of the vend system were retained, and some of its obvious disadvantages were removed, by the scheme of rationing that had been introduced as a pilot project in Sialkot and Jhelum districts prior to the 1979 Order banning all opium use. The rationing scheme worked thus: in place of the licensed vends selling opium in cake form, Government Opium Rationing Depots, run by private individuals on a commission basis, would dispense set numbers of strip-packed opium tablets to addicts who were registered with the district Excise Office. Three thousand opium users had been registered in Sialkot, and about a thousand in Jhelum—very close to the estimated numbers of addicts in the areas; and the government of Punjab was about to extend the scheme to other districts when the whole campaign had to be abandoned because of the Prohibition (Enforcement of Hadd) Order, 1979.

Although the rationing system was not of itself a medical maintenance programme, it did bring the registered addict to the attention of medical and social welfare workers, and thus increased the likelihood of treatment and rehabilitation. So far, this cannot be said for the system of supply of opium to addicts via the hospitals, which was evolving after the promulgation of the Order; because many addicts were experiencing severe and dangerous withdrawal symptoms as a result of the total cessation of supplies, hospitals were authorized to use their discretion in issuing opium tablets against prescriptions. However, at the time of writing, it is felt that the numbers of addicts so registered falls short of the estimated total in the country, and it is suspected that many of them have now become customers of illicit suppliers of opium—or heroin.

SRI LANKA

There have been no national studies of the pattern of drug abuse in Sri Lanka, and the published reports either describe specific hospitalized populations or give a general picture unsupported by detailed statistics.

Opium has always been a major commodity in the two-way illicit traffic between Tamil Nadu and Sri Lanka and it has been estimated that roughly five tons of opium is annually smuggled in via this route (Sundaralingam, *Colombo Plan Meeting on Narcotics and Drug Abuse Problems*, Colombo, 1973). Forty opium divans were reported as operating in Colombo, providing opium mainly to lower income individuals as well as to some hippies and foreign sailors. Consumption is via hookah pipes, opium cigars or cigarettes, and in liquid form diluted with coffee or tea. In 1978 it was estimated that there were about 15,000 opium addicts in Colombo and the suburbs (Satkunayagam, *Colombo Plan Workshop*, Penang, 1978).

Cannabis has been used in Sri Lanka from time immemorial in Ayurvedic medicine, for religious purposes, and as a euphoriant. Cultivation of cannabis is widespread in the country, and it has been estimated that about 3,000 people are engaged in its illicit cultivation in the 'Ganja Belt'. Various *ganja* dens exist in Colombo, and in the suburbs, and as cultivation increased the drug became considerably cheaper. Sundaralingam (op. cit.) estimates that a pound of *ganja* in the early 1960s would have cost Rs. 300; ten years later the same amount could have been purchased for Rs. 30.

In 1973, there was no indication that large numbers of young people in Sri Lanka were taking opium, or that it had become a problem in the university, but clearly there was more youthful involvement than there had previously been.

Ayurvedic drugs were considered by Pilapitiya (*Colombo Plan Meeting*, Colombo, 1973, p. 55) not to be narcotic, because compared with the other ingredients the quantity of opium used was negligible. He gave as an example the manufacture of *Buddharaja Kalke*: 75 herbs and other items are used, along with opium, which would represent only about five to eight grains in a pound of prepared drug.

At the time of the 1973 Conference, the participants could only speculate on the numbers involved in drug abuse, their reasons for use, and whether or not, as some participants believed, particular communities had affinities with particular drugs. By the 1978 Penang Conference, Satkunayagam was in no better position, although he could cite the numbers of addicts being treated in two hospitals providing a programme. Very few addicts came to the hospital until a press campaign and police, and customs enforcement activities increased the price of opium. Of these patients, two-thirds were over 50 years of age, with the oldest being 85 years old, and most had a history of drug use of twenty years or more. Only two had an age of first use of less than 21 years. Many had first taken opium for quasi-medical reasons. Fifty per cent denied taking any other drug, and the remainder admitted taking alcohol or *ganja* as well.

Interesting as this hospital population may be, it clearly represents those who found coping with the temporary opium shortage most difficult, and in no way may be presumed to be representative of the pattern of drug use in the country. (Thus, for example, not a single *ganja*-only user has presented himself for treatment, although it is known that the drug is used widely in the community.)

BANGLADESH

According to the Bangladesh Country Report to the Commonwealth Regional Working Group on Illicit Drugs (Kuala Lumpur, 1979), only cannabis and opium, among the traditional narcotic drugs, pose a problem. It is claimed that the consumption of opium has been severely restricted, and that there is no cultivation of the opium poppy within the country. The scheme of compulsory registration has identified about 1,600 chronic opium addicts, and official estimates are that it will take until about 1984 to end this pattern at the present rate of progress.

The cultivation of cannabis is permitted under full governmental supervision, in a compact growing area of about 100 acres, and the sale of cannabis is conducted through approved retail licence shops. There is no requirement that cannabis users should register, although there is a restriction on the quantity an individual may purchase or possess. The view is taken that, as the smoking of cannabis (*ganja*) is traditional in society the habit cannot be changed overnight. As a signatory of the Single Convention on Narcotic Drugs, Bangladesh is seriously contemplating the complete abolition of the cultivation of cannabis under licence, and its non-medical use thereafter. The intention is that this would be done gradually, so as to avoid other drug problems emerging.

There is some evidence to suggest that the traditional user groups have been joined by a youthful group of drug users. Formerly the users tended to be older people from the lower strata of society, but recently *ganja* has become popular with the younger generation.

So far, no country-wide surveys exist to assess the extent of the drug use pattern in the country, but a Colombo Plan Workshop is planned to be held at the time of writing.

BURMA

The main drug of abuse in Burma is opium, particularly in those areas where the opium poppy is being illegally grown, and changes in the pattern can be expected as a consequence of vigorous governmental action against cultivation and transport of the drug, and of the crop substitution programmes. Heroin use is now on the increase, particularly in the largest cities, Rangoon and Mandalay; this may be due partly to tourists (Ne Win, *Addictive Diseases*, 1977, 3:87–8). Marijuana and methaqualone (MX) have been reported as being used by some schoolchildren in senior classes, but L.S.D. and glue sniffing have not been noted. The use of cocaine has been practised by the rich, but with a negligible incidence (Ne Win, op. cit.).

Although there is a compulsory registration scheme for persons dependent on narcotic drugs, the numbers actually registered, and the proportion these represent of the total user population, vary widely in the published reports. Thus, whilst Ne Win, in 1977, states that 1,300 persons had registered by this date, and that there were approximately ten times this number of drug dependent individuals in the country, the *Far Eastern Economic Review* estimate in 1979 (16 February, p. 31) was that Burma had about 30,000 registered drug addicts, more than 80 per cent of whom were students.

CONCLUSIONS

The pattern of drug use in a country at any one point in time is affected by a range of factors: drug availability will be determined by, amongst others, commercial and legal factors, and the activities of particular drug rings; and demand may well be shaped by changes in, for example, the youth culture. Thus, whilst the general picture of a worsening-to-epidemic situation, with the diversification of substances, and the increased involvement of youth, is repeated in the recent history of country after country, the particular details of the pattern, the timing of epidemics, the substances available, etc., are in many cases closely relatable to particular events or factors. Recall, for example, the case of heavy advertising of stimulants in Japan after World War II; the very active anti-opium campaigns in Hong Kong, Thailand, and Laos, with the rapid development of a heroin market consequent upon the elimination of opium supplies; and on the sudden appearance and then disappearance of Rohypnol abuse during Singapore's Operation Ferret. The various control measures, too, are clearly having their effect upon the patterns of drug abuse: the very strict denial of all or some supplies, as in China and the Philippines, and the active rehabilitation and preventative education programmes, as in the case of Hong Kong's youth population.

The particular balance of factors in each country thus makes each country in many ways unique, and it is therefore possible to make only the broadest summary about the changing pattern of drug abuse in East Asia. One observation which can be made about many countries in the region is that, where there had been separate patterns of abuse characteristic of the different ethnic groups in a plural society, this is less and less true of the new, younger group of drug users. As was noted in Chapter I, opium use during the nineteenth and early twentieth century had been predominantly found in the overseas Chinese populations of South-East Asia; now, factors other than ethnicity are the indicators as to which of the youthful population are most at risk, although there may still be some ethnicities overrepresented in the older generation, who are the tail-end of the earlier pattern. Again, most countries in the region have witnessed the increasing involvement of girls in drug use: a marked contrast to the earlier, almost exclusively, male pattern. Similarly, there have been recent indications that initiation into drug use has been earlier, and experimentation has been wider: worrying signs among the younger adolescent age-group. However, as various surveys have shown, much of this early experience *is* experimental and likely to be short-lived, and this has implications for how society should treat the phenomenon.

Drug abuse has not yet become as widespread (and even normative) among college youth in East Asia as it has in America, with the possible exception of some colleges in India and in the Philippines. Several accounts mentioned earlier in the chapter lay stress on urban street-corner society as the origin of much of youthful drug abuse (for instance, accounts of the Philippines and of Thailand): yet the broader-scale Malaysian surveys found levels of drug use among rural youth to be comparable to that in urban areas. Perhaps, then, the concentration of some writers on an 'urban problem' is misleading: urban drug use may be more visible and more publicized, but it seems unlikely that in countries with good communications the problem would not have moved outward to the rural areas.

'Traditional patterns' of narcotic drug abuse have largely disappeared from much of the South-East Asian part of the region, but they remain in the opium producing areas of Burma, Thailand, and perhaps Laos, as well as in the North-West Frontier Province of Pakistan. The continuing tradition of cannabis production and consumption has received much less mention in the present chapter, largely because the major concern of the literature cited has been upon the opiates and other drugs. The collection and use of *kratom* leaves in Thailand has attracted some local attention, but the use of betel, locally produced and widely consumed in many countries, has received little or no mention in the literature: unlike the early European writers, whose disgust at the practice has been mentioned, contemporary writers on drugs used in the region seem to feel that the drug's effects are such as not to warrant a mention.

The Indian subcontinent represents a combination of the traditional patterns of cannabis and opium use, with, superimposed, the international youth pattern, involving a diversity of drugs. Heroin had not, at the time of writing, posed a problem in India, Pakistan, Bangladesh, or Sri Lanka, but we have recorded the fear that the introduction of strict anti-opium measures in Pakistan would lead to the traditional pattern's rapid replacement by the heroin pattern as in South-East Asia.

One cannot, however, make confident predictions on the basis of past trends: as stated at the outset, the pattern of drug use in a country is the resultant of many forces. However, one trend which has been noted recently in a number of countries is the poly-drug use of pharmaceuticals by the young drug users. Which substances are preferred seems to be much influenced by transient fashions in youth culture (as well as of availability): in Malaysia it was noted that younger and older adolescent drug users seemed to belong to somewhat different subcultures; and the situation appears to have reached its most diverse state in the Philippines, where one recent paper (Zarco and Almonte, op. cit.) lists scores of synthetic products which have been abused by the samples they studied.

III

The Adult Drug User

WHY do people begin to use illegal drugs? How far do these reasons remain important in maintaining the habit; or does continuance depend largely upon a new set of reasons? One approach that the researcher can take is to ask the users directly, and, by comparing their answers, to see the relative weight given to different possible reasons. Thus, some studies report a rank-ordering of reasons given by casual and by regular drug users. However, individuals do not necessarily see the whole pattern of forces acting upon their behaviour. They may be aware of the proximate causes—for example, they may report the influence and example of their friends, or their overwhelming problems—but they are much less likely to perceive, or at least mention, the background factors which increase their being 'at risk': many adults experience stresses, but only some respond to it by resorting to drug use. Thus, in addition to using direct questions, a second approach to the explanation of an individual's drug use concentrates upon background variables. These might include his social class of origin, present status, degree of health, and of satisfaction, and his social relations. However, the reader will see that underlying such a list of potential 'predisposing factors' there is a hypothesis about the nature and causation of drug use, namely, that it is to be seen as an aberrant behaviour brought on by circumstances or personal problems, or, alternatively, a coping strategy for such states. It is possible also to see drug use as being normative and, more simply, instrumental in some societies (just as, in the next chapter, we shall argue that it has become normative within some youth groups to smoke tobacco and cannabis): thus, in some traditional societies, opium is used socially, and is used in predictable situations by many adult members of a village; and in others, cannabis is used in religious rituals. In such cases, clearly, the explanations for an individual's use of these drugs lie at cultural rather than individual level. Other culturally sanctioned uses of drugs include various medical and quasi-medical purposes. Some of these involve the direct use of a drug to alleviate symptoms, or the taking of compounds which include the drug: for example, traditional preparations such as are used in the Ayurvedic system, and a range of modern pharmaceuticals. The Thai hill tribes' use of opium illustrates such patterns of usage; and, as we shall argue in the concluding chapter, any anti-drug campaign must examine the functions a drug performs in society. Where, as for the hill tribes, health care provision is meagre or lacking, opium provides a mainstay of local self-medication.

In such traditional societies, problems of drug *dependence* arise as individuals drift from occasional social or medical use to a frequency of use which sets up dependence: a commonly reported history is of a chronic illness being the occasion for use of opium over a long period, during which the individual becomes dependent upon the drug. Other individuals in the society may maintain an occasional non-dependent usage throughout adult life (Westermeyer, *Am. J. Psychiatry*, 1974, 131:165—70). This may be contrasted with many case studies of users of heroin and other drugs in non-traditional societies, where there is often a rapid translation to dependent status. (See, for example, Holzner and Ding, *Int. J. Addiction*, 1973, 8:253—63.)

How far an individual who is using drugs regularly can remain within society, retaining his job, maintaining his family relationships, and not experiencing disenabling psychological or physical symptoms clearly varies from case to case. However, the proportion of regular users in East Asia who do remain within society would surprise the observer who took Western drug dependants as his point of reference. Many dependants in America and Europe present themselves for treatment because they cannot function in society, or because they cannot cope with the psychological or physical effects of their drugs. The evidence seems to be that in East Asia, a larger proportion of those coming to treatment do so because they cannot afford supplies, or, in some countries where a successful denial operation has been mounted, cannot obtain supplies. The motivation for seeking treatment and for rehabilitation may in such cases be rather superficial: a point taken up in the chapter below on treatment and rehabilitation.

In the present chapter, the general social unacceptability of drug use is mentioned as one of the limiting factors; and in the next chapter, we shall see that adolescents often report that fear of parental disapproval had either curbed or entirely suppressed their possible use of drugs. Adults, too, are subject to powerful social pressures, from spouse and family, colleagues and acquaintances, as well as more generally from 'public opinion'; and becoming a regular drug user may lead to the individual's being cut off from those who could most effectively help him back, throwing him instead upon the society of fellow drug users and small-time pushers. Such a society of fellow users may be somewhat supportive, but there seems no evidence that there exists within it anything which positively encourages the use of drugs. Alternative views on society are commonly expressed by many drug users in America and Europe; but in East Asia, there is little evidence of a drug-using counter-culture.

Most of the research to be presented in this chapter concerns the characteristics which in general differentiate drug user from non-user. A topic accorded virtually no attention in the published research is the choice of particular drug types by particular users. One could posit a number of possible external factors: the general availability of the drug, specific commercial pressures and example of friends, etc.; and a number of personal reasons, most important of which would be attitudes towards and beliefs about the effects of the available substances. Only a few writers have speculated about the cultural roots of preferences for one or other drug substance; and here, it is the whole cultural pattern which is invoked, rather than individual preferences. Yet, even if such broad trends can be presented (for example, the contrasted attitudes of the Chinese toward alcohol and narcotics), nonetheless, there is considerable individual variation in preferences within a community.

The present chapter describes, country by country, what is known about the characteristics, background, and motivations of the adult drug user. (As has already been stressed, the information is more readily available in some countries than in others.)

MALAYSIA

The adult drug user who comes to the attention of the various agencies in Malaysia is almost certainly an opiate user. As has been described in the section on patterns of drug abuse in Malaysia, opium use has very largely given way to the use of heroin and morphine during the 1960s and 1970s; and the typical adult user is no longer the opium-den frequenting elderly Chinese reported all over South-East Asia up till the mid-twentieth century. The increasing involvement of Indians and, more recently, Malays in opiate use has been reported above, and has occurred at a time when youthful involvement in drug abuse generally has been growing. Many social commentators in Malaysia and beyond have explained the changing pattern in terms of rapid social and economic changes occurring in the country during this period (Tan and Haq, *Med. J. Malaysia*, 1974, 29:126—30; Parameshvara Deva, *Med. J. Malaysia*, 1978, 32:249—54). A different approach can be taken by considering the personal and social histories of individual drug abusers, and this has been done in a pair of studies from Universiti Sains Malaysia (Navaratnam and Spencer, *Bull. Narc.*, 1978, 30:1—7; Navaratnam and Spencer, *The Drug User and the Law*, Centre for Policy Research, Universiti Sains Malaysia, 1977). The first study examined the social and personal characteristics of drug dependants volunteering for hospital treatment; and the second examined equivalent variables among drug offenders before the courts and in prison. Both studies took as samples the total population of the institutions over the study period, and although each group clearly has its own characteristic reasons for coming into contact with the agency one can begin to depict the characteristics of the regular adult drug user in Malaysia.

The majority of drug dependant patients seen at the hospital were young adults (over 70 per cent of the group were aged between 21 and 35), but nearly 50 per cent of the total had commenced their drug habit between the ages of 10 and 20. The largest single group were manual workers (35 per cent), with, as next largest, shopkeepers or shop assistants (22 per cent). Most of these were working in coffee shops, which are known to be a major source of drug supplies. The unemployed formed the third largest category (19 per cent), with skilled workers, professional/managerial staff, and the retired making up the remaining 14.5 per cent, 3 per cent, and 2 per cent respectively. (The reader will perhaps appreciate that a hospital-based sample is likely to underestimate involvement with drugs by professional and managerial people, who are most likely to consult private medical practitioners.)

Unemployment and underemployment may either be seen as cause or as consequence of the use of drugs. Nearly 15 per cent of the respondents in the hospital survey had been dismissed from their job as a result of their drug habit; and where a comparison was made between the occupational status of the individual with that of his father, it was found that among the sample there were many who were downwardly mobile: a striking finding in a country where economic growth has made intergenerational upward mobility normative.

The prison population (in Navaratnam and Spencer, 1977, op. cit.) had as its largest single group the 20- to 24-year age-group, with two-thirds of the prison population being under 30. Manual workers comprised 36 per cent of the total imprisoned drug offender population, with skilled workers contributing a further 26 per cent to the total. There were 9.5 per cent of the population who reported that they had been unemployed at the time of conviction, and a further 21 per cent, who gave no details of employment to the interviewers, may well include many further unemployed individuals. Very few professional and managerial status individuals were imprisoned for their drug habit, but 6 per cent of the sample had *fathers* who were of such professional or managerial status. Of the remainder, manual and skilled workers' sons were equally common, and only 1.5 per cent of prisoners came from families where the father was unemployed.

The majority of the prison sample had received at least a primary school education, but fewer than 10 per cent had upper secondary education, and only one individual had any tertiary education. Almost invariably, prisoners had received as much education as their parents had done, and in many cases more; the same was true of the hospital sample, and indeed would be true of any randomly drawn group of adult Malaysians. There were somewhat more hospital patients who had upper secondary education (18 per cent), and fewer who had no formal education at all (4.5 per cent as opposed to 8 per cent of the prison sample).

Very few individuals in either sample had signs of any previous pathologies, although in both samples about 10 per cent had someone in their family who themselves had a history of drug abuse. This percentage is presumably much higher than would be found in a control sample of similar-aged individuals; and yet it means that 90 per cent of drug dependants in hospital or prison had no family contacts which could explain their own drug habit.

In contrast, the friends of drug dependants emerged as one of the major influences upon their habit. Virtually no drug offenders would appear to be isolates, knowing no other users, but a sizeable minority (25 per cent) know only one, two, or three other users. At the opposite end of the scale, 28 per cent claimed to know more than nine other users.

Although a combination of several reasons may prompt any particular individual into using drugs, the influence of friends must rate very high in most cases. Thus, in the prison and hospital samples, the most frequently given single reason for initiation was the influence and example of friends (53 per cent), of prisoners and of patients (47 per cent). Drug use for pleasure was mentioned by 24 per cent of prisoners and 17 per cent of patients. Patients were more likely than prisoners to cite problems as their reason for starting drug use, but not too much significance should be attached to the small differences between the samples in their memories of why they started drug experimentation.

The samples were, however, interestingly different in the reasons they gave for continuing to use drugs. Continuance was frequently associated with the pleasure that drugs brought by the prison sample (46 per cent); but, not surprisingly, only half as many of the patients (23 per cent) mentioned such a reason. These individuals, who were after all seeking treatment (as opposed to the prisoners, whose drug habit had been terminated less voluntarily), tended to mention the experience or fear of withdrawal symptoms as the most important factor in continuing to use drugs (35 per cent as against 26 per cent of prisoners), followed by the alleviation of mental stress or financial problems. The patients tended to play down the role of friends in their continuing to use drugs: only 8 per cent mentioned this reason, compared to 23 per cent of prisoners.

Further evidence on the great importance of the social network to the initiation of the drug habit was given by the dependants when they discussed how they had gained information about drugs in the first place. Eighty-five per cent cited friends as their source of knowledge, with 20 per cent considering that their own enquiries had made a major contribution. The role of the pusher who was not also an acquaintance was very small: only 4 per cent mentioned such a figure, and only 1 per cent mentioned a family member. Drug use took place equally commonly at home and at public events: a quarter of the sample reported that they used drugs at some meeting between friends, with a further 14 per cent specifying friends' homes or parties. Work (14 per cent) and night clubs (4 per cent) were much less important venues for drug use, although it is again necessary to stress that these may well be more important venues for experimental or casual users.

Three-quarters of the prisoners had at one time or another made an attempt to stop using drugs; and all the hospital sample were there as voluntary patients. Many, indeed, recorded repeated efforts to stop.

However, there was little evidence that the majority of respondents in either sample had strong motivations to seek treatment. Forty per cent of the hospital patients and 34 per cent of prisoners gave as their sole reason the increasing cost of drugs: a reason which indicates little more than an appeal to tide the individual over until his financial situation improves. More hopeful for chances of rehabilitation were some of the other reasons given: 33 per cent of prisoners were afraid that continued drug use would shorten their lives (as against only 10 per cent of patients mentioning health reasons), and the remainder reported pressures or encouragement from family and friends. Very few individuals indeed mentioned

lack of availability of the drug substance as their reason for seeking or wanting treatment.

Given the reported frequency of use, it is entirely credible that
the financial pressure of the habit was indeed the foremost reason
for wishing to stop: the average frequency of use among drug offenders had been between four and five times a day, and their
reported daily expenditure upon drugs at such a rate was clearly
outstripping their capacity to finance their habit.

The picture which one gains of the adult drug abuser when one
interviews hospital patients or drug offenders is of regular, generally
heavy, users who have been using drugs for some length of time.
Clearly, the reasons which bring a drug user to seek hospital treatment, or to the attention of the police, indicate that he is likely to
be somewhat unrepresentative of the adult drug user population as
a whole: this latter population will include many with less extensive
and less dependent use of drugs.

THAILAND

Ever since opium was introduced into the country some considerable time ago, the pattern of drug use in Thailand until 1960 must
have been relatively stable, and similar to that in neighbouring countries: an older, opium-using population, largely limited to the
urbanized Chinese and Thai, and more recently to hill tribes who
were themselves cultivators of the opium poppy. Some use was also
made of cannabis and of *kratom* for medicinal, herbal, culinary, and
recreational purposes. The use of opium, rather than of these latter
drugs, was perceived as a problem for containment and regulation,
but, until the 1958 and 1959 legislation, banning opium altogether,
official restriction changed little. For the first few years of the ban
it was clear that many of the former opium addicts were now using
heroin; but perhaps because of limited supplies of heroin, the urban
epidemic did not reach its height until the mid-1960s. Meanwhile,
the hill tribes continued to have access to opium, and thus did not
shift from their traditional patterns of use.

Discussion of the contemporary adult drug user in Thailand must
therefore consider separately the typical urban users of heroin (and
heroin in poly-drug use with other substances), rural users of *kratom*, and finally hill tribes users of opium.

The urban addict population presents various faces to the several organizations which deal with drug addiction. Drawing their
samples from different sub-segments, two surveys can give quite
different pictures of the addicts' social background: thus, Punnahitanond reported that 82 per cent of addicts at a treatment centre

were from the low income group; whereas Poshyachinda and his
colleagues found the average monthly income of their addicts to
be above average per capita income for the country. Another sample again, this time of 500 patients at Thanyarak Hospital, showed
that in terms of educational level, the addict population was not
significantly different from the rest of the population (Suwanwela,
Drug Dependence in Thailand: a Review, Chulalongkorn University, Bangkok, 1976).

Accounts of the reasons for drug abuse by adult Thai range
from those in terms of the Thai character and *sanuk*, the desire for
immediate pleasure within a circle of friends; to sociological reasons—the pressures of urbanization and the loosening of family ties;
to the individual's own self-reported reasons, including the influence of friends (see, for example, Khunying Amboorn Meesook,
'Cultures in Collision, an Experience of Thailand'; in I. Pilowsky,
1975, Australian National Association for Mental Health, Adelaide;
R. J. Schneider *et al.*, 'A Survey of Thai Student Use of Illicit
Drugs', *Int. J. of the Addictions*, 1977, 12:227—39; and Suwanwela, op. cit.).

The causes of addiction are, as Suwanwela so rightly states, complex and difficult to ascertain, but some information at least can
come from the addict's own opinions on why he started to use
drugs. There are a number of Thai surveys which put this question,
and the most frequently cited reasons were curiosity about the
drug's effect, and the influence of friends. Addicts were clearly
more susceptible to the example of their friends than were non-
users, given their answers to other survey questions. As few as 5
per cent of male convicts cited that they had been experiencing
mental stress when they first turned to drugs.

There are implications for prevention or control programmes in
these results: any such programme would have to consider how
drug use spreads and is maintained through the network of friends.
Genuine companionship and commercial considerations here are
mixed: interviews with addicts showed how introducing one's
friends to drugs could be used to gain supplies of drugs for one's
own need (Suwanwela, op. cit.).

How much had becoming an addict changed the individual's way
of life? Family bonds are traditionally strong in Thailand, and Suwanbubpa showed that of those who had been living with their
family when they became addicts very few left, although the family
members strongly urged them to stop the habit, or actually punished them. In the same study, it was found that over 50 per cent of
addicts charged with narcotics offences had been able to keep a
full-time job, and a further 13 per cent had some part-time employ-

ment (Suwanbubpa, *The Etiology of Heroin Addiction Among Narcotic Prisoners*, Kasetsart University, Bangkok, 1974). The raising of finance to purchase drugs is clearly a problem for many who remain in employment; for those out of work, the problem becomes acute. Yet Poshyachinda found that only 12 per cent of unemployed addicts undergoing treatment admitted obtaining income from illegal activities, as did 8 per cent of those in employment (*An Epidemiological Study of Addicts at Thanyarak Hospital*, Chulalongkorn University, Bangkok, 1976). Some clearly receive financial support for their daily expenses from members of their family, and in any case the market price of narcotics is relatively low in Thailand.

There are many studies on the nature of the urban narcotics problem, but one of the few published accounts of those who use *kratom* has been published by Suwanlert (*Bull. Narc.*, 1975, 28:21—7). Twenty-nine male and one female regular users of the *kratom* tree leaf were interviewed: all were over 30 years of age, Thai, and followed such occupations as market gardener or labourer. Almost all subjects in the sample said that they had started using *kratom* because they wanted to work more efficiently, in spite of the heat of the day. ('Addicts are, however, afraid of the rain, which causes them to catch cold easily'.) They also mention the initial euphoria, and the subsequent calmness of mind, which sets in after taking the drug. In contrast to the reasons sometimes given for opium or heroin use, no subjects mentioned chronic illness as a precipitating factor. One clear factor is the cheapness of *kratom* (100 leaves can be bought for 5 baht, and most addicts use fewer than 30 leaves a day) and its widespread availability. A second factor is its social acceptability in the rural areas: *kratom* users have a strong desire to work and to make more money.

The reasons for use given by hill tribes opium addicts frequently include references to its medicinal properties, or its power to alleviate pain and fatigue stemming from hard work in the fields. Opium's social use was clearly a major factor in introducing many of the hill tribes men to the drug in the first place, but by many accounts addiction only occurred when the individual felt a need to smoke opium for medicinal rather than social reasons (Suwanwela, op. cit., p. 9).

A medical survey team from Chulalongkorn University went to seven of the hill tribe villages to study the health status and opium use of the Hmong and Karen villagers (Suwanwela *et al.*, *The Hilltribes of Thailand: Their Opium Use and Addiction*, Chulalongkorn University, Bangkok, 1977). Some users they classified as addicted, and some as occasional users, and of the latter they stress that

the reasons for opium use may change with each use. The drug
may be used in the therapy of a whole range of ailments: abdom-
inal pain, headache, and backache were often-cited occasional
reasons for using opium. For a number of acute illnesses, which
subside spontaneously, opium may be used only once, or for a few
days, and discontinued as the individual recovers. Some illnesses
become chronic, and the continued use of opium leads to addiction: ulcers, tuberculosis, injuries, and a general continued pain
resulting from malnutrition are the most common chronic states
which were reported.

Opium was not, however, viewed just as a medicine: its tranquil-
lizing and euphoric effects were well known to the villagers, and a
number of them dated their use of the drug from a bereavement.
Opium was also used to relieve tension when the village experienced
some crisis, one key example of which was the anticipation of a
police narcotics raid on the village. The third type of reason for
using opium was for recreation:

In the evening villagers sit together around the fireplace in certain houses.
Men chat, drink tea or local spirits, and smoke tobacco via a waterpipe or cigarettes. Some who are opium addicts will also smoke opium in a nearby couch
or bed. Friends who are occasional smokers can join in for some reasons such
as illness or sorrow. A new experimenter might start in this way (Suwanwela
et al., 1977, op. cit.).

If there exists such widespread and casual social use of opium,
then one might ask why its use is not universal. In fact, the villagers
are well aware of the physical dangers that lie in opium addiction,
and a number of older villagers, some of whom were themselves
opium addicts, told the survey team that the younger generation
should be discouraged from opium smoking, for health, financial,
and religious reasons: the Hmong belief is that addicts cannot go
through the door to heaven after their death.

SINGAPORE

As has been described above, the patterns of drug abuse in Singapore, and with them the population of users, have changed dramatically since the late 1960s: from the opium smoking (with
occasional cannabis smoking communities) pattern which had per-
sisted throughout the colonial period, to the diversification of
drug substances, first to morphine and then (with the involvement
of youth for the first time in numbers) a small range of pills, to
the dramatic rise in heroin addiction and its containment during
1977 and 1978 by Operation Ferret.

In the main, the use of opium during the colonial period was confined to the older Chinese migrants for medicinal and recreational use (Krishna Iyer, *Report to the UNESCO/UNFDAC Fellowship Programme*, 1977): a pattern familiar throughout South-East Asia. The Indian and Pakistani community in Singapore recorded a number of its members who were users of cannabis, but as the habit was confined and undramatic, even if illegal, no studies of the users would seem to have been published. Morphine addiction was reported as the third pattern of use in post-war years, and Leong reports it to be confined in the main to mature Chinese, with some Indians and Pakistanis (Leong, *Addictive Diseases*, 1977, 3: 93–8). The majority of the morphine users were reported to be a decade younger, on average, than the opium addict (in his thirties, as opposed to late forties), and to have progressed from opium to morphine either under the influence of a morphine addict acquaintance, or a morphine den operator who introduced him to the new mode of injection.

The 'pot and pills' group (Leong, op. cit.) has been in the main a group of adolescents and very young adults, and will therefore be discussed in the chapter on the adolescent drug user. Many, too, of the heroin addicts in Singapore fall in this transitional age, and are, again, more appropriately discussed in the context of adolescent rather than adult drug abuse.

INDONESIA

Before Indonesia started to collect systematic information on its drug abusers, the social background of those involved in drug abuse, their personal drug history, and their reasons for using drugs were matters which each clinician, seeing only a small number of cases, could only speculate on. Thus, for example, in 1971 (*ICAA Conference*, Hong Kong, 1971) Setyonegoro 'suspects that the following few factors are relevant to the recent increase in drug abuse in Indonesian metropolitan cities': improved economic conditions, making drug purchases easier, loosening of family ties, and the development of street-corner societies.

According to Setyonegoro, Indonesian hospitals came to identify certain characteristics in the young addicts they were seeing. No longer was the typical addict an elderly Chinese opium smoker: he was quite likely to be younger and from a good, middle-class family, which may or may not have been disrupted by marital discord. The influence of friends was often cited in the first experimentations with marijuana, and then perhaps the desire to have 'real' experiences with drugs such as morphine or heroin. The individual became passive or apathetic to the daily routine of work, and this might carry over into a willingness to co-operate in the withdrawal programme. Most came voluntarily to treatment after prior consultations with the family physician.

At this stage, the drug problem in Indonesia had not reached epidemic proportions. Its peak was to come two years later, and the course of its rise and then containment was charted by the National Mental Hospital Reporting Programme (Salan, *Colombo Plan Workshop*, Penang, 1978). This monitoring system now enables clinicians to give a much broader-based description of the typical addicted individual, although, as Salan warns, it necessarily samples only those addicts who come for treatment.

The average drug abuser seen in the hospitals between 1971 and 1977 is almost certainly male (the ratio of males to females is 9 : 1) regardless of which part of Indonesia one discusses. Salan accounts for this in terms of the predominantly male-orientated nature of Indonesian society, which provides greater opportunity for males to seek diversion outside their homes, and to band together into groups. Girls, expected to take a more conservative outlook on life, and to stay closer to home, are thus less open to peer influence and to new fashions.

Most likely too, the drug user seen by the hospital lives in, or at least was born, in a major metropolitan area. (Data recorded from country hospitals indicate that some of their drug patients had recently arrived from Jakarta or Surabaya.)

In assessing the patients' income and social status, Salan notes the fact that in Indonesia obtaining reliable information about income level is difficult, as the quoted amount of earnings often did not reflect real income. For evaluation, other variables were also used: the presence or absence of signs of wealth in the home, family background, mention of additional jobs, etc. Based upon this cumulative index, 68 per cent of the patients could be categorized as medium income level (with a further 17 per cent who refused to give any information). Salan records that, during more recent years, a larger proportion of lower income level individuals were coming to hospital for treatment.

The educational level of patients again shows changes during and after the epidemic. In total, 80 per cent of patients had an education which was more than sixth grade, and 47 per cent more than tenth grade. Analysed year by year, it becomes clear that the epidemic was largely amongst those with secondary school education. With the waning of the epidemic, the involvement of the less well-educated became more apparent.

A considerable contrast between the Indonesian situation and that in many other countries was the lack of association between drug taking and crime, at least as shown in the records of those drug takers who were hospitalized. Most of the drug abusers were never arrested, and a very small proportion were arrested once or more. Clearly, the potential for crime is present, with the combination of low income level, the present endemic and more serious drug abuse, and rising street prices of drugs. Indeed, there were several notes on patients' records to indicate that they had stolen from family members to support their habit.

THE PHILIPPINES

Much contemporary discussion of the drug abuse problem in the Philippines centres on the adolescent user, and makes little mention of the adult abuser. This represents, as will be clear from the section on changing patterns of drug abuse in the history of the country, a reversal of the pattern which had been the norm until the 1960s, where drug abuse had been almost entirely a problem found amongst adults. As Zarco and Almonte state, the most outstanding feature of dangerous drugs control in the Philippines has been the decline and virtual elimination of criminal opiate addiction during the mid-1970s (*Addictive Diseases*, 1977, 3:119–28).

Few studies have been published of the remaining adult drug users in the Philippines. The pioneering interview study, *Street Corner Drug Use in Metropolitan Manila* (Zarco *et al.*, Narcotics Foundation of the Philippines, 1972) took two populations: 118 drug abusers at large, and 88 inmates of Manila City Jail. Only 15 per cent of the drug users at large were over 20 years of age, but half of the jail inmates were between 20 and 37 years old. The mean age of starting drug abuse was similar for both groups, 16.25 and 17.58 respectively, although there were some in the jail population who had been initiated in their early twenties.

Clearly, the pattern of drug abuse had been acquired in the company of existing drug users: 90 per cent reported that they had associated closely with persons using drugs before they themselves had started to use drugs, and 91 per cent of the jail inmates (and 50 per cent of the abusers at large) blame their gangmates (rather than schoolmates or friends) for their initiation. Friends, family, or other key figures in their lives had tried to intervene in the large majority of cases. Many of the lower class drug abusers came from the Tondo in Manila, a district of the city with a long history of opiate abuse and crime: 51 per cent of the jail sample were born within a few city blocks in the Tondo, 58 per cent spent their first ten years of life there, and 62 per cent resided there at the time of arrest. More affluent drug abusers in Metropolitan Manila showed, however, no such concentration of area, but were fairly evenly spread between the suburbs of the city.

As Zarco *et al.* remark, one very unusual finding was that in neither sample were there *any* middle-aged drug abusers. An official report covering the years 1950 to 1959 indicated that the mean age of persons arrested for using opiates was between 40 and 50 years. The probable answer, they feel, is that 'the average life expectancy of the drug abuser is lower than that of the general urban population ... the combined factors of drug abuse, poverty, and lack of personal discipline work against the addict of the urban slum, hence death at an early age is the consequence'. They warn, however, that the suggestion has yet to be empirically established.

LAOS

As noted in earlier sections, the history of drug addiction in Laos can be divided into a long period—certainly several hundred years——in which opium was the major drug of use; the four years from 1972 to 1976, when the heroin epidemic was at its height; and the years since 1976, under the fully Communist government, during which time drug addiction is reported to have been rigorously controlled.

During the first period, opium was used mainly on a regular basis by the elderly and the chronically sick, as a socially approved means of coping with old age and ill health. Powerful family and community taboos were (and remain) effective in keeping the majority of the younger, healthy members of society away from the habit.

Westermeyer (*Am. J. Psychiatry*, 1974, 131:165—70) presents an intensive survey of forty opium addicts, conducted in 1971 amongst refugee populations which had moved south into Vientiane province, a sample which he believes to be representative of the country as a whole. The addicts ranged in age from 27 to 70 years, with a mean age of 46 years, and in this and other populations reported there has in each case been a remarkably low male to female ratio, 2 : 1, as opposed to the 4 : 1 or 5 : 1 ratios normally encountered in American samples of addicts.

Most subjects were rural peasant farmers, but amongst the urban minority in the survey were members of all social classes, and indeed, in a few instances, Westermeyer argues that the use of opium may actually have enabled certain addicts to maintain their productivity in spite of disabling physical conditions.

There were several patterns of opium use before addiction. Some users had lengthy medicinal or social use before finally becoming addicted. Some came from families where use was common, and some had never used the substance before their addiction. The average age of onset of addiction was 31 years, and for the large majority of the sample the onset of addiction was related to illness or pain (both *tehaep* in Lao), and the remainder described stressful or challenging life events occurring at the time of their addiction (death in the family, refugee movement, etc.).

Although this study was of a non-patient, community-based addict population, Westermeyer reports that three-quarters of the group had made serious attempts to stop addiction. This resolve was, however, tempered with fear of stopping, and the prospect of losing former pleasures.

Not only was there a high proportion of women among the opium addicts but, as is shown by a study of Meo tribes people who were opium addicts, there were remarkably few factors which differentiated male from female users (Westermeyer and Peng, *Br. J. Addiction*, 1978, 73:181–7). Both sexes had the same average age at first usage, duration of non-addictive use, duration of addiction before admission to treatment at the National Detoxification Centre, mode of use, context of use, doses per day, and cost per day. The fact that there were 2.7 men to one woman in the sample indicates that socio-cultural factors (e.g., admission to social gatherings) gave unequal entry into the opium smoking habit, but that, once an individual has started the habit, the clinical course of addiction is the same for both sexes.

When the heroin epidemic began in Laos, Westermeyer and Peng (*J. Nervous and Mental Diseases*, 1977, 164:346–50) described the differences they found between the opium addicts and the heroin addicts coming forward for treatment at the National Detoxification Centre in Vientiane. Of the 503 patients, 51 were heroin addicts, all of whom came either from the administrative capital, Vientiane, or the nearby town of Tha Deua, whereas the remainder of the patients seen by the Centre were opium addicts from all regions of the country, including Vientiane. The striking geographical concentration of heroin users in the one heavily populated area might well have later dissolved as time went on, and as heroin supplies reached the rural populations, but it might equally well have maintained a disturbing level had the change of government not taken place in 1976.

HONG KONG

As in many other countries, the main reasons given by drug addicts in Hong Kong for their initial experiments with drugs are the influence of their friends, curiosity, and an urge for fun and 'kicks'. Some addicts surveyed also mentioned that they had used heroin to escape from the frustrations of life, to allow them to cope with pain and disease, to relieve fatigue, or to increase their sexual ability and pleasure (on this last, see below). As the *Hong Kong Narcotics Report* for 1976 states, however, these are but the direct, perceived causes: also important are the indirect causes, such as the loosening of family ties, the generation gap, and other social problems including unemployment, poor housing, crime, and corruption.

Given that many individuals in society face these personal and social problems and seek a solution in some form of intoxication, what determines the choice of intoxicant among the Chinese? Singer, a Hong Kong-based psychiatrist, attempts to answer this question in terms of the Chinese cultural background (*Br. J. Addict.*, 1974, 69:257–69). Why, in particular, he asks, is the Chinese prevalence pattern that of high narcotic and low alcoholic dependence, when exactly the reverse is true of Europe and America? The general consensus of those studying the prevalence of alcoholism in the Chinese has been that while they drink fairly copiously, there is a very low rate of alcoholism. Singer notes that the Chinese in Hong Kong traditionally drink at meals and at banquets; they tend not to drink without food; and the main aims of drinking are to promote conviviality and to improve health. Social custom sanctions social drinking, but strongly disapproves of drunkenness.

In contrast, the consumption of opium was so widespread in China that it became 'a social activity interwoven into the ideational systems, customs and practices of culture' (Singer, op. cit.). Opium smoking came to have many recognized functions: to promote sociability at gatherings such as weddings and funerals; to solve family problems (Singer cites rich families wishing to keep sons at home, away from gambling, or to keep widows away from trouble); to prolong sexual activity; and as a remedy for innumerable ailments. But, one may still ask, why should opium use have become traditional in the first place, and why did it not do so in the West?

Opium smoking may now largely have been replaced by the use of heroin, but this, too, is in the main smoked or inhaled. Now, because the consumption of opiates by smoking is less intoxicating than by injection, because it produces less physical dependence, and because there have been many who have smoked opium for many years without apparent social or physical effect, then, one can hypothesize that the habit could gain its social acceptability and thus widespread use. (Note, as further confirmatory evidence, that Chinese society nowadays condemns the injecting heroin addict.)

Singer's discussion concludes with a scholarly analysis of the greater attraction of opium over alcohol in terms of the fulfilment of traditional Taoist ideals, which sanction the passive and yielding traits, and abhor rowdiness and boisterousness; of Confucian ideology, which stresses order, behavioural limits, and a fairly puritan way of life; and of traditional beliefs about the properties and effects of opium and alcohol. Modern Chinese beliefs about alcohol have been studied by Sargent (*Br. J. Sociology*, 1971, 22:83–96), and show some continuance of these traditional views. She contrasted Chinese beliefs with those of Australian, Jewish, and Japanese samples. The Chinese students she questioned heavily endorsed the statement, 'To get drunk shows a lack of moral stamina', a view opposed by all three other groups. They also believed that drink too often causes fighting and other unpleasantnesses (her sample were Chinese students studying in Australia!), and they did not believe that 'Drinking improves the way people get on together (although all three other groups strongly agreed with the statement). Sargent's data backed up Singer's case with respect to alcohol, and it is a pity that her study did not also include beliefs about drug taking within its scope.

One recurring theme in the account of Chinese beliefs about opium use is that of its presumed aphrodisiac qualities. Ding (*ICAA Conference*, Hong Kong, 1971) quotes survey figures for Hong Kong which indicate that approximately one in five male addicts took a narcotic initially for sexual reasons—primarily, to prolong their coitus. A large portion of the sample made their drug experiments for reasons of curiosity, or because of the influence of friends, but soon discovered the changed quality of their sexual relations whilst under the influence of the drug, and this in itself contributed to their addiction. Finally, Ding discusses the important role sex may have as a reason for relapse: many addicts become preoccupied with their narcotic and lose interest in sex; this interest returns during treatment, but its fulfilment is hampered by premature ejaculation—a frequent symptom in the post-treatment state. To prevent this, the ex-addict resorts again to the narcotic, which had worked so well before, and the cycle is complete.

Although drug abuse in Hong Kong is mainly a male phenomenon, there are some female addicts. Comparison of male and female addicts reveals some significant differences in their social history and general patterns of addiction (Ch'ien, *ICAA Conference*, Hong Kong, 1971). Both male and female groups contain a majority of individuals who were born in China (only among those under 25 do the Hong Kong-born predominate), but among the males, Cantonese and Chiu Chau are the largest groups, whereas the largest single group among the women comes from the Shanghai district.

The majority of the male addicts in Ch'ien's sample (of nearly 1,800 patients seen by SARDA clinics) had primary education, and only 7 per cent were illiterate, but nearly 40 per cent of the women were illiterate. Nearly half the male patients were still bachelors, but nearly 90 per cent of the women had been married.

Only 24 per cent of the men, and 5 per cent of the women, reported themselves to be unemployed, although many addicts had a history of deteriorating activities, having started in skilled work before their addiction, and changing to less skilled when addicted. The majority had criminal records, but most of these were for the offence of possessing dangerous drugs.

The sexes differ slightly in their drug histories: the females on average started to use narcotics later than the males (27 rather than 25 years), and wait slightly longer before seeking treatment (13 instead of 12 years' duration). They differ substantially in their mode of consumption: men seldom injected (10 per cent in the 1970 sample), whereas this was the single commonest pattern among the women (42 per cent). Ch'ien speculates that women are more conscious of their facial appearance than are men, who would rather lose some teeth than show needle marks on their arms (men being apt to wear short sleeves in Hong Kong).

Why did the addicts first start using drugs? Again, there are striking differences in the reasons given: men primarily cite the satisfaction of their curiosity, whereas women saw drug taking as a panacea to treat an illness or injury, and only secondarily was curiosity their motive.

Self-reflective reasons figure prominently in the reasons given by both sexes for seeking treatment ('I feel there is no future. . . .'), with, next for the males, sheer economic hardship, and, for the females, worries about health and premature death. The women, at 35 per cent, had a somewhat better prognosis for voluntary abstinence after treatment than the men, at 25 per cent, although many more women than men came from homes where there was multiple addiction in the family (59 per cent as opposed to 6 per cent).

INDIA

Social sanctions and beliefs have in the past contained the use of India's traditional drugs of abuse. Cannabis, generally in the form of bhang, has normally been 'considered a vice of the lower orders and the depraved' (Dubé and Handa, *Br. J. Psychiatry*, 1971, 118: 345—6), although bhang drinking has been widespread in a religious context in east India, and *ganja* smoking is common among unskilled labourers and peasant cultivators (Wig and Varma, *Addictive Diseases*, 1977, 3:79—86).

In the early 1970s, before the youthful drug abuse peaked, Chopra conducted a study of 1,000 cases of drug addiction in the urban and rural areas of West Bengal, Punjab, Bihar, Uttar Pradesh, and Orissa (*Int. J. Addictions*, 1972, 7:57—63). His object was to assess the role of narcotic or habituating drugs on the social and economic life of regular users, and he makes no claim that his voluntary patient sample is representative of all users, although it does indicate the greater prevalence of drug use in urban areas.

Chopra suggests that with developing industries in the urban areas come new psychological stresses, and that 'such pressures have induced certain individuals to search for artificial means of fortifying themselves against depression and frustration'. Some support for this is given by an analysis of occupation, average working hours per day, and income of the addicted individuals: drug dependence is more common among individuals who work long hours, and who receive more than a minimum wage, and are thus better able to sustain the habit. (Chopra does not speculate on what the lowest paid do in response to their frustrations.) When interviewed, many workers stated that the drugs ameliorated fatigue and were used to insure a restful sleep. Others mentioned the alleviation of hunger, or of physical ailments or the effects of hard labour. Indeed, there were reports that in some rural areas of Punjab, 'pep pills' were sometimes offered to agricultural labourers during the harvest season in addition to wages, because they could then continue to work for longer periods without rest.

Chopra's early study remains one of the few studies to examine the social causes of drug abuse amongst adults in India. Most of the subsequent studies have examined the consequences—medical, psychological, and social—of such drug abuse. Thus, Dubé and Handa (op. cit.) have shown an association between drug use and mental illness in their house-to-house survey of Agra; and Mehndiratta and Wig (*Drug and Alcohol Dependence*, 1975—6, 1:71—81) compared the physical and mental health of 50 heavy cannabis users with 25 non-user controls, matched for age, sex, and social class.

The majority of the drug users were in considerably poorer physical health than were the controls: they reported weight loss, coughs, and lack of sleep; physical examination showed them to be in a poorer nutritional state, and with more chest and eye problems than the non-users. Few individuals in either group had family histories of mental illness, or had themselves shown any strong signs of disturbance (although more of the drug users had vague anxiety or depressive symptoms). Although the cannabis users more often reported disagreements with their parents, their own marital and sexual adjustment was no worse than that of the controls. Work adjustment appeared to have been significantly affected by the drug habit, as had the drug users' general social behaviour: several reported getting into violent quarrels when under the influence of cannabis.

The psychological correlates of long-term heavy use of cannabis in the same sample was reported by Mehndiratta, Wig, and Varma (*Br. J. Psychiatry*, 1978, 132:482–6), who subjected their cannabis users and controls to a battery of psychological tests. The drug users had slower reaction times, were poorer at time estimation, had higher neuroticism scores, and showed greater perceptual errors under disturbance. The tests were performed, the authors assure us, 'as far as possible' whilst subjects were not under the influence of their drug.

As the reader will have gathered, there is a need for more information on the background and motivations of the average adult drug user in the Indian community. The adolescent (and especially the student) population is much better served in this respect. Many authors speculate and presume upon the causes—industrialization, the strain of rural labour, etc.—without demonstrating that drug users have in any way been more subject to these than their non-drug-using peers. Clearly, such factors cannot be sufficient to explain drug use, as many individuals so affected do not use drugs; nor yet are they even necessary conditions for drug abuse, because individuals higher on the social scale are also reported as drug users.

PAKISTAN

The adult drug users whose background and reasons for use are most fully known are those who have come to hospitals for treatment; otherwise, there exist in Pakistan at present only general observations about the broad characteristics of the drug user.

One of the earlier studies published was of hospitalized drug dependants in the Punjab: Ijaz Haider interviewed one hundred first-time admissions to the General Mental Hospital, Lahore (*Colombo Plan Workshop*, Rawalpindi, 1975). The majority of patients in this area of the country were cannabis users (note that important regional differences in drug availability within the country might limit the generality of the study's findings).

The population was almost entirely male (96 per cent), and was single (48 per cent) more often than married (32 per cent) or separated, with a bias towards the uneducated (54 per cent), but also with 14 per cent graduates and professionals. Although there was a preponderance of lower class individuals, the skilled and professionals were not absent from the sample. (Indeed, some drugs—most especially pharmaceuticals—have had a reputation of being the drugs preferred by the affluent, although nowadays this pattern is found throughout the different levels of society.)

Among the youngest users, the most commonly given reason for starting their drug habit was to enjoy meeting challenges and facing risks. Many reported that they had been motivated by rebellion or hostility, and that they had responded by breaking society's rules. A minority said that they used drugs as a means of escape from the stresses of life. Peer group pressure—especially where that group contained friends who were pushers—was mentioned by a quarter of all subjects. Increasing one's sexual potency and changing one's personality were also hoped for by a minority of drug users, many of whom would be among the older users.

The free availability of drugs in Pakistan is illustrated by the openness of respondents about the sources of their drugs: the synthetic drugs were most often purchased legally at the chemist, and opium was available at the vends. The vend system, together with the shrines, were in fact the main source of introduction to drugs; though, as experimental use gives way to regular use, drug pushers became the source of supply for one-quarter of the total.

Perhaps the most detailed portrait of a segment of the drug using population in Pakistan resulted from McGlothin's interviews with 105 opium customers at vends in Rawalpindi and Peshawar, and 42 opium users in two villages, one to the north of Peshawar, and one in the Buner region (*Opium Use in Pakistan*, WHO, Geneva, 1976). Interviews covered family drug use patterns, own reasons for initiation, subsequent drug history, and effects of the drug upon health, sexual performance, work, family relations, and finances.

Virtually all customers were opium eaters, eating a regular daily average of one gram. (It is generally believed that the eating of opium is considerably more effective than smoking the drug.)

The median age of initiation was 28 years, and the most common reason given for starting was for the self-treatment of coughs, dysentery, and other illnesses. Among other reasons mentioned were the enhancement of sexual performance, pleasure in general, improved work capacity, and coping with bereavement. The majority of respondents feel that opium is bad for their health—an interesting observation, coming as it does from an 'at large' rather than treatment-seeking or hospitalized sample. (In fact, when questioned, the majority said that they *would* wish treatment if it were available.) Furthermore, a large majority experience family disapproval of the habit, many having been able to hide their use for a long period, and, indeed, they themselves felt guilty about their habit, and would not want their children to follow their example: it would, amongst other things, hinder them from making a good marriage.

Most of the opium users whom McGlothin interviewed at the vends were illiterate, and were of lower social class, but the customers were not by any means only from such a background and status: several were shopkeepers, or had some other source of substantial income.

This urban, vend-centred sample of users can be contrasted with rural patterns in the growing areas of the North-West Frontier Province (McGlothin, op. cit.; and Siddiqui, *Survey of Opium Smoking in North-West Frontier Province*, Pakistan Narcotics Control Board, 1975). In these areas, a common pattern is that if a large landowner becomes addicted, there is a strong chance that his tenants and servants on the estate will also become addicted. On the estate surveyed by McGlothin, there had been, as well as this pattern of opium use, also an epidemic of barbiturate and Mandrax use, leading to some deaths as a result of overdoses. Opium came direct from nearby cultivation areas, rather than from a vend, and clearly the pattern of use was a social, pleasurable one, inducing much greater lassitude than was evident in the urban vend customers.

The influence of a single, influential opium addict on a locality was even more strikingly demonstrated in Siddiqui and McGlothin's other rural study village—Kuria, in Swat. Forty years ago, a single addicted individual moved into the area, and currently the percentage of male adults who are addicted is probably in the order of 50 to 75 per cent. Half of these cultivate opium poppies themselves (and supply the remainder), and there is no use of any other drugs in the village.

CONCLUSIONS

One cannot sum up the typical adult drug user in a few phrases. The extent of drug abuse varies considerably between countries in the region, and so, accordingly, adult drug users may represent a significant minority in one area, and be only a small and unusual group in another. A pattern of use which was typical in one country might be atypical in most others. Cultural and social factors, as well as the extent that drug use has penetrated society, cause considerable differences in what is the 'typical drug user in each country'. Consider, for example, the very different circumstances conducive to drug use in, for example, rural North-West Frontier

Province, Pakistan, and in urban Hong Kong. In the former, the single factor which best predicts whether an agricultural labourer will be an opium user is whether his landlord and estate owner is himself a user (rather than any personal variable); in the latter, the predictors of drug user status are a low level of education, job instability, being an immigrant rather than Hong Kong-born, and membership of a particular linguistic group.

Some generalizations can, however, be made. In most countries in the region, drug abuse by adults is very largely a male phenomenon (although, as the next chapter will show, increasing numbers of female adolescents are becoming involved). The more traditional the area, the more exclusively male is the use of drugs; and only in the international cities are small female groups of users found: in Hong Kong, for instance, among the *demi-monde*, or among some professionals. For an explanation, we need to consider the social circumstances of initiation and of continuing use of drugs. In a traditional society, women are more sequestered, and thus are less exposed to the purveyors of drugs, or less able to participate in drug use with others: café society and other meeting places are more exclusively male. In a major city, where women are altogether more involved with such society, there are more opportunities. Even here, however, it seems that women have less access to street drugs. Ease of access remains a major factor in determining the individual's chances of becoming a drug user. Thus, consider an example quoted from Malaysia, where one of the occupational groups overrepresented among the drug users were workers in coffee-shops—these places being one of the main sources of drugs.

Drug abuse among adults may then be a predominantly male phenomenon. Is it, as it has often been portrayed, also predominantly a lower class phenomenon? Such a stereotype is reported to be strongly held in India, for example. Yet, as the example of eighteenth- and nineteenth-century China shows, drug use may well occur throughout all levels of society. During much of the nineteenth and early twentieth centuries, drug use in South-East Asia was indeed largely confined to older manual workers, but it has since then become more widespread, such that professional middle-class and skilled workers are found among those seeking treatment. The unskilled may still predominate, but so do they in the population as a whole.

Many studies, as well as examining the individual's social background, have also sought his reasons for drug use. The influence of friends is one of the most frequently given reasons for the initiation of drug use; and several writers, most notably in the Philippines and Indonesia, have stressed 'street-corner society' as indeed being a major source of contagion in recent drug epidemics. Not all classes of urban society, however, participate in such street-corner activities; and yet, as just observed, there are some individuals in every social class who are drug users. Initiation to drug use may thus involve the more subtle, less publicly observable influence of friends, meeting in the greater privacy of middle- and upper-class society.

The reasons given for starting and for continuing drug use are wide-ranging, as will have struck the reader to this chapter, and include: recreational, medical, problem solving, aphrodisiacal, and as a work aid. Higher enlightenment is seldom mentioned, in contrast to studies of Western users. The aphrodisiac use of drugs is mentioned by strikingly few researchers, but those who do come from the very different settings of Pakistan and Hong Kong. One suspects that the belief about drug effects upon sexual pleasure is much more widespread, but has seldom been elicited by the coy scientist.

Given that there is such a variety of reasons, one cannot usefully attempt to summarize, or to make much of the relative weightings of each reason for use, across different populations. Some features are of course common, for example, the obvious functionality of stimulant drugs for heavy manual workers, but cultural differences make it as difficult to describe the 'main reasons for drug use' as it is to portray a single 'typical adult user'.

What effects do regular drug use have upon the individual's pattern of life? The effects are, according to many studies, rather less disruptive than an observer familiar with the American literature might presume. Being a regular drug user does not necessarily entail worse job performance or poorer social relations. Certainly, the rate of unemployment in samples is often low. However, many individuals have reported that, although they still remain in work, they are gradually taking less skilled jobs, and may be downwardly mobile as a result of their habit. The extent to which individuals become alienated from their families varies considerably in the reports from different countries: in Hong Kong there is much evidence that drug use has a disruptive effect on family life, whereas some Thai reports claim that the strength of the family in this country is sufficient to provide a restraining influence upon the drug user. Indeed, many clinicians try to build on, or restore, the support of the family in the later stages of rehabilitation, and in aftercare.

Work, family relations, and health may be the major casualties of drug use. Accounts of prolonged casual drug use without apparent damage to health are occasionally given, yet regular heavy use may well produce signs of ill-health fairly rapidly. Poor health, or fears for one's health, are often given as reasons for seeking treatment. Financial inability to support the habit, however, is a more commonly given reason in many studies.

IV

The Adolescent Drug User

DRUG abuse amongst adults is a social problem recognized by all, but drug abuse by adolescents captures much more public attention and concern. It is in a way easier for the man in the street to rationalize away the problem of adult drug abuse as being a property of unfortunates, or of the marginal in society (however inaccurate this impression may be); faced with the epidemic among youth, it is much less easy to dismiss the problem: many people will know, or know of, perfectly ordinary adolescents who have become regular social drug users or who have become fully dependent upon drug substances.

Virtually the whole region experienced an epidemic of drug use among adolescents and young adults in the late 1960s and in the 1970s. This was an unprecedented involvement of a whole segment of society which had previously been entirely outside the drug world; and it happened at a time when a range of new drugs were first being abused on a major scale. The situation was indeed alarming; but there is a danger in overreacting, if, as could be shown in some areas, the predominant pattern among youth is for brief periods of experimentation, with then a permanent cessation of drug use. If society's response is alarmist and heavy-handed, treating these experimenting users as 'addicts', and equating their behaviour with that of a proselytizing drug dependant, then the situation might well be worsened. As the present chapter will show, many youthful users of drugs appear to take them in some spirit of rebellion and self-assertion, and society's well-meaning but authoritarian response may well reinforce this rebellious spirit.

The very fact that there was, right across the region, an upsurge of youthful drug use of epidemic proportions is in itself an indication that the main explanations for adolescent, as opposed to adult, drug use should be sought at the social and cultural level, rather than primarily at the level of the individual and his problems. During the past twenty years, the general life-styles of (especially) urban youth have changed quite considerably, and there has been much discussion of the emergence in both the East and the West of a youth culture where individuals were more independent of their family, and more closely identified with their peer group than had been the case in earlier generations. This general change could then provide a background for the emergence of drug use as one among a number of new forms of behaviour amongst youth. There are, of course, clear national and urban-rural differences in the extent to which youth has adopted this culture, and the Philippines perhaps can claim to be the most Americanized. But, as we have already argued in the introduction, the worlds of American and East Asian youth still remain importantly different in many respects, and we must not assume greater similarities in the motivations towards drug use than can be proved to exist.

Talk of an epidemic of youthful drug abuse tends to obscure the fact that, as Chapter II showed, drug use (and especially *regular* drug use) is very much a minority behaviour in most societies: youthful use of drugs is way behind alcohol use, and even further behind tobacco use. Even if a 'youth culture' exists as a background, which may suggest the existence and the attractiveness of drugs to the individual, we still have to enquire what makes one particular person adopt such possible behaviour, and another one not adopt it. The research emphasis has almost always been upon the drug-using segment of the population, and the factors which motivate non-users is an almost universally unresearched topic; yet it is clearly one of considerable potential importance to those who design drug education programmes. Are they consciously avoiding a known possibility, or are they merely unaware of it? If they are actively choosing against drug use, is their decision well-based in knowledge of drug effects, or does it stem from vague and dispellable fears?

If individuals are aware of the existence and availability of drugs, what are the precipitating factors which lead them to experiment with the substances? What role do personal problems, insecurity, worry over work or study, play—these being the classic reasons advanced to explain drug use. Or, taking a different approach, is the difference between drug-using and non-using adolescents the degree to which the individual is an adherent of a youth culture which promotes drug use amongst other behaviours?

There may well be considerable differences within the age-group in the same area, and especially between those who remain within the school system (and are thus being socialized towards jobs of some status within society), and those, their contemporaries, who have dropped out to unskilled labour or unemployment. It might well be that the latter in reality face more personal and social problems than the former, and that seeking one predominant explanation for all adolescent drug use would therefore be inappropriate. This point should be kept in mind when reading discussions of research into the topic: is the researcher talking of student or street-corner populations?

MALAYSIA

In the late 1960s, in common with most countries in the region, Malaysia witnessed the beginnings of adolescent drug abuse on a scale large enough to cause considerable public concern. In the years which followed, all indicators—drug seizures, arrest records, hospital admissions—showed a continued upward trend in drug abuse by young people, and an increase in use of heroin, morphine, and synthetic drugs, alongside cannabis (*ganja*) and opium. Public and governmental concern was great, but the lack of information about what was going on led to many presumptions being presented as facts, and the causes and nature of the drug problem amongst youth were often discussed as if it were self-evident that drug abuse was a social problem like many another, characteristic of the lower and deprived sections of society, or of those individuals who were personally maladjusted. Estimates of the numbers of young people involved with drugs were necessarily based upon guesses, and were often alarmist. The estimates also tended to lump together individuals who had brief experimental use of an illicit drug, those whose use was more regular, and those who were truly dependent, under the emotive and misleading title of 'drug addicts'. Definite information was clearly needed if policy were to be formulated effectively, and towards that end the Drug Abuse Research Group at Universiti Sains Malaysia (the forerunner of the National Drug Dependence Research Centre) conducted three surveys to investigate the extent of drug experience in that section of the general population believed to be most at risk—the adolescents.

One in ten representative samples of the entire secondary school populations were taken in three of Malaysia's thirteen states, Penang, Selangor (including Kuala Lumpur), and Kelantan, giving sample sizes of respectively 5,803, 10,358, and 4,646. The three survey states were chosen to sample the range of background whence Malaysian youth came: Penang is a predominantly urban state, with a Chinese majority; Selangor contains both rural, urban, and metropolitan areas, and has more of a balance between Malays and Chinese; while Kelantan is a predominantly rural Malay state. The three states also differ with respect to the pattern of drug trafficking in the country. Kelantan adjoins the Thai border, whereas Penang has sea and air connections with supplying regions, and Selangor receives its illicit drugs either overland or via Kuala Lumpur's airport. As the chapter on patterns of drug abuse has indicated, the survey found remarkable consistency in the incidence and nature of use across all three states: somewhere over 11 per cent of the secondary schoolchildren in each state had had some experience of illegal drugs, with a smaller proportion who reported a continuing use; and in each state, younger users had, as drugs of preference, sedatives, amphetamines, and tranquillizers, with older users preferring *ganja* to these drugs; with, in all areas, the opiates being less frequently reported. Given this similarity between rural and urban, east and west coast, Chinese, Indian, and Malay samples, the analysis presented below will consider the Malaysian adolescent sample as a whole. (Separate detailed analyses are given in Spencer and Navaratnam, *A Study of the Misuse of Drugs Among Secondary Schoolchildren in the States of Penang and Selangor*, Universiti Sains Malaysia, 1976; and Spencer, Navaratnam, and Lee, *A Study of the Misuse of Drugs Among Secondary Schoolchildren in the State of Kelantan*, Universiti Sains Malaysia, 1978.)

The surveys did more than ascertain the extent of drug experience among the adolescents. By taking representative samples of the secondary school population, and by asking a large range of general questions, the study was able to compare the minority of 'drug users' (those who have at any time tried an illegal drug) with the majority non-user group in terms of their social background, their educational progress and aspirations; social relationships, self image, social and general attitudes, and their beliefs and knowledge about drugs.

As already mentioned, public opinion within Malaysia had tended to assume that, as drug abuse was seen as a social problem, so the users of drugs must come largely from those sections of society which are in other ways problematical. Yet the study shows that such reasoning cannot be supported; a social deprivation explanation for adolescent drug abuse in Malaysia seems entirely inappropriate for a phenomenon which is so evenly distributed throughout society. Rather, the findings of the survey indicate that the main characteristics which distinguish youthful users of drugs from their non-using contemporaries are their social attitudes, precocity, and membership of drug using friendship groups. As will be reviewed below, social indicators such as social class, size of family, religious or ethnic background, etc., were found to be of little or no predictive value for discerning an 'at risk' group, whereas depressed educational aspirations, reported desire to be up with adolescent fashion, cigarette-smoking (and, to a lesser extent, drinking), knowledge about the local availability of drugs, and having as one's acquaintances numbers of drug using adolescents were all much more frequently found to be characteristic of drug users than of non-users.

If just over 11 per cent of the total sample had ever used illegal drugs, then the percentage of children from any particular social class within the sample who were 'ever users' varied very narrowly round this average. (Social class was here assessed with reference to the father's occupation.) There were slight variations within particular sub-samples—for example the children of teachers were slightly overrepresented in one state and underrepresented in another. But rather than taking this as the basis for recommending that teachers with adolescent children seek transfer from State A to State B, one should recognize that this is what would be expected within the sampling error of such a survey, and that these minor differences are of no significance. Approximately 40 per cent of the drug users come from families whose head was either a manual worker or was unemployed: this again is capable of misinterpretation, and is not evidence for a social deprivation hypothesis of drug abuse, for approximately the same percentage of non-users are drawn from these classes. To repeat, there was no significant difference between the social class structure of the drug using and non-using sub-samples. Thus, far from being a phenomenon confined to children of socially deprived families, the experience of drugs was found in a minority of individuals at each social level, from the unemployed to the professional.

Were the drugs a manifestation of social pathology, one would predict, as well as an uneven distribution across social classes, a relatively even distribution with age. Instead, in all three states, there were found to be two peaks in the number using drugs: at first- and second-form level (ages twelve to thirteen) and again at sixth-form level (eighteen). If drug abuse were primarily a response to difficult social circumstances, then one would not expect to find such marked peaks and troughs with age. (A slowly rising trend with age might perhaps have been expected, with increasing age making for easier access to drugs.) The existence of a young secondary school wave (using predominantly synthetic drugs rather than *ganja*) would rather indicate that the pattern of abuse reflects changing fashions in youth culture. When the sample is further broken down by race and locality, it can be demonstrated that the levels of penetration of the habit varies considerably between local communities. Thus, for example, in one area Indians are overrepresented, and in another, underrepresented, with Malays or Chinese predominating among the local drug using group. The picture that emerges is of particular face-to-face groups having either a relatively low or a relatively high degree of involvement with drugs, and it is this which has the most influence on whether a particular precocious adolescent expresses himself through the use of drugs or in some other way.

Given the heavy preponderance of males amongst the adult drug dependants seen by the drug treatment centres in Malaysia, it is particularly striking to see how much closer are the sex ratios in the school age drug users. In the upper three forms of secondary school, males do predominate (13.9 per cent of the boys, but only 5.4 per cent of the girls, admit to any experience with illicit drugs); the ratio is much more even in the lower three forms (12.6 per cent of the boys and 10.2 per cent of the girls admit to such experience). Thus, there is evidence of a rapid change occurring—from about seven years ago (the modal initiation year of those being seen in treatment centres at the time of the survey), when very few females would appear to have been involved sufficiently to become dependent, through the group who were in the upper secondary school, who still show some male predominance, to the youngest and newest experimenters, where the percentage of girls experimenting has nearly approached that of the boys.

Spencer and Navaratnam (op. cit.) argue that, although undoubtedly some Malaysian adolescents clearly do turn to drugs because of the problems they face, more individuals have experimented with drugs and perhaps taken up the habit during the course of self-assertion, in precisely the same way that previous (and present) generations of adolescents have used cigarettes, alcohol, fashions, and music to mark out their identity.

In a minority of cases, the drug habit was found to be associated with personal problems, and with a level of unhappiness which is entirely uncharacteristic of non-users. Thus, 21 per cent of the drug users, but only 1 per cent of the non-users, report themselves to be in poor health; more users than non-users reported frequent minor medical and nervous upsets; and an overall 46 per cent of users rated themselves as being generally unhappy, as compared with 25 per cent of their non-using contemporaries.

Many items on the questionnaire were designed to elicit a detailed self-description, and again it was found that an appreciable minority of the drug users presented a picture of themselves which was consistently different from that given by the majority of adolescents. Thus, a higher proportion of drug users than non-users (but by no means a majority of all users) see themselves as *isolated* (not feeling close to their friends, lonely, bullied, feeling bored much of the time, wishing to be alone); as *in rebellion* (their parents do not understand them, they want to leave school and earn a lot of money, they feel grown up, they wish to try new things, and they believe that one does not have to obey laws if one does not agree with them); as *reliant upon their peers* (a whole range of items attest to this); and they hold a rather fatalistic view of their situation (believing that, in order to succeed, one needs luck rather than hard work, and that people like themselves have not much chance to be successful).

Relations with parents are perceived to be good by the large majority of children in the sample, drug users and non-users alike, with, at each age, some of the drug users manifesting something of the shift in reliance upon parents onto friends, which is characteristic of the next age-group.

Aspirations with regard to school are strikingly high throughout the Malaysian secondary school population, with an unrealistically high 72 per cent hoping to go to university. Drug use is, however, associated with some slight dampening of such aspirations: only 55 per cent of users were seeking university entrance, with, at the other end of the scale, 10 per cent of drug users who expressed themselves unconcerned with passing any examination (compared with 0.5 per cent of non-users saying this).

The older drug users are much more likely to see their school as being too authoritarian: 65 per cent of users as against 35 per cent of non-users. But there are few differences between drug users and non-users in seeing their time at school as worthwhile, and feeling able to express themselves freely at school. A much more striking difference is found with regard to absenteeism: consistently across the states, only 21 per cent of non-users are away from school for more than a day or two a term, whereas 46 per cent of drug users report such absences. This may indicate both a greater actual level of sickness *and* a level of disenchantment with school.

The findings of these sections of the questionnaire support the contention that social deprivation or personal problems explain fewer cases of drug use than does social precocity. Whether they are talking about themselves, their relations with their parents and friends, their aspirations, and how they respond to school as an institution, drug users frequently give the impression of being young people trying to be older and more independent than their contemporaries. For them, youth culture and peer group are major influences.

As in many peer surveys in other parts of the world, drug users

were found to hold more favourable attitudes towards drug substances and their use than do those who have never experienced
them. Interestingly, it was also found that the drug users tended to
hold as negative a picture of the typical drug user as did the non-
users.

Drug users were more likely than non-users to see occasional use
of *ganja* at parties as being acceptable: very few of the latter would
countenance it. Again, many more drug users believed that drugs
help one to relax, make one feel good, may help one to do things
better, and to make many friends. It was also found that drug users
were more likely to underplay the chances of addiction, and to
believe that only some drugs were harmful.

Non-using adolescents emerged as having a very stern code of
beliefs about illegal drugs, whose even occasional use would seem
to them almost inevitably to cause harm. This transfers to a disapproval of the regular use of alcohol, and the use of sleeping pills
without a doctor's prescription. It would seem that the Malaysian
government's anti-drug campaign has had considerable effect among
the non-users in shaping their beliefs about drug substances. The
campaign's portrayal of degeneracy of the typical drug user, furthermore, had been accepted by both non-user and user alike. The
rather unattractive composite image of the 'typical drug user' held
by Malaysian schoolchildren showed him to be tough (a desirable
attribute in itself) but to the point of being anti-social, and seeking
to achieve precocious adult status, but in a rather maladjusted way.
Young drug users seemed well able to differentiate themselves from
the public image of the individual who was fully committed to the
habit.

One of the major concerns about drug education is its possible
effect in heightening interest in the substances. The importance of
the media (all of which take a strongly anti-drug line in Malaysia)
was clear in the survey findings. They were the predominant source
of information for non-users of all ages (58 per cent of whom ranked the media above all other sources), and they were also the major
source for younger users (41 per cent). However, amongst the
older users of drugs, only 24 per cent rated the media as their main
source of information, with 48 per cent indicating their source to
be people of their own age—friends, brothers, and sisters.

Only a very small number of the non-user sample admitted that
they had been made more interested to try drugs by the information received, but 10 per cent of the drug users did admit to such
an effect. A public educator would need to balance this against the
much larger proportion who stated that the effect had been to
make them *more* afraid of trying drugs (53 per cent of non-users,

and 25 per cent of users, said this). If one places confidence in these findings, then the overwhelming effect of the information received had been to create a negative and off-putting picture of drugs and drug taking. (The media, at the time of the survey, had been using scare tactics as well as straight information.) However, when respondents were asked about particular drug substances, then there was a worrying level of interest expressed by those who had never experienced any drug. 'I have not tried (the substance) but would be interested to do so', was the response given by as many as 15 per cent of the sample with relation to sedatives, 10 per cent with relation to amphetamines, and 8 per cent with relation to tranquillizers, but with relatively few giving this response for heroin (5 per cent) and morphine (3 per cent).

What explanations did drug users give for their starting with and continuing to use drugs? And what inhibitions on the use of drug substances, if any, acted upon users and non-users?

Combining the users of all drug types, there emerged a hierarchy of reasons for drug use, which was found in all three states. The questionnaire had listed a number of possible reasons, some of which had been cited in the literature as the motivations most likely to be given by casual and experimenting young drug users, and others which were more frequently given by longer and more dependent users. The drug users in the present study overwhelmingly cited the former type of reason.

Curiosity and the influence of friends were the main reasons cited by 68 per cent of the drug using sample: the pattern which would be predicted of a young, non-dependent group (and which contrasts with the reasons given by voluntary hospital patients and adult drug offenders in the other Malaysian surveys: see the earlier chapter on the adult drug abuser). Only 16 per cent of the young users gave coping with their problems as their main reason, with a further 12 per cent citing the use they made of drugs as an aid to studying. Few identified with the more rebellious reasons which were provided as possible responses: to be independent, to be different, for enjoyment, or for self-understanding.

Those drug users who had only ever tried one substance almost exclusively cited curiosity as their main reason. The poly-drug users somewhat more often mentioned the influence of friends, the forgetting of problems, and sheer enjoyment. (One might contrast the very low proportions of young Malaysian drug users who see drugs as a means of increasing self-awareness with the numbers that would be expected in a comparable Western sample: there is no drug-oriented 'underground press' in Malaysia.)

If these, then, were the reasons for starting and continuing drug use, what were the inhibitory factors as the sample perceived them?

Very largely, the inhibitions which operate were the same ones for users and non-users: for the younger adolescents, the main reasons given were parental disapproval of the habit (48 per cent gave this reason) and fear of loss of energy (40 per cent). The older individuals were much more likely than the younger to cite the dangers of addiction; with, the next most frequently given, principle ('it is against my beliefs'), and only then the fear of parental disapproval. (Individuals were allowed to cite more than a single response: the respective percentages for these three reasons were 48 per cent, 45 per cent, and 35 per cent.)

The potential for friends not only to influence the initiation of the drug habit but also to maintain it was illustrated by the comparison of drug users and non-users in terms of the number of people each individual knew who were themselves drug users. The average non-user was found to be very much isolated from the drug culture; strikingly few (10 per cent) of the younger non-users knew *any* individual who used drugs (and, in later informal discussions, some such individuals expressed disbelief that anyone in their school had ever used drugs). Older non-users had somewhat greater knowledge of drug use among their contemporaries (25 per cent knew one or more drug users).

Drug users in the sample were much more aware of others who use both their own drugs of preference and other drug substances, with the older users showing somewhat more such knowledge than the younger. A fairly close-knit drug-using community seems to be indicated, which, at present, the majority of non-users are only remotely aware of.

To summarize: the three representative surveys furnished no evidence to support a social deprivation explanation of the incidence of drug use among Malaysian secondary schoolchildren, and only limited applicability for a personal problem explanation, although such explanations have been found to be more applicable to the adult drug dependants coming to the attention of hospitals and the police in Malaysia. The differences in level of drug abuse and in the types of drugs preferred between lower and upper forms in the secondary schools indicated that drug experimentation in schools should be seen as a matter of fashion: in some friendship groups, drug use is an approved and encouraged behaviour, whilst in most it is fairly strongly disapproved of. The surveys, whilst not designed to map actual drug using friendship group networks, nonetheless demonstrated in the analyses of the sample by ethnic group, by geographical locality, and by age, that such mapping would be quite feasible.

Within drug using groups, if expressed attitudes are taken at face value, there was found to be considerably more positive attitudes towards drugs, and more complacent beliefs about their properties, than are to be found among non-using groups. Thus, attitudes rather than demographic variables are *better* predictors of which individuals in a population would be those who have experienced drugs. However, this does not mean that there was a polarization of views between users and non-users. Indeed, the two were capable of holding very similar images of the 'typical drug user', and many individuals who had had some experience of drugs were now capable of expressing anti-drug attitudes. One cannot necessarily deduce from the overall finding that drug users hold the most positive attitudes towards drugs, that they now use drugs because in the past they came to hold such attitudes. Many seemingly 'causal' attitudes are in fact *post hoc* rationalizations for behaviours performed for other reasons, the example and pressure of friends being a major factor in the case of initiation to drugs. And the reasons why an individual chooses one group of friends rather than another (and thus comes under their influence) is in part a matter of the self-image and more general attitudes and values the individual holds. Hence, the surveys examined the aspirations, self concepts and social attitudes of the drug users, and found them to be, in general, indicative of a more assertive, occasionally rebellious, and precocious approach to life. Social precocity, it is therefore argued, best predicts those individuals who will experiment with drug use at a time when the youth culture includes such drug use among the repertoire of potential behaviours that the young can adopt.

The surveys have been carried out with the more accessible section of the youth population, namely, those who remain in secondary school. Clearly, by sixth-form level, this sample has become fairly unrepresentative of the age-group in the country, and the aim is to survey next the non-student youth in Malaysia. Nonetheless, the findings of these surveys of school-attending adolescents have been presented in some detail because, it is argued, many of the observations are likely to apply to the whole of the adolescent population, whether at school, at work, or unemployed.

THAILAND

The changes in Thai society, and in particular the increasing urbanization and the drift to Bangkok from the countryside, have been described by Khunyung Ambhorn Meesook (*Cultures in Collision*, I. Pilowsky (ed.), Adelaide, Australian National Association for Mental Health, 1975). In the past, she argues, each village could be regarded as a large extended family, and all problem solving, for example, dealing with bureaucracy, was dealt with via personal contacts. The *wat* provided more than just the religious centre of the village; its monks also educated the boys of the village, provided psychological counselling, resolved conflicts between individuals, and gave some basic medical attention. Now, these roles are more and more being taken over by other institutions, and the *wat* has become less of a focus. In the central region of the country, as many as 70 per cent of the young people of the villages are moving away to Bangkok, and it is suggested that this represents more than just a physical distancing from their past. In the move to the city, belief systems change, the support of the family is weakened, and sex roles converge and become more 'international'.

The use of drugs amongst urban youth is *not* limited to those who have personal, social, or economic problems, but would seem better described in terms of the life-styles of youth culture in the capital and other cities. Thus, in the Thammasat University's study of young drug users at three treatment centres (*Repeated Drug Addiction*, Thammasat University, Bangkok, 1977), it was found that the large majority of young addicts considered that they had good or at least average relationship with their family; the majority kept in close touch with the family; and they were either in full-time employment, or were students. Thus, as the study concludes, the circumstances of homelessness, helplessness, and of poor family relationships cannot be said to explain drug use amongst this population. Much more to the point, three-quarters of the addicts reported that they lived in those areas of the city where drugs were sold, and that perceived availability was high. This is in contrast with the 8 per cent who stated that they had used the drug to combat medical or work problems. From the interviews, social influences, rather than personal problems, were clearly at the root of the drug use.

A further piece of evidence points to the social rather than personal origins of the habit. In his review of many studies of student populations in Thailand, Suwanwela comments that the rate of drug experience varies considerably between different types of school; not only are there changes of rate across the age range but, for example, private vocational schools have an average double the rate of experience that the technical schools have (*Drug Dependence in Thailand: A Review*, Chulalongkorn University, Bangkok, 1976). One might postulate that particular schools within a classification would themselves vary considerably, such that whether an individual teenager was or was not experienced with drugs would be better predicted by knowing which school he attended than by knowing anything about his home circumstances or personal problems.

Schneider, Sangsingkeo, and Punnahitanond surveyed 1,506 Thai schoolchildren in 37 schools throughout two northern provinces (*Int. J. Addictions*, 1977, 12:227–39). The schools and classes were selected as being representative of students by grade, sex, kind of school, and subject specialization, and the average age was 16 years. Nearly one-quarter of all students reported having ever used some illicit drug, but only 6 per cent reported current use, a figure much lower than suggested by the rather dramatic treatment given to the 'youth drug problem' in the Thai press.

Marijuana was the illicit drug most frequently reported to have been used (16 per cent of the sample had used it but had now stopped, and 5 per cent were continuing); next were barbiturates (3 per cent ever, 1 per cent current); and for other drugs, *including* opiates, 1 per cent or less had ever used them, and none were current users. Where is the youth epidemic, ask the authors? One possible explanation which they discuss is that their sample was overwhelmingly rural. There are differences between, on the one hand, their findings in Chiang Mai and Nakorn Ratchisima provinces, and, on the other, the Bangkok surveys summarized by Suwanwela (op. cit.): some of the Bangkok student figures for 'ever experienced' are half as large again as those for the rural students. But in both rural and urban schools the rate of current use is comparable, and is considerably lower than that of 'ever experienced'.

Whether the technique for assessing experience and rate of use is by self-report or by urine sample, the range in the published studies is between 1.5 per cent and 8 per cent. Schneider *et al.* conclude that it seems clear from their survey findings that the easy availability of illicit drugs does not necessarily lead either to their experimental or chronic use.

School students, then, do not seem to constitute the bulk of Thailand's 'youthful drug epidemic': rather, we should look to the tertiary education students for this. Shaowanasai states that a 'big proportion' of the heroin addicts he was treating at the Phra Mongkutkrao Army Hospital were in fact student drug users of 'a rather amateurish type', whose treatment needs were somewhat different from those of the older, hard, street addicts: typically they came for treatment with high motivation.

Suwanwela concludes his review of youthful drug use (op. cit., p. 8) by stating that the information on the student population remained very fragmentary and inadequate, and that further epidemiological studies were needed, together with an assessment of the role of education in the prevention of drug abuse amongst youth.

SINGAPORE

Drug abuse in Singapore was traditionally a feature of the older members of society until the early 1970s, when clinicians such as J. H. K. Leong (*Addictive Diseases*, 1977, 3:93–8) began to see the first of what he calls the 'pot and pills' group of adolescents and young adults come to a drug dependence clinic. Mainly from middle-class backgrounds, and themselves either students, servicemen, or in a variety of jobs, these young Singaporeans were taking cannabis and MX pills. The age range in the clinic for this pattern of abuse was 12 to 23 years of age.

Experimental poly-drug abuse did not long confine itself to these soft drugs. As C. C. Leong (*Youth in the Army*, Federal Publications, Singapore, 1978) records, hard drugs, especially morphine and heroin, began to replace them from 1973. He quotes official statistics to indicate dramatically increasing arrest rates (up 40 per cent per year from 1974 to 1978), with 65 per cent of the arrested drug takers falling within the 14- to 29-year-old age-group. At the time of writing, the bulk of the young drug users were using heroin.

Although Malays form about 17.2 per cent of Singapore's population, they accounted for 25.5 per cent of all drug takers arrested during the period, with corresponding underrepresentation of the Chinese and Indian populations.

C. C. Leong's book, *Youth in the Army*, is a fascinating and unique portrait of the youth of an Asian nation, based on interviews and case studies by Leong and his colleagues in the Psychological Service of the Singapore Armed Forces. As national service with the Singapore Armed Forces involves all males at the adolescent-adult transition stage, Leong's sample therefore comprises a complete cross-section of the age-group most at risk (and, indeed, as he remarks, undergoing the additional strain of accommodating to life in the armed forces).

Within the army, as well as in civilian life, there was a steep rise in the number of drug arrests since 1973–4, with, one must presume, a corresponding increase in the numbers unarrested and unknown to the authorities. Leong's interviews allow him to state that some addicted soldiers were spending close to S$1,000 a month on drugs, and, to get this money, were resorting to theft, robbery, and other crimes. Almost one in two of the drug taking soldiers is also guilty of committing some military offence, e.g., being absent without leave, sleeping on duty, or gambling. In the opinion of their officers, such individuals do not just make ineffective soldiers: they move into a limbo crowded by the malingerers, the 'poor disciplinary cases', the 'trouble makers', and the 'incorrigibles'.

Leong is quick to distinguish the factors conducive to drug use in Singapore from those operative in the West (as he sees them):

In some of the communities of the West, where girls lose their virginity as merrily as they abandon the boys who cause the loss, indulgence in marijuana and other drugs has become a fad ... a form of hedonism, the followers of which spend their time in pursuit of new forms of experience and stimulation. For them, drug taking is not a mindless self-indulgence: it is an avenue towards liberating the mind and expanding the possibilities of living! Only a small segment of Singapore's population of youths succumb to such beliefs and eagerly submit themselves to being initiated into drugs for the sake of novel experiences, of experimenting with living, or simply just for 'the kicks'. The more bored a youth is, the more likely he is to seek a passage to sweet oblivion.

Leong's Singaporean army researches revealed that far more common than the bucolic hedonism he believes prevails in the West is the direct imitation of friends' behaviour as a cause for inducing the drug habit. If an individual's closest acquaintances are taking drugs, *and* he is dependent upon the group for his emotional needs, then he is likely to follow suit when persuaded. In many cases, the individual had been initiated into the habit before he joined the forces, when his reference group had been other schoolchildren.

Having presented an overall picture of the drug-using adolescent becoming adult in the forces, Leong then asks if the hard drug user, compared with his peers, shows any particular pattern of delinquency or of personality problems.

His findings are based on two studies of drug users within the Singapore Armed Forces. Many of the drug users had been drop-outs from English-medium primary schools, and had had, before national service, a record of unsteady employment. They were found, independently of their drug abuse, to be significantly more delinquent or emotionally unstable than the average soldier.

Comparing the personal data in the files of 655 self-confessed drug takers with those of a sample of 500 non-drug-users randomly drawn from the population of soldiers, Leong and his colleagues found that significantly more drug takers than non-drug-takers were of low educational attainment. There was again indication of much greater delinquency: 21.4 per cent of the drug takers, but only 4.6 per cent of the non-drug-takers, had committed civilian offences prior to their enlistment in the army.

Low education attainment, delinquency, and drug taking are convincingly tied together by Leong's statistics, although as always, assessing the pattern of cause and effect between them is not straightforward. Do the drug takers come from more deprived circumstances, socially or emotionally, than the non-drug-takers? Leong takes a strong stand on this—asserting that they do—but his statistics here do not really bear him out, and his argument is left dependent more upon his clinical judgement and his impressions from interviews.

In both his studies, about 23 per cent of the drug users had lost at least one of their parents, *but* so had 21 per cent of the non-drug-using control group. Leong concentrates his conclusions upon the quality of home life: 'What really matters is the texture of home life: whether the parents are constantly wearing each other out by relentlessly bickering, yelling and banging doors; or are busily making a living from dawn to dusk, tending a chicken rice stall, or slaving as an assistant in a provision shop.'

A youth from the former background, he believes, has more need to seek solace in the easy, accepting, convivial company of a group of drug takers. 'From them, the offer of a puff of heroin is the offer of friendship, and how could he turn it down, especially when the offer is made repeatedly?'

Thus begins the familiar progress from the initial pleasurable effects, especially when smoked in convivial company, through the use of the drug to suppress one's earlier anxieties, to the often solitary continuance of the drug for fear of the onset of withdrawal symptoms.

INDONESIA

The modern, as opposed to the traditional, pattern of drug abuse in Indonesia has so much involved the adolescent-young adult transitional age-group that many of the observations of Setyonegoro and Salan, cited in the chapter on drug abuse among adults, could equally well be applied to the adolescent user: their predominantly urban, middle-class background, and their lack of involvement with the police, though with some indication of stealing from parents and other family members. Most were boys with good secondary education, especially in the years of the drug epidemic leading up to 1973–4.

Some of the authors' observations are particularly pertinent to the adolescent drug abuser. Thus, Setyonegoro (*ICAA Conference*, Hong Kong, 1971) notes changes in youth culture. Young Indonesians, wishing to be more independent of their parents, began to use 'extravagantly bright colours', long hair, and distinctive clothing, in their 'drive towards freedom'. Drug use was, for some of them, just another element in this way of life.

This led, in some parts of Jakarta, to the development of youth gangs out on the streets, defiant of adult authority, and often engaged in rowdy behaviour and inter-gang fights. This, Setyonegoro seems to imply, was a fertile breeding ground for the spread of drug abuse.

The abiding impression left with the clinician, after contact with the adolescent users in the earliest years of the drug epidemic, was of an escapist and hedonistic philosophy of life. Setyonegoro links this especially with those who had moved on from experimental to sophisticated, regular use. In trying to understand their approach to life, he concludes that the very concept of pleasure varies enormously from one individual to another, and may include what to the outsider appears to be perversities. He notes that some of the drug abusers show signs of depression or psychopathology as a result of their habit, and suggests that the compulsion to experience again and again the euphoric effects of morphine, heroin, etc., cannot simply be explained in terms of physical dependence: there is an element of a search for solutions.

Many of the younger drug users were at the experimental or casual phase of the habit, had not been using drugs for a long period, and, the clinicians reported, exhibited only mild or no withdrawal symptoms at all (Salan, *Colombo Plan Workshop*, Penang, 1978).

Can one then summarize the reasons why youth in Indonesia took drugs during the mid-1970s? Setyonegoro has been quoted above; Salan also suggests that the answer will lie in an analysis of the problems faced by the adolescent, in his education, family relationships, adaptation to changing circumstances, and personal relationships. The data provided by the Hospital Reporting Programme can provide some clues, but, in Salan's opinion, what is needed is diligent interviewing by clinicians to extend the questionnaire-derived information: indeed, 'The fact that the problem encountered by one teenage patient may differ extremely from another patient, is a strong rationale for an individualized approach towards treatment and rehabilitation.'

THE PHILIPPINES

Adolescents dominate the discussions on contemporary drug abuse in the Philippines, and the main research effort has been to describe and explain the rise and continuance of the youthful use of drugs from the mid-1960s to the present.

Zarco and Almonte (*Addictive Diseases*, 1977, 3:119–28) attribute the increasing involvement of youth in drug abuse to changes both in drug availability and in youth culture. From its introduction into the Philippines in 1955, marijuana had been ever more widely grown, until, at the present day, it is cultivated in all areas of the country, and is very easily obtainable in urban centres and school campuses alike. Unlike the opiates, which have always had Chinese crime syndicate associations in the Philippines, marijuana is seen as distinctly American. Westernized Filipino youth culture models itself upon American youth (or at least its image of American youth), and the youths who use marijuana employ the same rationalizations for their behaviour and the same drug slang and drug habits as do American marijuana users.

Drug use amongst students in the early 1970s was investigated by Zarco and associates (Narcotics Foundation of the Philippines, 1972). They selected a college within the University of the Philippines which had the reputation of having the highest incidence of drug use in the University, and, in a quota sample from all four undergraduate years found that approximately a third had ever used marijuana. Only 6 per cent of the students, however, used the drug as often as once a week, and, of the other drug named, benzedrine was the next most frequently used, often as a study aid at examination time. Mandrax, L.S.D., and other drugs were mentioned by fewer than 5 per cent of all students. The authors claim that the regular users of marijuana were also users of other drugs, and that 'a progression into the use of a variety of amphetamines, depressants, and opiates is certain'. This alarmist conclusion is neither borne out by the evidence presented, nor indeed was there a massive move towards opiate use amongst students in the years after the survey was conducted.

Marijuana users were found to be more likely to have had premarital sexual experience, and/or homosexual experience, and have lower course grades than non-users. Church attenders, church society members, and students who live in supervised university accommodation are on average less likely to be marijuana users than sorority and fraternity members, or students who live at home.

Four years later, when Cudal and her associates conducted their nation-wide study (*Youth and the Use of Drugs in the Philippines*, UNESCO, mimeograph, 1976), fewer than 3 per cent of these schoolchildren and young workers admitted taking prohibited or regulated drugs, four-fifths had never taken alcoholic drinks, and two-thirds had never smoked cigarettes. Hence, the main value of the study is as a review of the general youth population's knowledge about and attitudes toward drugs.

There was a very high awareness of the drug problem, largely engendered, the children reported, by media campaigns. Typically, they viewed (correctly) the drug problem as affecting all strata of society, and they see the street corner as the spawning ground for drug abuse, because it is there that the *barkada*, or peer group, spend much of their free time. Many stressed the health consequences of the drug habit (again, reflecting the stress laid on this aspect by the media), and were familiar with some of the physical symptoms of abuse. Consistent with this, many individuals say that, if they found a close friend or relative to be using drugs, they would seek help from a physician.

The image that the large majority had of the drug abuser is of a person who withdraws from the company of others and wants to be left alone, who shows little concern for his personal appearance and is not interested in any activity. (There is little mention of membership of a counter-culture of the type Zarco and Almonte (op. cit.) described as characterizing contemporary Filipino drug using youth, although half describe drug use as an act of rebellion against parents and other adults.)

Consistent with the health (rather than legal) problem in the perception of youthful drug abuse, the majority of individuals in the survey believed that drug users, once discovered, should undergo compulsory treatment, and they see the jailing of drug abusers as unhelpful. Most believe that the peer group is the largest single influence in the initiation of the drug habit, but feel that if they themselves were offered a drug by a friend, they would refuse the offer, and perhaps report the friend to the authorities.

HONG KONG

Although very far from solved, the problem of youthful drug abuse would seem to have been contained in Hong Kong by vigorous preventative education measures: all media facilities are used to their utmost, with their main target audience being youth. The estimates of the numbers of young people abusing drugs are necessarily imprecise, but one can gauge the situation from the falling numbers being treated in the main programmes: the Prisons Department recorded in 1969 that 25 per cent of the inmates in their drug addiction treatment centres were under the age of 21; by 1976 this had dropped to 8.6 per cent (*Hong Kong Narcotics Report*, 1976). Estimates from Ley (*Commonwealth Regional Working Group*, Kuala Lumpur, 1979) indicate that the downward trend continues: the youth addiction rate (under the age of 20) was less than 3.5 per cent of the total number of addicts. In the population as a whole, as opposed to detected individuals, only 0.28 per cent of the 15 to 19 age-group were shown as addicted to drugs (Central Registry of Drug Addicts, quoted in *Hong Kong Narcotics Report*, 1976).

One might well query whether the stresses and strains which lead to at least some of the youthful drug abuse have also diminished over the period, or are being met by the youth activities prog-rammes, or perhaps whether the problems remain, but are responded to in other ways. The literature on drug abuse largely exists in a vacuum, and is *not* integrated into a broader account of patterns of social life and social pathology.

Ch'ien, for example, suggests that one of the main reasons for youth choosing drug abuse as its mode of coping was the ready availability of drugs: if they become scarcer, then he suggests they would switch to alcohol. Other powerful environmental factors include the strength and volatility of youth culture: not only the influence of peer groups but also the criminal-commercial activities of the triads, and what Ch'ien calls the 'abundance of misinforma-tion about drugs'. A study which he quotes showed that one-third of young people interviewed in Hong Kong believed that if one was healthy and reasonably strong-willed, one could smoke heroin safely without becoming addicted (Ch'ien, *ICAA Conference*, Bang-kok, 1975).

Clearly, if such environmental factors were to change, then much of the impetus towards drugs (rather than alcohol, for example) would disappear. Yet the susceptibility to such influences remains, and it is wishful thinking to see drug abuse as merely a manifesta-tion of the present (and passing) phase of youth culture. One of the published studies which brings this home most clearly concerns young women drug addicts, and the forces attracting and keeping them in the Hong Kong drug subculture (Holzner and Ding, *Int. J. Addictions*, 1973, 8:253—63). Fourteen case studies are present-ed, rather than a broad representative survey, in order to get close to the individual's own account of her personal history, and drug experience.

All fourteen subjects were undergoing treatment for narcotic addiction; half were found to be under 20, the other half over; and most were Hong Kong-born. All had histories of frequently changing places of residence, and many had contracted what the authors describe as not very stable common law marriages. Few had had stable employment: changing from factory work to being a dance hostess or prostitute was a common pattern; and poverty had also characterized their parental families.

Many girls added that their family life had not been happy . . . the frequency of financial stress, moving of homes, and the lack of one or other parent. Where the family had remained together, it was not usually a warm, cohesive unit. From examining all the information about family relationships, in only three cases could we surmise that there was any real attachment to the family or any degree of strength and support derived from the family. The pattern of family disintegration seems quite clear, especially as compared to the traditional very strong Chinese family.

The case is an entirely plausible one, but given that there is no comparison group of non-drug users of similar social status, one cannot in fact conclude that these factors are the major ones precipitating the drug use pattern. [A cautionary note from a study conducted in Singapore (C. C. Leong, *Youth in the Army*, 1978): one might have cited the absence of the father, in the parental homes of 23 per cent of the drug abuser sample, as a likely factor; but Leong also found the same absence of the father among 21 per cent of his matched non-user sample.]

Why had the girls first experimented with drugs? Each gave several answers during the course of the interview (a point in itself to be pondered by the researcher who instructs his questionnaire respondents to 'check one'). Almost without exception, they said that they had been associating with others who were using drugs; curiosity, fun, and excitement were mentioned by a minority; and fewer cited the escape from worries as their reason. More than half said that they had been aware of the dangerous nature of drugs before they took them but—the 'abundant misinformation' at work again—they had not expected to become addicted so quickly. (Six of the fourteen had become addicted within a month of first experience.) Most preferred to smoke in the company of other addicts, and preferred to keep to a maintenance dosage even though they could afford more, since an increased dose would lead to sleep.

The girls were asked to describe their attitudes about themselves and their lives: they saw their main life goal as being a solid family life, and 'success' (however one defined it). Twelve of the fourteen saw themselves in a poorer light now that they were addicted, and had lost the respect of their former friends. Few had any clearly formulated life plans, and most found that the quasi-legal and illegal professions they now follow are likely to afford them a better standard of life than the mundane alternatives they see as available. But being a dance hostess or prostitute means continuing in a subculture closely tied to drugs.

INDIA

If there are few good studies of drug abuse among adults in India, the adolescent, and especially the student population, has been somewhat better surveyed (being, one suspects, a far more accessible and amenable group).

Reasons given for starting drug use by Indian students—curiosity, for relaxation, to help study for examinations—have much more in common with the reasons given by students elsewhere in the world than they have with the reasons given by adult, largely lower-class, Indians. The difference between student and adult patterns reflects the very different life circumstances of the two groups, and shows student use to be generally experimental and hedonistic, or, if instrumental, then, only to cope with an immediate problem—most often an examination—whereas the average adult drug user reported that his drug use was almost entirely instrumental, and helped him cope with stressful work circumstances or illness (Varma and Dang, *Indian J. Psychiatry*, 1978, 20:318–23; and 1980, in press). Drug abuse, it seems, became fashionable in some Indian universities, and it is to such fashions, rather than to any deep-seated personal reasons, that one should turn to explain prevalence rates, such as the 76 per cent rate found among male medical students at Agra (Dubé, Kumar, and Gupta, *Acta Psych. Scand.*, 1978, 57:336–56). (Note that, in these studies, alcohol is included among the list of drugs whose use was investigated, and contributes a considerable proportion of the reported 'drug use'.) Although the drug use found amongst the Muslims at Agra was as high as 40 per cent, it was less than the Hindu or other religious groups. Students from urban backgrounds have a higher rate of drug use, and Dubé *et al*. suggest that this may be because in rural areas drugs may be less available or less well-known; stresses and strains may be fewer; and there will be little or no impact of hippie and drug cults in rural areas. (Non-users, when asked why they abstained, reported a lack of interest or curiosity.) Stated reasons for use, as might be expected, related closely to the type of drug abused: thus, all tranquillizer users mentioned tension relief (and indeed, many had been introduced to the drugs by their physician in the first place); bhang, *ganja*, *charas*, and Mandrax using students tended to give enjoyment as their reason; with Dexedrine being used as an aid to studying.

In the older students surveyed by Dubé *et al*., attitudes towards drugs and their use reflected whether the student was himself a user or non-user. Varma and Dang (*Indian J. Psychiatry*, 1980, in press) have shown that, among students of the broad age range 10 to 24, the large majority disapproved of the use of most drugs, perceived that most were difficult to obtain, and saw most as involving great risk. Their disapproval discriminated between cigarettes and barbiturates, on the one hand, and the much more pronounced disapproval of cannabis, heroin, and L.S.D., on the other. The public image of the drug taker in the eyes of these young students was

fairly to strongly negative: he was seen as likely to be less ambitious than the average, and to be anti-social, emotionally unstable,
conforming, weak-willed, and sexually permissive.

The majority of these young school students had little exposure
to drugs apart from alcoholic beverages, and so they can be contrasted with the older students of the Dubé *et al.* study reported
above, who were fully exposed to drugs and alcohol, and, if users,
much more approving of their use than were the younger students.

PAKISTAN

Although the under-20 age-group are undoubtedly represented in
the hospital and clinic drug dependent populations, the larger proportion of drug users in contact with these agencies are adults, and
it is almost entirely upon the adult drug user that the scant research
effort in Pakistan has been concentrated.

Malik Mubbashar (*Colombo Plan Workshop*, Rawalpindi, 1975)
summarized the psychiatric evidence he has accumulated in his
clinic, and appended to his brief paper were the following observations on 56 teenage *charas* smokers who attended a psychiatric out-
patient clinic. Family income spanned all economic levels, with
some concentration in the middle to higher income groups. Half
of the youths reported that their parents had a poor relationship
with each other, and that they themselves had poor relations with
their parents. Although many had left school, or had poor performance at school, over a quarter reported better than average academic
performance. Again, about a quarter were known to the police.

The sample consisted mainly of regular *charas* users. Drug availability was perceived to be easy by the majority, who were on
average customers of a pusher rather than of a friend. The most
frequently cited reason for first trying the drug was to relieve tension, and very few reported that curiosity or excitement were their
reasons.

Clearly, the self-referred adolescent attending a psychiatric clinic
is unlikely to be representative of the whole adolescent population;
and the reasons these adolescents gave their psychiatrist are indeed
likely to have been elicited under circumstances where the doctor's
own beliefs about the origins of drug abuse are clear, and thus likely
to act as demand characteristics in the clinical interviews.

For this age-group of drug users even more than for the adult,
there is an obvious gap in the socio-medical literature of Pakistan.
The proposed Drug Dependence Monitoring Scheme for Pakistan
will provide much useful data on the patterns of, and reasons for,
adolescent drug abuse in the country.

CONCLUSIONS

Youth culture emerges as an important factor in the explanation of adolescent drug use in many studies cited, and its effect is notable in student groups (as shown, for example, in several Indian studies). However, as studies of urban youth in Thailand and the Philippines, for example, have shown, one can extend this explanation to much of the age-group. The pattern of at least some of the results reported in this chapter does parallel findings of surveys conducted with youth in America and Western Europe. Thus, adolescent drug users in East Asia have been found to be somewhat further towards the freer, more rebellious end of the spectrum of behaviour and beliefs than their non-drug-using contemporaries. They may be also somewhat less dependent upon parents, and more upon their peer group as sources of approval for their behaviour, they may be rather less religious and more hedonistically inclined. But such differences are of emphasis rather than of kind: one must not exaggerate the extent of the differences which have been found.

Studies which have investigated deprivation, personal problems, or misfortune as precipitating factors have, in general, tended to indicate that such factors are not very important. Thus, the reader will recall the Singaporean study which found no difference in the proportion of drug users and non-drug-users who came from homes where one or both parents had died, and the Malaysian study showing no disproportionate representation of children from poor homes.

Why, then, if drugs are easily available (as, at least, the adolescents who *are* drug users perceive them to be in many countries) do some individuals use them and others do not? Differences in perceived availability might, of itself, be one such explanation; there is also evidence that beliefs, knowledge, and attitudes about drugs and drug taking are important in determining the individual's response. One major difference between East Asia and—at least the well-publicized portion of—the American adolescent drug culture is brought out in Leong's interviews with Singaporean drug users. He found that it was the boredom of life rather than the glamorous or mystical image of drugs and drug experiences which led nearly all of his users to start their habit; and one suspects that interviews in other countries would yield similar stories. (However, some Indonesian and Filipino observers *have* stressed not only local youth's escapism, but also their extravagant life-style, as conducive to drug use.)

Many researchers speak of the easy availability of drugs as being the key to the control of youthful drug abuse, and, by implication, suggest that, just as an epidemic can sweep through a population, so also can it be subdued. It might well be—as some countries in Europe are now finding—that a behaviour rooted in the shallow soil of youth fashion may well be replaced by other, perhaps less damaging, behaviours. However, such an analysis does not take into account vested criminal-commercial interests in the maintenance of this 'fashion'.

A recurring theme of researchers working with young populations is what one has called the 'abundant misinformation' they possess about drugs. Appropriately enough, the next chapter deals with what society can, should, and is doing about providing preventative education.

V

Preventative Education and Information Campaigns

THE first part of the book has described the evolution of the current drug problem in East Asia, and the present pattern in each country in the region, and it has summarized what is known of the individual adult and adolescent drug user. The second part of the book is devoted to society's response to the drug problem, and will review preventative measures via education, the treatment and rehabilitation of drug dependants, and the legal and enforcement measures taken to control the supply and use of drugs.

Studies reported in the last chapter, on adolescents in East Asia, indicate how ignorant is the population most at risk. Thus, for example, one study found that approximately one-third of the youthful sample interviewed in Hong Kong believed that, providing one was strong and in good health, one could regularly smoke heroin without becoming addicted. The widespread currency of such a dangerously misleading belief, and other 'abundant misinformation', might prompt the easy response that society's first duty was to provide much clearer information about drugs and their effects. Yet the issue is not so straightforward: some of this misinformation, when further investigated (as, for example, in the Malaysian surveys of adolescent beliefs), turns out not to be erroneous, habit-promoting beliefs, but erroneous, habit-inhibiting beliefs. Some adolescents have been scared off drugs about which they were curious because they believed the substances would have immediate and devastating effects, and such beliefs were not challenged by the experience of meeting users of those drugs who had not suffered such effects. Thus, the 'simple' campaign aimed at replacing all misinformation with factual information about drugs and their use might sweep away more habit-inhibiting than habit-promoting beliefs, and the effect of the campaign would thus be to increase rather than to reduce drug experimentation among the target population. Drug information education programmes in schools, and information campaigns directed at adult audiences, have sufficient risk attached that a number of countries—for example France, Iran, and the United States—have at one time or another declared a moratorium on their use. How far have countries in this region been aware of the danger when planning their response to the drug problem?

Before considering the published aims and the achievements of each country, it would perhaps be useful to have as a touchstone a number of points made in various international publications on drug education (e.g., *UNESCO Courier*, May 1973; G. Birdwood, *Drugs and Society*, 1972, 1:4—12). Those countries quoted, which have, as policy, dropped drug education in schools, have done so for fear of provoking curiosity. Excessive publicity, it is felt, might well encourage the spread of drug taking. Where there is an agreement that some such education is needed, there should always be reservations about saying too much, saying it badly, or having ill-prepared teachers.

There have tended to be two, rather opposed, strategies in drug education. In the first, the concentration is very much on the dangers of drug use, in an attempt to balance one-sided pleasure-orientated communications the audience will already have had from peers, youth culture, etc. The second attempts to dispel the somewhat magic aura of drugs by putting drug education into health education classes, and not tackling it in a way which glamorizes drug use. Above all, whichever strategy is used, there is a need for objectivity and accuracy. Supposing between 10 and 20 per cent of students have some drug experience, then in an audience of fifty, there will be from five to ten individuals carefully measuring the teacher's words against empirical knowledge. If they note any discrepancies, they are likely to let their friends in the audience know, and the effect will be to breed distrust of the *total* presentation.

What effect can we expect from well-considered campaigns? To quote Birdwood (op. cit.): the supposedly preventative education about pre-marital sex in Britain and alcohol use in Sweden, for example, seems to have done as much to popularize the 'product' as to improve the balance between use and abuse. Effectiveness surveys on drug education which are adequate in their methodology are few and far between. However, there exist a number of teacher's manuals based on the experience gained in various countries, which offer fairly detailed advice on the pitfalls to be avoided, and the types of presentation which seem to be received best by different types of audience. (A few examples from one such manual: do not put on star performers by outsiders—it may lead to excessive curiosity and interest; do not give sets of factual instructions—these may act as a manual of drug use; do not stress dangers—risk-taking may be attractive to a portion of the audience, who can protect themselves by thinking that 'it can't happen to me'; and do not use ex-addicts—the message which may get across is that it is easy to kick the habit because they have done so.)

MALAYSIA

In the mid-1970s, when the Dangerous Drugs Ordinance of Malaysia was being amended to cope with the rising tide of drug abuse, steps were taken by a number of government departments and private agencies to launch a major programme of preventative education. Three levels were identified by Mrs Ann binte Abdul Majeed, the Chief of Preventative Services, Ministry of Welfare Services in Malaysia (speaking at *Colombo Plan Workshop*, Nathiagali, Pakistan, 1977):

1. Primary prevention education, aimed at providing information and education to those who are vulnerable to drug abuse, and providing services to meet these needs;
2. Secondary prevention education, aimed at providing information and assisting those at the experimental stage of drug abuse, and providing them with alternatives;
3. Tertiary prevention aimed at helping rehabilitated drug dependants, and providing them with adequate after-care services, in order to prevent them from returning to drugs.

Target groups were to include educational establishments of all levels, the 'world of work', and the general public; and information was to be delivered by 'suitable persons', so that 'the message can be efficiently delivered'. No details were given on the selection or training of such suitable persons; nor was there any indication that a systematic evaluation component would be built into the preventative education programme, as it had been in several countries in the region. Mrs Ann binte Abdul Majeed concluded that it was 'too early for us to assess the extent of success we have achieved, but we strongly believe that the family which prays together stays together'.

By 1979, the official review of national efforts to combat drug abuse (*The Problem of Drug Abuse in Malaysia*, Cabinet Committee on Drug Abuse, Kuala Lumpur, 1979) could speak with greater conviction about the programmes which were now well established.

The Ministries of Education and of Information were developing and implementing programmes which were the lineal descendants of those being discussed in 1977. There was now, within the Ministry of Education, a panel responsible for developing drug education curriculum for schools, both using special courses and also introducing the topic via the normal educational subjects. Guidance counselling services were also to be improved in schools. The Ministry of Information, for its part, was about to launch a nation-wide campaign, using all available media, to inform urban and rural audiences alike of the dangers and consequences of the illicit use of drugs.

The very existence of a Cabinet Committee on Drug Abuse is evidence of the seriousness with which the drug problem is taken in Malaysia; and the recommendations of the Committee have more and more stressed the importance of preventative education; gradually, the drug problem has been recognized as the human problem that it is (Krishna Iyer, *UNESCO/UNFDAC Fellowship Report*, 1977). The decision-makers (who are very much those who sit on this Committee) have come to recognize the value of educational approaches as a long-term measure in the campaign against drug abuse.

What, then, do the educational programmes consist of? One notable and intentional absentee from the campaigns in schools is any attempt to supply information to pupils on the various drugs or their deleterious effects. Campaigns are persuasive and general rather than informative and specific. Schools have been advised by the Ministry of Education on the use of a multi-disciplinary approach in drug prevention education: there is a pamphlet on the do's and don'ts of launching a drug abuse prevention scheme; another one details the actions required if a secondary schoolchild is detected smoking cigarettes; and a third provides guide-lines for the school's procedures, to be observed if a pupil is identified as a drug abuser. The Ministry of Education requires all secondary schools to submit returns not only of all confirmed cases of drug abuse among their pupils, but also of pupils identified as at high risk of becoming drug abusers (Krishna Iyer, *Proceedings of the National Seminar-Workshop on Strategies for School-Based Drug Abuse Prevention Education Programmes*, Bulacan, Philippines, 1978).

The Ministry of Education puts on courses for guidance personnel, giving them appropriate approaches for primary prevention, and it has also had these trainees design and evaluate posters relevant to a prevention campaign. The Ministry's guidance unit has also produced two tape-slide presentations aimed at youth audiences:

these have been found to be a convenient way of stimulating a non-threatening discussion on drug abuse with the adolescent audience.

Malaysia, like the Philippines and Hong Kong takes the position that an important part of the anti-drugs campaign amongst youth consists in the organization of alternative activities—'worthwhile activities for those pupils most in need of something to counter boredom', writes Krishna Iyer (1978, op. cit.). Thus, there have been a number of career guidance work-experience programmes for the school holidays, and a few pilot work-camps. Many other governmental programmes are officially cited as auxiliary to the main drug education campaign: thus, the free textbook scheme for the poor is quoted as a service which will improve the quality of life (which it undoubtedly will), and with the implication that drug abuse occurs because the quality of life is low for some pupils. Again, the official line is that 'it has been found that in all instances of drug abuse among adolescent pupils, factors operating in the home or the community have predisposed them to drug abuse' (Krishna Iyer, 1978, op. cit.); and, on this basis, programmes are being developed for parents and community. Again, such programmes are undoubtedly an excellent thing if done well; but such a description of the origins of drug abuse amongst youth keeps on forcing it back to a social deprivation or personal problems model when, as has been discussed in 'The Adolescent Drug Abuser' section above, there is evidence that an adolescent precocity model fits the majority of cases much better.

In fact, the case studies included in the packages sent out to schools and parents' discussion groups *do* acknowledge both broad models of the origins of youthful drug abuse. Evaluation of the materials currently used in the various campaigns is under way, and the results are due to be published during 1980/1.

As mentioned earlier, there are, in addition to the official programmes aimed at the school-age audience, preventative education campaigns for the general public in Malaysia, put on by both official and voluntary bodies. Thus, for example, one of the largest states, Selangor, has undertaken a variety of activities under the auspices of the Selangor Anti-Drug Abuse Committee. These include district publicity campaigns, distribution of posters in Malay, Chinese, Tamil, and English, organization of exhibitions, and courses of religious sermons. There have also been courses specifically designed for particular groups—youth leaders, village headmen (*penghulus*), and neighbourhood committees (*Rukun Tetangga*)—many of whom may be asked to be on the alert for signs of drug abuse in their communities. Voluntary organizations, such as the Lions Club, have been much involved in organizing particular local campaigns, and indeed have been responsible for producing some clear and level-headed publicity material. In addition to all such efforts, the national voluntary body against drug abuse, PEMADAM (National Association Against Drug Abuse, Malaysia), was launched in 1976, with the objective of bringing Malaysian citizens into the prevention of drug abuse, and co-ordinating voluntary activities in the country, both information campaigns and rehabilitation ventures, such as half-way houses, etc. PEMADAM's national campaign had, as its first priority, the training of staff for each state, so that there would be a consistent approach, common content, and concerted effort in the implementation of the later stages of the education programme. Programmes include contests to involve young people in designing posters and slogans, lectures, exhibitions, and public meetings, and the production and distribution of audio-visual materials. Krishna Iyer (1977, op. cit.) concluded his review of preventative education in Malaysia thus:

While there are a number of agencies involved in drug abuse prevention education, their very number implies duplication and need for co-ordination. It is also important to note that, to date, with very few exceptions, objective evaluation of the approaches and contents of the drug abuse education programme has yet to be carried out.

On both fronts, one can report progress.

THAILAND

In Thailand, preventative education and anti-drugs information are co-ordinated by the Narcotics Board, which, through its sub-committees, also formulates policy on enforcement, treatment and rehabilitation, crop replacement, and community development. Krishna Iyer, reviewing the basic philosophy of Thailand's anti-narcotics campaign, saw it as a calculated mix of the moral-legal, the psycho-social, and the socio-cultural approaches (*Education Concerning Problems Related to the Use of Drugs*, UNESCO Fellowship Programme Report, 1978). Thus, where the Board's target group comprises the current users of drugs, then the moral-legal approach is seen as being just as relevant and valid as the other approaches; and the creation of fear, the threats of arrest, and the mobilization of public opinion against the addicts is deemed as relevant as the changing of undesirable cultural beliefs (in, for example, the efficacy of opium as a panacea) and the denial of supplies of drugs via enforcement activities; where the target group consists of those young people who have no drug experience, then the Board takes what Krishna Iyer characterizes as a more clearly psycho-social approach, in developing appropriate anti-narcotics attitudes in their audience, as well as by pursuing environmental improvement programmes to alleviate what are felt to be root causes of drug abuse in the community—the socio-cultural approach.

According to official publications, considerable importance is attached to the preventative education part of the Narcotics Board's programme of action, begun in 1976 (see, for example, Thailand's *Country Report*, UNESCO Regional Meeting on Education, Penang, 1977). Many governmental agencies and private organizations are involved for example, in training programmes for public health officials, education officers, and some volunteers. One-day or two-day courses are held to explain dependence-causing drugs and their effects. Many educational establishments now have staff who have received some training in seminars, workshops, and courses organized by the Ministry of Education, which also collaborates with the Police Department in the training of teachers, who liaise with the police on law enforcement in the schools.

The report states that information was also disseminated via the media, but gives no details of the programme, or of any research on how effective it might be. Clearly, from the remarks of some observers, the Thai press had previously over-dramatized the problem, and thus any more carefully considered information programme was welcome (see, for example, Schneider *et al., Int. J. Addictions*, 1977, 12:227–39). Nor is there mention made in the Report of any central provision of teaching materials for health education in schools, or of any public information campaign such as, for example, Hong Kong and the Philippines have used with considerable apparent effect.

Indeed, one must ask of any education and information programme how effective it has been. Punnahitanond, in his *Survey of the Attitudes of Thai Youths about Drugs* (Chulalongkorn University, 1977), records that general drug use had increased in the four-year period from 1972 to 1976, even in those areas where (prior to the 1977 national campaign) there had been organized drug education and prevention programmes. Asked about their opinion on the effectiveness of anti-drug exhibitions, about 25 per cent did not think that they served any useful purpose; only 7 per cent believed them to be very effective; and the majority gave the rather grudging answer of 'moderately useful'. Asked why they thought that exhibitions were not more effective, the majority of individuals evaluated preventative education not so much in terms of what techniques it was (or was not) using, but rather in the context of the whole national anti-narcotics policy; and they characteristically remarked that such campaigns ignore the roots of the problem, and that the authorities should act against the powerful syndicates behind the drug scene. Most people, in other words, perceived the real causes of drug abuse to lie in the general conditions of society, and not in individual maladaptation.

SINGAPORE

In 1977, funded by a UNESCO/UNFDAC Fellowship, G. Krishna Iyer visited Singapore, Thailand, and Malaysia to document and assess programmes of education in these countries concerning problems related to the use of drugs; and his report to the funding agencies was published in the following year (Krishna Iyer, *UNESCO/ UNFDAC Fellowship Programme Report*, 1978).

After describing the pattern of drug abuse in Singapore, he turns to describe the education component in drug abuse prevention. This is carried out by a number of agencies, and 'there does not appear to be a clear-cut policy with regard to approaches and/or content of such campaigns, nor is there a clear delineation as to the target groups that should be addressed a particular message'.

The Central Narcotics Bureau has published brochures to give information to the general public, covering topics such as cannabis, narcotics, methaqualone (MX pills), and the role of parents in preventing drug abuse. It has also initiated campaigns to increase awareness, by placing anti-drug slogans in public places. (Singaporeans are accustomed to many such campaigns on a wide range of public concerns.)

The parental role has also been one of the concerns of the mass media, which issues 'discreet low-key messages to parents urging them to exercise responsibility in the welfare of their children'. Cigarette advertising is not carried in the media, and there is a concentration on recreational and sports activities.

The voluntary Singapore Anti-Narcotics Association has also been active in increasing public awareness of the medical and legal consequences of drug abuse. The Association's programme makes little mention of the social and psychological implications of drug abuse. Future plans include programmes aimed at specific segments of the population, e.g., factory workers and school-leavers.

The Ministry of Education uses health education and general 'education for living' programmes in schools, to develop and change attitudes towards drugs and their use via the inculcation of social, cultural, and moral values which would be inimical to drug abuse and delinquency in general. There is no special emphasis, or the highlighting of any particular problem, in the drug education programme: the curriculum merely provides forums on the responsible use of drugs in general, and makes some mention of the medical and social-psychological implications of drug abuse. The teachers in charge received no specific training (Le Thanh Khoi, *Working Paper EPDRAS/2*, UNESCO, 1977). Within the Ministry, there is a unit responsible for identifying and helping problem children, and it tackles drug abuse amongst other problems via group work techniques. Krishna Iyer notes that, initially, there was only limited support for this work from school principals, and his final conclusion is stern:

Overall, in Singapore, what appears remarkable by its absence is, that despite its smallness of size, despite the recognition of the seriousness of the drug abuse problem, there appears to be a marked lack of co-ordination with regard to the education component in drug abuse prevention. Whilst enforcement, detection, treatment, and rehabilitation appears to be well organized and systematic, programmes aimed at primary prevention appear to be ad hoc, pragmatic, and occupy a low priority in the total scheme of drug abuse prevention.

Le Thanh Khoi (op. cit.), however, concludes in a rather more sombre fashion, stating that the empirical data gathered from work carried out among drug abusers in schools reveal that preventative education 'had no effect in preventing drug abuse among students who are drug prone'. Rather, its effect has been counter-productive, generating interest amongst those most at risk. Those individuals who 'want' to get involved are normally already aware of the dangers of drug abuse, and are influenced much more by peer than by adult-authority pressure.

INDONESIA

Reviewing regional educational programmes on drug issues, Le Thanh Khoi (*UNESCO Document EPDRAS/2*, Penang, 1977) stresses that the weight attached to such programmes varies widely across South-East Asia, and cites Indonesia as a country where, since 'the phenomenon of drug abuse is not important', programmes and activities are limited and sporadic. Even if drug education is included in the school curriculum, it is unlikely to be effective, he concludes, because the teachers are not given training for it, nor are there any books on the subject available to them. Where drug education occurs, it is included in health and sports education for grades six to twelve.

Various other agencies, the police, health departments, hospitals, etc., have also conducted public education programmes (Widjono, in *Drug Abuse in Indonesia*, Jakarta, 1975). The first campaign was conducted by the police force, which sent information teams to different parts of the country, with the aim of increasing public awareness of the dangers arising from drugs, and of involving the public in the solution to the problem. Educational groups, community leaders, civil and military agencies, and religious leaders also participated in the programme.

Refresher courses for medical doctors, run by the University of Indonesia Medical School have, since 1972, included panel discussion on problems of the non-medical use of drugs, and some similar courses have been held for teachers and for social workers.

The Jakarta Metropolitan Health Department has, since 1973, organized an Annual Narcotic Campaign Week, with high school students and their teachers as a major target group. There are, in various official publications, references to the use of the mass media in the campaign against drug abuse, but problems of style and of the media's penetration may militate against their effectiveness. Thus, for example, Salan (*Colombo Plan Workshop*, Penang, 1978) comments rather sadly that, as a result of the massive newspaper coverage and mass communication time devoted to the drug problem, there was some panic among the public and governmental authorities, and some wild exaggeration of the numbers involved. It is doubtful, however, whether this panic spread beyond the urban areas, because, according to Sundardi (in Widjono, *Drug Abuse in Indonesia*, Jakarta, 1975), in the areas outside Jakarta, only one person in 116 reads a newspaper, and there are only 2 million radio sets and one-third of a million television sets in a nation of 125 million inhabitants.

THE PHILIPPINES

Opiate dependence may have been unrecorded in the Philippines since 1974, but, according to Mrs Aurora Cudal, a leading official concerned with preventative education, the government was not being lulled into complacency, and it continued to use large-scale, organized preventative education campaigns as a major part of its anti-drug strategy (Cudal, *Bull. Narc.*, 1976, 28:1–9).

The traditional practice of giving stereotyped lectures to undefined target audiences has been discouraged, and lectures to young people on the different drug substances, their history, and their effects have been abandoned altogether, because the education campaign now conceptualizes the drug abuse programme as being 'not merely a problem of drugs but a problem of people' (Cudal, op. cit., p. 2). Drug education has now been officially defined as the creation of awareness of the underlying causes of the drug problem in order to generate individual, group, and community involvement in formulating social action patterns to minimize those perceived causes.

Thus, in place of the more usual educational packages used in some countries, the policy in the Philippines is to employ social discussions, study sessions, and the development of individuals' ideas about the role they could play in the solution of the drugs problem. Such a policy might sound hollow, and the ideals difficult to translate into action, but the various documents produced, which describe in some detail how the policy has been implemented, would repay examination by those in a position to influence preventative education and community development programmes in their own country. Cudal (op. cit.) summarizes much of this campaign's aims and initial stages, and more detailed accounts are given in the two Colombo Plan Workshops on Drug Abuse Preventative Education (Laguna, 1974, and Manila, 1976), and in *Educational Programmes on the Prevention and Control of Drug Abuse in the Philippines*, Dangerous Drugs Board, 1977, as well as much further publicity and campaign material. Reports on the campaign are included in the *Philippines Country Report* to the UNESCO Conference, Penang, 1977, and in a paper by San Pedro to the Colombo Plan Workshop, Penang, 1978. The following is an (necessarily much abbreviated) account, drawing on all these sources.

The campaign, initiated at the first of the Colombo Plan Workshops (Laguna, 1974), can be very broadly divided into those programmes which are educational and those which seek to prevent, by providing alternative activities and facilities for young people.

Educational programmes for youth have been designed to stress the value of physical and mental health; the building of spiritual and moral values; personal and social development; the medical use of drugs; and the Dangerous Drugs Act of 1972.

The programmes aimed at parents contain much more material on the particular drugs currently abused: the causes, nature, and extent of the drug abuse problem; and they also include dialogues on relationships within the family (including parent-child communication), growth, and personality development.

Community leaders receive yet another emphasis in the programmes designed specifically for them: here, there are discussions on law enforcement, treatment and rehabilitation, preventative education, and research and statistics.

Education programmes can be based in the schools, or can be community-based. To illustrate how thoroughgoing these programmes are in the concept of preventative education, consider an example of a community education project at San Antonio, Singalong (cited by Cudal, op. cit., p. 4). Community leaders at San Antonio initially requested a seminar on drug abuse prevention and control; the seminar took place, and as a result the community leaders decided that there should be a planned programme, to be integrated with existing community development projects; and a community co-ordinator was then appointed.

Thus, out of an initial seminar grew a project which studied the total community, its cultural and demographic characteristics, patterns of leadership, and pre-existing resources and facilities available for a community education programme. The project showed what the existing needs of the community were, and, in response to these, youth organizations were brought together, study groups for parents and young people were formed to focus on topics ranging from family planning to the Green Revolution, and sports and cultural events were organized, especially for the young. Contrast all of this with a pre-packaged information programme, standardized and unaware of the local situation and the needs of a particular community.

Many other programmes with the same kind of philosophy could be cited: youth leadership seminars (with the participants then organizing events and programmes themselves, once they returned to their own communities); the Department of Education and Culture's requirements that every college student should give 120 hours of civic service before graduation; and the Boy Scouts of the Philippines Drug Abuse Preventative Education Programme: 'a busy and active boy following the scouting ideals will not resort to the use of drugs'. It has been made part of the role of relevant law enforcement agencies that their officers should be available as resource speakers at seminars.

Finally the media, through the National Media Production Centre, have been organized to supplement existing programmes in the community, and to initiate information campaigns of their own. Thus, for example, the media gave much publicity to the nationwide Celebration of Drug Abuse Prevention and Control Week, which falls on the third week of November.

How effective are all of these concerted efforts? As Cudal says, although each project contains an evaluation component, it is difficult to separate the effect of a particular campaign from the general 'favourable moral and social climate brought about by the imposition of Martial Law'. However, several of the research projects attest to the effectiveness of the campaigns in shaping and developing attitudes amongst youth towards drugs and drug taking. Thus, for example, Cudal and associates (*A Study of Youth and the Use of Drugs in the Philippines*, UNESCO, mimeograph, 1976) examined the attitudes of young people in ten areas throughout the Philippines, and found everywhere a very high level of awareness of the drug problem, as well as knowledge about drug abuse in the

Philippines, which matched the research data upon which much information in the campaigns and the media is based. Again, the widespread knowledge of the physical symptoms of drug abuse can be traced to their portrayal in the media, and their general perception of drug abuse as primarily a health problem reflects the stance taken in many campaigns. Altogether, the study shows how strong an influence the mass media can be in communicating information and attitudes about a topic of which many of the audience do not have any direct knowledge.

In the Philippines, preventative education, where it is aimed at a youthful audience, could be summed up by saying that it avoided over-emphasizing drugs and their effects; it contrasts drugs and their use with a positive, value-centred way of life; and it seeks to promote activities for youth which offer a positive alternative to drug use.

HONG KONG

In his report to the Commonwealth Working Group of the Asian and Pacific Regions on Illicit Drugs (Kuala Lumpur, 1979), Ley attributes the ever-diminishing numbers of young people among Hong Kong's large population of addicts to the strength of the Colony's preventative education programmes.

Prior to 1976, the audience at which such preventative education and publicity was directed was largely undefined; but the programmes contained messages appropriate to the public at large, the special risk groups, and those who were already dependent upon drugs. In 1976, the Action Committee Against Narcotics (ACAN) formulated a new strategy for anti-drug education and publicity, with separate aims for the general public (involving them in the fight against drug dependence), young people most at risk (identifying them as those with least education, and who are in contact with existing users), and existing drug dependants (to inform them of the voluntary treatment and rehabilitation facilities available, and to encourage them to come forward).

There has been a much increased use of the media in the campaign: television advertisements, films and documentaries, radio jingles, local district campaigns aimed at the young people of the area, advertisements and posters in places where most drug dependants would see them, and a telephone drug use inquiry centre (Le Thanh Khoi, *UNESCO Conference*, Penang, 1977).

The Action Committee Against Narcotics' strategy, described above, was designed to be cost effective, and thus from the start, it has included some evaluation of its effectiveness. Thus, when one of the first major local campaigns was launched in Kowloon, a survey was undertaken to evaluate its impact. One thousand eight hundred local residents were interviewed, with 75 per cent of the 15 to 60 age-group saying that they had been aware of the campaign, and 10 per cent having actually participated in the campaign activities (*Hong Kong Narcotics Report*, 1976). Sponsorship of sports events (e.g., an inter-district basket-ball tournament) has been another way to reach the young public, who, coming to watch basket-ball, also receive anti-narcotics pamphlets, and see plays on anti-narcotics themes in the intervals.

A further example of a campaign aimed at a specific audience can be given. In June 1976, a methadone detoxification programme was launched; an intensive publicity campaign was mounted, using all media; and 6,600 addicts had registered within the first year (*Hong Kong Narcotics Report*, 1966).

At one stage in this campaign, it was discovered that the drug pushers were organizing their own word of mouth information campaign, to scare the addicts off the programme by misinforming them about 'side effects' of methadone. As a result, a counterblast to this misinformation was included in the official campaign, and the methadone detoxification programme became generally known to addicts in Hong Kong.

A conventional criticism of the way in which education campaign successes are evaluated is voiced by Le Thanh Khoi (op. cit.): that what is generally measured (as here in Hong Kong) is people's *awareness* of the campaign, rather than the actual *behaviour changes* induced by it. However, the Hong Kong position on this is that each particular campaign (and, indeed, the whole of the preventative education and publicity effort) is only part of a co-ordinated public and official response to the drug problem, and should only be judged as such. Thus, it is argued, there have been manifest changes in behaviour during the period in which the campaigns have operated, but these are attributable to a chain of events. First, law enforcement pushes up the prices of illicit drugs, thus compelling addicts to seek treatment. Second, this demand for treatment is met by the provision of a range of treatment facilities (in-patient, out-patient, etc.). Third, education and publicity play their part in preventing the addict population being augmented by young people. Therefore, one cannot assess the success of the educational programme, let alone a single campaign in isolation.

PAKISTAN

At the first Colombo Plan Workshop on the prevention and control of drug abuse to be held in Pakistan (Rawalpindi, 1975), it is perhaps significant that most of the discussion was about what needed to be done, rather than of programmes already in action, and nowhere was this more true than in the field of preventative education. Only two papers were devoted to health education—one, by Muzaffar Shah, a general discussion of the aims of such education; and the other, by M. A. Kazmi, looked at the specific role of radio in prevention. By the second conference, held in Nathiagali in 1977, the focus was much more upon preventative education, but here the substantive papers tended to come from visiting experts: Eddie So, from Hong Kong, Mrs Ann binte Abdul Majeed, from Malaysia, and several speakers from the United States and the United Nations.

In the earlier conference, Muzaffar Shah stated that health education must be made an important subject of the school curriculum: 'exhibitions of films on the ravages of drug abuse should be displayed periodically'; emphasis should be given to moral and spiritual values within education; and also sport, folk dances, arts, music, and community social work must be provided. This offers an indication of what was *not* being done in Pakistan at the time: indeed, the tenor of the whole Workshop was that the drug problem in the country was not being taken seriously enough. However, the papers presented did not suggest how these desired educational changes were to be brought about: there already *was* a health education division in the Health Department, and yet there was little evidence of an effective programme.

The experience of Hong Kong, Malaysia, the United States and other countries in co-ordinated preventative education programmes was presented to the Second Workshop two years later, and this time, more detailed proposals were forthcoming: there should be an expert committee to draw up syllabi for schools; guide-lines should be provided for the Ministry of Religious Affairs, and for existing organizations within the community; and in-service education on drug abuse should be instituted for the medical practitioners of Western, Ayurvedic, and Tibbi systems of medicine. Similarly, there were positive proposals about the establishment of information centres; the writing of preventative education material; the holding of seminars for journalists; the establishment of counselling services in the universities, etc. (*Final Statement and Recommendations, Colombo Plan Workshop*, Nathiagali, 1977).

Some of the writers on preventative education in Pakistan conceptualize drug abuse as a sinful action, and thus see the role of the helping professions in an essentially religious light (see, for example, the paper to the Nathiagali Conference by Shaik Said-ud-Din Ahmad, who quotes Koranic authority for many of his recommendations). These are, however, backed up by some of the techniques suggested by the secular writers, so that his 'ten commandments' for those dealing with drug abusers include both spiritual exercises and the use of film shows.

CONCLUSIONS

Several countries in the region have committed considerable resources to preventative education and information, whilst some countries, at the opposite extreme, have little or nothing to report. Some of the education campaigns which are being mounted in the region are extremely impressive, well thought through, and clearly informed of the pitfalls described earlier in the chapter. Other countries may, however, be making the position worse with each campaign.

One characteristic of the well-constructed campaigns is their clear realization that there is more than one target audience, and that for each, a separate sub-campaign is needed. The Philippines has gone further than most countries in shaping the campaign for each group, and in getting community involvement in programmes. Rather than relying upon lectures to passive audiences, the policy has been to form discussion and action groups, and to use the *barangay* leaders and other established community figures to influence fellow citizens. Education campaigns can be, as suggested, too passive, allowing the target audience to escape mentally or physically; or, if active, they can be somewhat irrelevant to the issue in hand. Youth galas, painting competitions, and so on have what one might call a 'fun today, gone tomorrow' quality about them. Information campaigns which relate to the *continuing* existence of the problem and the resources to meet it, offering help to parents and out-reach to addicts, are a better prospect, and in the long run, we feel, are more likely to change community responses to drug use.

Drug education should be seen as a long-term rather than an immediate measure in the campaign against abuse. The challenge to proponents of such education has always been: how effective can it be in preventing drug abuse?, and the answer must be that its effectiveness can be evaluated only in context and over relatively long periods of time. A subtle and consistent campaign may aim to counter the seductive pro-drugs aspects of youth culture, and eventually to turn that very culture around: this aim is not achieved easily or rapidly. Existing worries about drugs, which the target audience may have, need to be given a stronger informational base, whence the individual can reject possible future temptations. Countries have varied in how this is to be done in practice. Malaysia, for example, has explicitly *not* included specific information about drugs and their effects in campaigns aimed at schoolchildren: the policy here is to use only general persuasion against drugs. This contrasts with a number of countries in the region, whose policy is to include factual information to schoolchildren as well as to community leaders. One way of avoiding glamorizing drug use, and appearing to claim special importance for it, is to embed drug education campaigns for schoolchildren within general health education. One can, by allying the topic to discussions of adult-youth relationships, self-development, and social ideals, appeal to the individual's sense of responsibility.

Publicity and education campaigns have been discussed in the present chapter mainly in their preventative role. But, as the example of Hong Kong indicates, information campaigns can have major importance in the recruitment of existing drug users to treatment programmes. Drug users, who are otherwise reliant upon word of mouth information on the treatment facilities available, can be directly informed about new facilities, as they become available, by the media acting in this service role.

As conceptualized in the most thoroughly thought through published policy documents, preventative education and information campaigns have, however, attitude formation and change as their major role, and this they can do effectively only in conjunction with other measures to reduce supply and demand, and to provide treatment for dependent individuals. Education is not a panacea by itself: as some of its perspicacious 'consumers' told the researcher in one study reported above, drug information campaigns cannot be expected to have much effect if governments do not tackle the major traffickers and pushers.

VI

The Treatment and Rehabilitation
of the Drug Dependant

THE development of facilities for the treatment and rehabilitation
of the drug dependant has lagged some way behind the emergence
of the drug problem in East Asia. Where drug use and dependence
existed in traditional societies, then there were some treatments
evolved by folk experience: some of these survived and will be discussed both in the present chapter and in the concluding chapter.
Where the problem was on a larger scale, as in opium smoking
by city dwellers and industrial labourers prior to the 1950s, then
the treatment and rehabilitation facilities tended to be rudimentary. Initial treatment, if it was available, might well be successful:
the main problem was the lack of after-care. The League of Nations
Commission Report of 1930 summarized the situation thus:

The concensus of opinion expressed before the Commission by doctors and
experts such as officials dealing with the opium question, and directors of prisons, was that the cure of opium addiction is not only possible, but comparatively easy, with the exception of inveterate addiction, which is considered
incurable. . . . As a rule, young addicts and moderate users are more easily
cured than others. . . . In order to make a cure possible, and to prevent the
former addict from relapsing into his old habit, it is necessary to keep him
from coming into contact with opium smokers. Experience proves that, though
the cure itself as a rule is successful, the majority of the cured relapse into
their old habit by succumbing to temptation from contact with smokers. To
prevent this, it will be necessary to adopt measures of a social character, aiming at keeping the cured addicts in favourable surroundings, preventing their
contact with smokers, and providing them with moral support to withstand
temptation.

The epidemic spread of drug abuse among new groups in the
population during the late 1960s, and the greater international dis-

cussion of the means of dealing with the problem, have led to a considerable growth in resources for both treatment and after-care. New techniques of treatment and therapy have been developed and imported from outside the region. The concluding chapter of the book, in its discussion of society's responses to drug abuse, will consider how these international approaches and the surviving traditional methods can be brought together, and it will stress the need for comparative evaluations of the effectiveness of all approaches. This issue will therefore not be further dealt with here.

Much of the present chapter is spent describing the various policies and administrative structures chosen for the implementation of these policies, and the relative roles of state and voluntary organizations in the provision of treatment and rehabilitation. Situations vary considerably in the region: what is required in urban Hong Kong may well be very different from that needed in the rural areas of Indonesia. The very drugs abused, the degree and extent of dependency in the community, the support from the family which the clinician can depend upon, may all differ.

The reader will notice variations in the philosophy and practice of the countries in their definition of drug use: some lay more emphasis upon the habit as behaviour needing treatment; others tend to stress its criminality. Some legal codes have instituted the requirement for compulsory treatment for detected drug dependants. This has the effect of bringing to the treatment programmes individuals whose motivations for cessation are not strong. (Even where a treatment is described as being for voluntary patients, the reality may be somewhat different: such patients may have been presented the alternatives of seeking treatment or facing legal action.) Now, many researchers have stressed the importance of strong commitment to obtaining cure: good motivation is a predictor of favourable treatment outcome. Thus, the route by which, and the state of mind in which, patients present themselves for treatment should receive careful consideration.

The 1930 League of Nations Report stressed the relative ease with which one can detoxify the patient, compared with the problem of rehabilitation and after-care. The reader will note how seldom, in the descriptions which follow, is it possible to find a fully-operative rehabilitation and after-care programme in operation in East Asia half a century later.

MALAYSIA

Malaysia has entered into the field of drug treatment and rehabilitation relatively recently, although, as will be discussed below, traditional medicine in the country has been involved in the treatment of addiction for a longer period, and there is currently an investigation into how the two systems might be used together, with some patients receiving traditional and some the modern modes of treatment, according to suitability.

It is now officially recognized that any sound therapeutic approach must allow flexibility in the modalities, because there are many human differences between one drug user and the next (*The Problem of Drug Abuse in Malaysia*, Cabinet Committee on Drug Abuse Control, Kuala Lumpur, 1979). Legal provisions seek to encourage early case identification and intervention, medical treatment with psychological support, and restoration to society through supervision and after-care. Legal provision was made for the rehabilitation of drug dependants for the first time as recently as 1975, when the Dangerous Drugs (Amendment) Act was passed. Under the Act, the Ministry of Social Welfare Services was mandated to establish and administer a rehabilitation programme, with the Ministry of Health providing detection and detoxification facilities.

Three existing welfare institutions were modified to provide residential rehabilitation for drug dependants. At the time of writing three centres, plus a fourth one, provide total accommodation for 600 rehabilitees. This number is planned to be doubled by the development of a further two centres. Each major area of Peninsular Malaysia will then have a relatively accessible rehabilitation centre.

It is also intended that there should be at least one detoxification centre in each state in Malaysia, and several hospitals are building additional facilities. There has been a sharing of responsibilities between the two Ministries, which Adnan bin Haji Abdullah, the Director-General of Social Welfare, described as being somewhat odd, but which has turned out to have satisfactory results (*Colombo Plan Workshop*, Penang, 1978). It might well be, he argues, that ideally detection and detoxification should be built-in functions of a comprehensive rehabilitation centre, but economic necessity compelled the country to make the best use of existing structures in the implementation of the new law.

One must distinguish among the suspected drug dependant, the convicted offender against the Dangerous Drugs Ordinance, and the drug dependant who volunteers for treatment.

The suspected drug dependant may arrive at treatment via the following route: a social welfare officer or police officer may produce him before a magistrate for remand to a detection centre. If he is certified there to be a drug dependant, and social welfare reports indicate him to be suitable, the court may have him admitted to a rehabilitation centre. (The court may, alternatively place him under the non-institutional supervision of a social welfare officer for two years, if he enters a bond of good behaviour: breach of the bond is an offence under the Ordinance.)

The drug dependant who has been convicted of a criminal offence under the Ordinance may, if he is under 21, be admitted by the court to a rehabilitation centre for six months (or committed to the two-year supervision described above). The court may, however, impose a fine or a term of imprisonment.

Finally, any drug dependant may voluntarily apply for admission to a rehabilitation centre, and his admission procedure would be similar to that for a suspected drug dependant, including becoming subject to the provisions of the law.

Clearly, as Adnan (op. cit.) and other writers have suggested, the provision of facilities at each stage has not been equal to the needs, and the *Third Malaysia Plan* (1976–80) includes various improvements which are now being implemented, such that the target figure in respect of accommodation, for the end of 1980, will be for 1,393 rehabilitees.

The underlying principles of rehabilitation in Malaysia are as follows:

(1) place the responsibility upon the resident to derive the maximum benefit from his stay at the centre;

(2) provide psychological counselling to back up therapy;

(3) isolate the residents from concentrated urban centres, by planning the centres away from their possible influences;

(4) offer 'purposeful activities' designed to aid the residents' return to a self-confident and meaningful life; and

(5) strive to be completely drug-free yet un-prison-like in atmosphere.

After-care, although it is recognized as an essential complement to treatment and rehabilitation, is only at an early stage in the country, and much of the existing effort comes from the voluntary body PEMADAM (National Association Against Drug Abuse, Malaysia), which is establishing half-way houses and day-care centres in the major urban areas. A private centre in Perak has been running for a number of years, subject to the rules of the Ministry of Social Welfare. Data on the incidence of drug dependence in the country are being collated from the returns made by the Ministry of Health, the Ministry of Social Welfare Services, the Police, and the Central Narcotics Bureau to the Central Data Bank operated by Universiti Sains Malaysia. This, plus data from all registered medical practitioners, will permit the formulation of reliable statistical data on the patterns of drug abuse in the country, as they are known to the separate authorities.

In Malaysia, as in practically every other country, there has not been any systematic evaluation of the various treatment and rehabilitation approaches actually or potentially used in the country. Malaysia has recently become, however, one of the five countries world-wide participating in WHO organized trials of a standardized international methodology for such evaluation (Hughes; Navaratnam, Sushama and Hughes: both papers in *Colombo Plan Workshop*, Penang, 1978). In each of the pilot studies, the collaborating organization developed its own research protocol to meet the particular needs of its study-population; but, strikingly, all five countries chose to emphasize different detoxification procedures. Later phases will emphasize the evaluation of after-care and rehabilitation. The pilot work in Malaysia suggests that it will be applicable to other countries in the region (Hughes, op. cit.).

In the Malaysian pilot study (Navaratnam *et al.*, op. cit.), subjects were randomly assigned to three different types of treatment and rehabilitation services available to heroin users. This assignment procedure was chosen in order to eliminate any sample biases likely to affect the results of the treatments. Thus, subjects were randomized, so as to balance out treatment-relevant factors such as age, educational level, criminal record, and previous treatment failures.

All subjects were followed up one month, six months, and twelve months after assignment to treatment. After twelve months, 24 out of the pilot sample of 53 had moved away and were untraceable. Missing cases were, however, fairly evenly distributed across conditions.

The three treatments compared in the study were: out-patient withdrawal; in-patient withdrawal, with follow-up out-patient counselling, and institutionalized social rehabilitation after in-patient withdrawal. Based upon the results from the small pilot group, the authors very cautiously suggest that a rather high percentage of relapses occurred both among the out-patient (42 per cent) and in-patient withdrawal (58 per cent) groups by the first post-admission month. Thirty per cent of the social rehabilitation group also admitted drug use at the one month follow-up (and then absconded). The very tentative conclusion offered was that, if the trends found with the social rehabilitation group were observed in larger samples, and over longer periods of the follow-up, then prolonged removal of drug addicts from the community, and the spending of additional monies on such programmes, could result in higher abstinence rates.

The decision as to which approach to pursue remains, clearly, one for policy-makers rather than social scientists. One further approach exists, and has recently excited interest among both social scientists and policy-makers: the treatments being offered privately to drug dependants by traditional Malay practitioners, *bomoh*. The research questions have been: what are the techniques used by the *bomoh*, what do their medicaments consist of, and how effective are their treatments? Policy implications might then flow from any indication that such treatments were effective. The following account is drawn from Heggenhougen and Navaratnam (*UNESCO Courier*, August 1979); and Heggenhougen and Navaratnam (manuscript in preparation).

There are in Malaysia approximately 2,000 full-time and as many as 20,000 part-time *bomoh*, to whom a substantial proportion of the population turn for the treatment of many ailments. A few of these *bomoh* have an established reputation for treating addicts, and draw clients from well beyond their local area. In August 1977, more than 100 *bomoh* met with cabinet-level government officials to discuss their potential role in the national anti-drug campaign. One of the consequences of this meeting was the formation of the Malaysian Association of Traditional Medicine.

Treatments vary between *bomoh*, but certain similarities are notable in the treatment of drug addiction. All healers use one or more medicinal 'teas' during the detoxification phase, although the period over which they are administered may be as short as three days or as long as a month. Many healers also include a spiritual component in their treatment programme, although this again varies considerably, some giving regular Islamic religious teaching in regular evening sessions, and others relying on lengthy incantations from the Koran, or the writing of Koranic verses on the chest and stomach of the patients on particular specified days of the detoxification. (Interestingly, the latter ritual is used with no concern as to whether the patient is Muslim or non-Muslim.)

Some of the healers perform *pembenci*, hatred charms, against the narcotic drugs. One *bomoh* observed by Heggenhougen used the following *pembenci*: crosses were cut in a medicine pot, whilst chanting the patient's name; four stones were then placed in a pot as the name was called out again; and then for three successive nights, the *ratib*—the constant repetition of the name of Allah, to create an almost ecstatic trance—was performed. *Pembenci* are usually used by *bomoh* for wives wanting a charm to keep their husbands away from mistresses, or for landlords wanting to drive out undesirable tenants. The remainder of the treatment (the herbal teas, etc.) approximates the treatment the *bomoh* would use to deal with mental illness.

The composition of the herbal teas is usually kept secret by the *bomoh*, but appears to be a compound of herbal leaves, roots, and tubers. (Again, there is a wide variation among the preparations used by different *bomoh*, from fairly simple compounds, to ones consisting of a large number of substances.) The therapeutic value of these teas is still not clear. Interviews with clients who have undergone treatment by traditional healers indicate that the consumption of these teas does indeed suppress the severity of withdrawal pain. Preliminary pharmacological analysis of specimens of these herbal teas indicates that they might well have the ability to suppress withdrawal in addicts: they have a depressant effect upon motor activity in experimental animals, as well as having a marked analgesic effect. No traces of opiate were found in the samples, although it is possible that some treatments do indeed use reducing doses during the course of detoxification.

Most *bomoh* seclude their patients away from their usual home environment during the treatment (although some do sell herbal teas to what might be described as their out-patients). In this way, they can create an atmosphere for change and for healing, using direct counselling, religious instruction, and near-magical techniques during the period of rehabilitation.

There are a variety of techniques used to ensure the continued success of the treatment: one *bomoh* discharges patients after two weeks, his cure being 'guaranteed or money back' *providing* that patients undertake to keep away from the smell of drugs for two months. Another makes patients swear on the Koran at discharge from treatment: they vow not to go back to drugs, or to mix with people they know to be drug users for at least three months.

Research is currently taking place on the effectiveness of such treatments by traditional healers. The clients of five *bomoh* drug treatment programmes have been followed up to twelve months (and in some cases longer) after treatment, and their abstinence rates checked. Inevitably, many former patients were untraceable after such a period, and, if one were to presume the worst, that all of them were back on drugs, one may set a 'worst possible' abstinence rate for each *bomoh*. This varies considerably among the five, from approximately 8 per cent for the least successful, to the two most successful, whose patients have (at worst) 30 to 35 per cent abstinence rates after one year. To presume that all those who were untraceable were back on drugs is to impose the harshest test of success, and there is reason to believe that some were untraceable because the *bomoh* had in fact wrongly recorded the patient's home address. (Seventy to 80 per cent of those patients *traced*, in the case of the two most successful sampled *bomoh*, were abstinent.) Even if the rate of success is within the range of 8 to 35 per cent abstinence after one year, this places *bomoh* treatment of drug addiction at least on a par with the other treatments now being offered in the country (and indeed, world-wide), and indicates that it is certainly worthwhile investigating this system further with a view to its incorporation in the national programme. The results of this research will be published in the near future. The reader will appreciate, however, that such comparatively high success rates (in a field where long-term success is depressingly infrequent) may well reflect a self-selected population, which might well consist of those most suited to such treatment.

THAILAND

The regional and ethnic differences in the pattern of drug abuse is reflected in the various treatment programmes offered. Thus, in Bangkok, heroin addicts constitute almost all of those who sought treatment facilities, whereas in the provinces, and especially in the rural areas, the addicts coming forward for treatment still include a number of opium users, and, among the hill tribes who cultivate the opium poppy, opium addiction remains a serious problem. At present, the country's resources are inadequate for the proven need: in total, there are less than 1,000 in-patient beds for the treatment of drug addicts; few patients continue on after detoxification in those rehabilitation programmes which exist; and in the three outpatient detoxification centres operating, rehabilitation and aftercare were only at the planning stage when the Thai Country Report was written for the UNESCO Regional Meeting on Education (Penang, December 1977).

The religious institutions should also be considered as part of the national provision of treatment: a number of Buddhist *wat* have provided herbal treatments for addicts, together with spiritual advice and support; and the most notable *wat*, Tam Kraborg, has a programme which will be discussed below.

Provision for the hill tribes is limited to a 50-bed treatment centre, which has been established at Chiang Mai University jointly by the Ministry of Public Health and the UN–Thai Programme for Drug Abuse Control.

Set against an estimated population of narcotic-dependent individuals not less than 50,000 strong, the present facilities for treatment are far from adequate (Suwanwela *et al., Colombo Plan Workshop*, Penang, 1978). Restructuring of the Narcotics Control Board in 1976 meant that all its activities, including treatment and rehabilitation, came under the Office of the Prime Minister, and a new impetus has now been given to a somewhat flagging and uncoordinated programme.

In the past, herbal treatment had been available for opium-dependent individuals from *wat* and practitioners. These herbal remedies, although widely known and used both by hill tribes and Thais, have not been tested for their efficacy, although Chulalongkorn University's Institute of Health Research has begun to evaluate the treatment offered by the Tam Kraborg (*Retrospective Statistics, 1963–1977*; and *Evaluation of Treatment Outcome, Tam Kraborg*; both published in 1978, Chulalongkorn University, Bangkok).

Considering the traditional caring role of the Buddhist *wat*, it was a natural response to the drug problem for some of these temples to assume the role of a drug dependence treatment centre, the best known of which, Tam Kraborg, is in Saraburi province, northeast of Bangkok. The three basic principles of its treatment model are:

(1) a strong voluntary motivation to seek treatment;

(2) a herbal medicine which is used as a purge of all physical taint from drugs, through vomiting and sweating; and

(3) a voluntary pledge of complete drug abstinence for life made to Buddha by religious ordeal, under the guidance of a priest.

A batch of heroin and opium addicts, arriving at the *wat*, take the religious vow, and then are detoxified *en masse* in a specially designated area of the temple. Herbal medicines are administered in diminishing doses for the first five days of a ten-day treatment regime. Some ex-addicts choose to stay longer, and may themselves assist in the treatment of others, whilst some, wishing to be ordained, stay on in the *wat* for a considerable period.

During the Chulalongkorn team's four-month study period in 1976–7, over a thousand cases came to Tam Kraborg, and the research team assessed the progress of each case over a period of twelve months, by postal questionnaire and by out-reach team, checking a sample of responses by conducting urine tests. At six months after the treatment, the abstinence rate of the heroin users was approximately 30 per cent, and of opium users 60 per cent, regardless of whether they lived in urban or rural settings. At a treatment cost of US$10 per case for the ten-day treatment, the Tam Kraborg programme seems extremely cost-effective, although many questions remain about the factors which affect treatment outcome. As much of the treatment—initial vow, explanations of the herbal purge's action, evening discussion groups, and final ceremony—is based on Buddhist beliefs and practices, this programme may prove more suitable for some cases than others.

Conventional hospital treatment of addiction has passed through several stages. In 1959, when the smoking of opium was made illegal, a special hospital was set up at Rangsit for the treatment of opium addicts. As it became clear that heroin was rapidly replacing opium as the main drug of addiction, then further treatment programmes were established to offer a variety of methods, the main one of which is in-patient detoxification, with methadone to decrease withdrawal symptoms. Some hospitals supplement treatment with psychiatric counselling, or group psychotherapy sessions, and religious instruction is also offered in some programmes. Few patients stay on to take advantage of the occupational rehabilitation offered at Thanyarak Hospital.

Out-patient methadone treatment for heroin dependent individuals has been available at four hospitals since 1976. Patients are required to report twice daily to their centre, to take liquid methadone for two to three weeks, and a psychiatric counselling service is available. The main criticism of this programme has been that too many of the patients are being re-admitted to the programme on an almost regular basis (Suwanwela *et al.*, op. cit.).

Acupuncture treatment, although shown to be effective by Showanasi, has been considered too time-consuming to be practised on a regular basis, and its use has been abandoned.

The treatment programme for the hill tribes people dependent upon opium was established in 1976 in Chiang Mai. Patients are treated with reducing schedules of tincture of opium, together with symptom treatment and tranquillizers. No rehabilitation programme is available, and, given the cultural context to which the ex-addicts return, the prognosis is not favourable. As Suwanwela *et al.* noted, ridding the hill tribes of their opium habit is a difficult and complex task, given their reliance upon the drug for medical and social reasons. Even if more medical teams were available, their presence would not persuade many of the tribes people to use modern medicine (Suwanwela *et al., The Hilltribes of Thailand: Their Opium Use and Addiction*, Chulalongkorn University, Bangkok, 1977).

The effectiveness of traditional and Buddhist treatment programmes was discussed earlier in this section. How effective has modern medical practice been in Thailand? The rate of relapse at the Thanyarak Hospital was shown to be fairly similar to that at Tam Kraborg temple (Suwanwela *et al.*, op. cit.).

Comparison of the drug addicts receiving treatment at Tam Kraborg with those at Thanyarak Hospital and at another conventional hospital, Phra Mongkutkrao, has indicated some of the relative strengths and weaknesses of the Buddhist and the conventional international approaches. Pornsiri Chatiyanonda and colleagues from Thammasat University compared the opinions of patients in each treatment facility, as well as assessing staff satisfaction in all three settings (*A Study of Circumstances of Repeated Drug Addiction*, Thammasat University, Bangkok, 1977). All patients selected for interview had previous experience of other treatment centres, and, looking back, 38 per cent had at the time felt their treatment to be successful because it rid them of drugs, with another 14 per cent being somewhat less enthusiastic, and as many as 45 per cent feeling that the treatment had left them with the same cravings, or at least that it had not fitted them to go back into society. Indeed, 38 per cent reported that they had resumed using drugs as soon as they had reached home after treatment, or even on their way home. Conventional hospital treatment centres were viewed as humane, with staff who were attentive to one's needs, and some recreational facilities which made the sojourn bearable. However, there were criticisms: medication seemed to be administered on a general basis, rather than according to individual requirements, during detoxification, and the hospitals were vulnerable to the activities of drug pushers. The Buddhist mode of treatment, using herbs to bring about vomiting, and herbal baths, seemed to have worked well, as symbolic of cleansing and purification, for those who had been to Tam Kraborg; so too had the support and example of the ex-addicts and monks who had assisted in the detoxification process. Some addicts, however, found the procedure too dramatic and unnerving, and the vigilance of the staff too severe. In both kinds of treatment programme, many respondents felt that more attention should be paid to the psychological side of treatment, and to providing a continuing after-care. Very few indeed had received any follow-up from social workers or from the monks, and yet, as some of this group of repeated drug abusers attested, they experienced considerable anxieties on leaving the treatment centre. Principal worries were related to their acceptance by family and friends, and of their being able to resist social pressures to use the drugs again.

Staff in the various programmes wished for legal powers to keep addicts until the end of the treatment period, and to make addicts pay a forfeitable deposit upon entry into the programme. The monks, in particular, were concerned to establish more spiritual bonds, and to introduce new values into empty lives. Staff in all three centres saw their work as in some ways undermined by the lack of success of the drug enforcement programme in society beyond the clinic.

SINGAPORE

During the period when Singapore's major drug abuse problem was confined to elderly opium smokers, their treatment and rehabilita-

tion was the responsibility of a single centre. This government centre widened its scope during the early 1970s, in response to the
new 'pot and pills' group of young abusers, for whom a clinic for
walk-in treatment was considered the most suitable facility. The
Misuse of Drugs Act of 1973 made drug use a criminal offence, but
those arrested, or volunteering for treatment, were treated as sick
individuals rather than as criminals (Leong, *Addictive Diseases*,
1977, 3:93–8).

This approach, coupled with public campaigns to increase awareness of the problem, failed to stem the rapid tide of new heroin
abuse, and because of this attitudes have hardened. In 1975–6,
changes in the law included corporal punishment (caning) becoming mandatory for certain offences, and also the death penalty for
trafficking or manufacturing heroin or morphine. The law now
empowers the Central Narcotics Board to order six months' compulsory treatment at an approved institution for addicts, to be followed by a period of supervision, including urine tests every five
days. In 1978, second-time offenders became liable to imprisonment for three years or more.

A total of 5,776 addicts were admitted to the drug rehabilitation centres in 1978, of whom 87 per cent were heroin addicts.
Replacement therapy was the method of treatment used in earlier
programmes, but now the addict is detoxified without supportive
medication, unless it is necessary to save his life. (The medically
unfit, and those over 55, are exempted from this 'cold turkey'.)
The second stage of the programme consists of a week of recu-
peration and reorientation to the remainder of the rehabilitation
programme. This consists of one week of 'intensive induction to
drive home to the inmates the evils of the drug habit, the realities
of life, and the contribution they can make in society', with the
freedom to attend weekly religious classes; 9 weeks of a military
form of training, designed to inculcate discipline and promote physical well-being via physical exercise, parades, and chores; and a
final three months of industrial training in the rehabilitation centre's workshops, to prepare the ex-addict for steady employment
in the community. Early release from the programme, or alternatively continued detention for up to two years, can be ordered by
a review committee appointed by the Minister of Home Affairs.
There were, in 1979, six rehabilitation centres, with accommodation capacity for 3,698 males and 143 females (*Singapore Country
Report*, Commonwealth Regional Working Group on Illicit Drugs,
Kuala Lumpur, 1979; Ng, *Colombo Plan Workshop*, Penang, 1978).
Although neither of these official reports contains any full evaluation of the programme, Ng notes that the rate of recidivism is 44

per cent, which compares favourably with the estimated 90 per cent relapse rate before compulsory after-care was introduced.

The need for prolonged supervision and after-care has been recognized in some of the legislation introduced in 1976: compulsory supervision for a period of two years was introduced for those released from the drug rehabilitation centres. Supervision officers—who may be either probation officers or special constabulary national servicemen—maintain frequent contact with their charges, and exert some powers of authority over their movement and activities (Ng, op. cit.; Krishna Iyer, *UNESCO/UNFDAC Fellowship Report*, 1978).

INDONESIA

Although there has been the abuse of opium and other drugs in Indonesia for a considerable length of time, there were few facilities available for the treatment of dependent individuals, either under the Dutch colonial or the Indonesian government after Independence. It was in 1969 that the state and private mental hospitals in Jakarta began to admit teen-age morphine or marijuana users, and gave them detoxification and preliminary rehabilitation. Many young people were also treated on an out-patient basis by these hospitals, and, according to Widjono (*Colombo Plan Workshop*, Penang, 1978), a substantial number were handed over to the police by their parents for 'cold turkey' treatment. The police considered this to be the best treatment method, assuming that they would in future avoid drug abuse upon recalling the intense pain of withdrawal. Many parents, too, were reported to have taken their drug dependant adolescents to traditional- and faith-healers, often without the individual's consent or even his knowledge.

As Widjono notes (op. cit.), there was some initial conflict between those who saw drug abusers as delinquents who needed punishing, and those who saw them as mentally sick individuals requiring treatment. Setyonegoro (*ICAA Conference*, Hong Kong, 1971), for example, wrote emphatically in favour of the supportive, therapeutic approach: withdrawal should be done under close supervision, and the young addict should be allowed to talk to his psychiatrist at unscheduled times. He preferred that addicts should come voluntarily rather than being referred by police: voluntary patients showed greater endurance during treatment, and had better prognosis than referred ones. Whereas the hospital treatment for withdrawal was seen as 'relatively easy', the rehabilitation of the ex-addict back into the community was much more laborious and difficult, and required continuing team effort from psychiatrists, social workers, parents, and friends.

This attitude towards drug abusers contrasts with the rather punitive approach taken by other agencies (Widjono, in *Drug Abuse in Indonesia*, Jakarta, 1975). Thus, for example, one finds that the Jakarta Raya Regional Government has established a body to co-ordinate activities dealing with the non-medical use of drugs, whose chairman is the head of the Jakarta Metropolitan Police, and whose other responsibilities include action against smugglers, counterfeiters, and subversive elements, and 'the control of foreigners'. As Widjono cautiously understates it: 'towards the illicit drug traffic, all agencies have the same opinion, while towards the users they differ somewhat.'

There is, in the treatment and rehabilitation of drug addicts currently practised in Indonesia, a conscious diversity of approaches, both between institutions and within, according to patient's needs and available resources (the latest review is by Widjono, *Colombo Plan Workshop*, Penang, 1978, from which the following summary is drawn).

When patients report to a specialist drug dependence unit (either the prototype unit at Fatmawati Hospital, Jakarta, or the others patterned upon it throughout the country), their drug use history, present state of dependency, motivations for seeking treatment, and future life plans are discussed with them in detail and also with their family. Where parents have forced a dependant to attend against his will, the physician explains the difficulties likely to be encountered in such compulsory treatment, and may try to persuade the parents that temporary ambulatory treatment would be more effective. For patients proceeding to treatment, the next phase is a thorough physical and psychiatric examination. Individuals who have been long-term drug users then receive detoxification.

Various detoxification procedures, ranging from abrupt withdrawal to gradual withdrawal, are employed. Depending upon the state of dependency, and the physical and mental state of the patient, symptomatic drug therapy may be used: tranquillizers, analgesics, antispasmodics, etc. Acupuncture therapy is also used by some units (see below for further discussion).

Post-withdrawal treatment may include individual supportive psychotherapy, individual counselling, group therapy, recreational activities, sports, language classes, art, and music sessions. There is an attempt to involve families at this within-hospital stage, either through family therapy or other structured family involvement, as well as in the post-discharge phase. After-care may also involve continuing individual or group counselling and therapy, social service support; and the encouragement of the ex-addict to participate in activities such as the Youth Red Cross.

The Police (Child, Youth, and Women Section) have recently opened Wisma Parmardi Siwi, a 250-bed correction centre for narcotic addicts. Admissions are on parental request, and detoxification is generally by abrupt withdrawal, unsupported by drug replacements. Rehabilitation concentrates on training the inmates in skills such as carpentry, hairdressing, and sewing, with psychiatric and social work evaluation and support. A success rate of 74 per cent was claimed in the first year of operation (Colonel (Mrs) Mandagi, in Widjono, *Drug Abuse in Indonesia*, Jakarta, 1975, p. 97), but this seems extremely optimistic.

Acupuncture has, as mentioned above, been included in the treatment of drug dependence by some centres, and Anggraini (in Widjono, *Drug Abuse in Indonesia*, Jakarta, 1975) has summarized the Indonesian experience. A preliminary study of acupuncture as a treatment was sponsored by Widjono at the Drug Dependence Institute, Jakarta, in 1975. In place of the drugs usually given to alleviate withdrawal symptoms, Widjono gave acupuncture to four volunteer addicts. Needles were inserted into the auricular lung areas bilaterally (as these had been reported the most effective needle points by Wen and Cheung, in Hong Kong), and 50 Hz frequency electrical stimulation given for a period of about 30 minutes, once a day up to 7 days. Withdrawal symptoms subsided, and three of the volunteers completed the programme (and the fourth, though benefiting, dropped out because his ears were still sore). Encouraged by this, Anggraini urged that further experimental work should be done, followed, if successful, by widespread use of the method in place of drug replacement therapy. However, reviewing the treatment situation several years later, Widjono (*Colombo Plan Workshop*, Penang, 1975) described the current use of acupuncture in therapy as sporadic.

THE PHILIPPINES

Under the Dangerous Drugs Act of 1972, the voluntary submission of a drug dependant to confinement, treatment, and rehabilitation relieves him of criminal liability for illegal possession or use of dangerous drugs. If an individual who is accused of any kind of drug offence is found to be a drug dependant by the court, then he will be compulsorily confined in a private or government centre for treatment and rehabilitation, in addition to any penal sanctions which the court may impose.

There are in the Philippines two types of rehabilitation centres: those that are general, and those that are specifically operated for the care of drug abusers (Zarco and Almonte, *Addictive Diseases*,

1977, 3:119–28). These are located mainly around Manila and Baguio City, the two cities with the largest concentrations of drug users in their population. In general, states Zarco, private rehabilitation centres have better facilities than government operated centres. Almost all are drug-free therapeutic communities, where most of the patients live in. Perhaps the rehabilitation centre which has the most thoroughly worked out philosophy of rehabilitation is DARE, which operates an admission centre and four other facilities, patterned after Synanon and Daytop in the United States, and which use encounter groups, confrontation, the authoritarian 'haircut', guided learning experiences, and a whole range of therapies during rehabilitation, with a social re-entry programme after the training phases are successfully completed. Government centres such as the NBI Centre also use counselling and psychotherapy, and spiritual, vocational, and recreational therapies (*Philippines Country Report*, UNESCO Conference, Penang, 1977).

The range of treatments available include the psychological, therapeutic community, day-care, and detoxification. According to Maravilla (*Colombo Plan Workshop*, Laguna, 1974), detoxification, although still used, is much less frequently needed than in the late 1960s and until 1972 (the declaration of martial law), as a result of the rapid decline in heroin addiction since 1972. Day-care facilities are provided by the Outreach Programme, for clients who are not regular drug users, and for those who only have emotional problems. Clients follow a structured programme in which they receive direction and guidance, and regular progress reports are made. Vocational rehabilitation is also offered in the day-care centres. Therapeutic communities in the Philippines, as in similar centres elsewhere, provide a protective and remedial environment for drug dependants. Total abstinence is imposed; the 'here and now' is emphasized, rather than past events, which may have contributed to the development of drug dependence; encounter groups confront the individual with his own behaviour; and peer and former addict pressures are used to modify conduct. (The therapeutic style of these centres is clearly much influenced by American practice: to take just one example, the therapeutic community at Olongapo City specializes in primal scream therapy.)

Psychological treatment on an in- or out-patient basis is available in a number of psychiatric units in government and private hospitals. Some psychiatrists and clinical psychologists now specialize in treating patients who have had 'bad trips', or who have exhibited unusual behaviour as a result of their drug dependence; and such treatment is intended to modify the patient's behaviour in the desired direction.

The very diverse pattern of therapies available in the Philippines, and, in particular, the great involvement of private agencies in the programmes, resulted from public concern, which was felt during the late 1960s, about the numbers of young people being arrested for drug offences (Cudal and associates, *A Study of Youth and the Use of Drugs in the Philippines*, UNESCO, mimeograph, 1976). Sensational newspaper reports appeared, the government was slow to establish treatment and rehabilitation facilities, and so the community became involved in the setting up of centres. From this period dates the Narcotics Foundation of the Philippines, which acted as a pressure group to amend the law on narcotics, and also the Drug Abuse Research Foundation (whose DARE centres have already been described above). At this time, there were a large number of other programmes to combat drug abuse: telephone hot-lines were opened, a newspaper columnist ran a 'Turn In A Pusher' scheme, and so on.

Since that period, governmental action has been increased, and the Dangerous Drugs Board has worked to co-ordinate the various programmes now provided by public and private agencies.

LAOS

A country with as lengthy a history of drug use as Laos is likely to develop a variety of methods of treatment for addiction, and Westermeyer (*Br. J. Addict.*, 1973, 68:345–9) has catalogued several such traditional treatments. The opium addict might, within his home community, be given massage, a thin rice gruel, and have sweating induced, especially in the toxic phases of withdrawal. Herbal medications (often containing some opium or alcohol) were known among all ethnic groups, and many addicts moved from one nostrum to another. Under economic pressure, the addict might switch from smoking to eating opium, which is not only less expensive (because it is less wasteful of the drug) but also less debilitating. He might decrease his dosage: experienced opium smokers, especially, are reported to be able to reduce their intake by removing themselves from the social surroundings in which they normally smoked. Thus, in one case reported by Westermeyer,

A. K., a 50-year-old Meo man decided to stop opium usage so that he might be more successful at his work. With enough opium to wean himself gradually off the habit, he went off into the forest to live alone for a few weeks so as to remove himself from the temptation to smoke in familiar surroundings. He remained abstinent for about two months, but subsequently became addicted during an illness, for which he used opium.

Various persons and places offered treatment for addiction:

thus, for example, some Buddhist monasteries have become noted for their successful treatment of opium addiction, by abruptly withdrawing the drug, within a supportive psychological milieu, and with spiritual inspiration. Lao village addicts tended to go to such withdrawal centres in groups, thereby to reinforce their own commitment to treatment. Westermeyer reports that such groups, once returned home, might act as an informal self-help group, to maintain their resolve and to help those who resumed the habit. He also records the existence of at least one private sanatorium, run by a Lao who had been a monk, who gave religious and psychological instruction to addicts. Upon discharge, his clients continued to return at weekly intervals to receive exhortations and ritual blessings.

Most traditional treatments tended to be combined, rather than employed alone, and they resemble in many ways modern 'Western' techniques of treatment. Thus, the withdrawal-within-supportive-milieu of the *wat* has its analogues at Synanon: the religious sanatorium with follow-up visits resembles supportive psychiatric care; and oral opium, with its slow onset and prolonged action, has many pharmacological similarities to methadone.

Against this background of folk treatments, the National Narcotics Treatment Centre was set up in 1972, as a 40-unit clinic, using detoxification and methadone substitution. In their report of the first year's experience, Westermeyer and Soudalay (*Proceedings of the ICAA Conference*, Bangkok, 1975) noted that the re-admission rates were high when opium addicts were given only a short withdrawal period before release: there was a much better success rate when the period was three weeks or more. They also noted the extraordinarily low death rate (4 out of 800 patients), considering how many had been seriously ill and had refused hospital treatment. Finally, they recorded that less than 2 per cent had signed out of the programme before completion.

Comparison of modern with traditional treatment success is notoriously difficult. Suffice it to say that Westermeyer (*Am. J. Psychiatry*, 1974, 131:165—70), in his representative survey of opium addicts in the community, records that, although most of his sample had made serious attempts to stop their addiction, they had had 'manifest lack of success in achieving and maintaining withdrawal', and showed considerable interest in asking Westermeyer what treatments he would recommend.

How did opium and heroin addicts compare in treatment via modern methods? Westermeyer and Peng (*J. Nerv. and Mental Diseases*, 1977, 164:351—4) used a study of pairs of patients, matched for sex, ethnicity, and age. The type of drug did not appear to be an important factor in determining the *outcome* of treatment, but it was noticeable that heroin addicts sought treatment much sooner *after* their addiction than did opium addicts. (There may have been an economic rather than a medical reason for this.) The two groups, however, did not differ for duration of narcotic use *prior* to becoming addicted, suggesting that heroin was not of itself more or less likely to produce addiction as compared with opium, although heroin addicts required higher detoxification doses of methadone.

The authors conclude that opium addiction is not a 'benign' or 'social' form of addiction. However, in comparison to heroin, it costs less, requires fewer doses per day, and has (at least initially) a less toxic withdrawal. Moreover, as already noted, opium apparently takes longer to produce life crises which motivate the addict to seek treatment.

Details of treatment techniques under the current regime are scarce, and estimates of effectiveness are not based on available statistics.

HONG KONG

In the 1950s (and before) a drug addict wishing to be treated would have gone to his private physician, received some short-term means of withdrawing from his physical dependence upon narcotics, and become re-addicted almost immediately. Some, according to Ch'ien (*Addictive Diseases*, 1977, 3:99–104), would in desperation surrender themselves to the police with a pack or two of heroin, in order to secure a court conviction and thus be committed for treatment at Tai Lam Prison's treatment centre.

The Prisons Department now operates three such centres for convicted addicts. After admission to the centre, an addict receives counselling from his after-care officer, with particular stress being laid upon re-establishing family relationships. Lodgings and employment are found for rehabilitees before their release, and a number of back-up services exist (Hollinrake, *Colombo Plan Workshop*, Penang, 1978).

Voluntary treatment for drug addicts has been provided since the early 1960s by SARDA (the Society for the Aid and Rehabilitation of Drug Addicts), which started a rehabilitation centre on Shek Kwan Chan island, to receive patients who had been withdrawn from physical dependence in hospital. SARDA now has its own registration and pre-admission service in the urban areas, and took over the withdrawal treatment from the hospital. It now can accommodate 500 male patients (with facilities elsewhere in Hong

Kong for 30 female patients). The usual pattern is for a voluntary patient to receive detoxification, 5 to 6 months of institutional treatment, and 2 years of rehabilitation in the community. Half-way houses and hostels have been established to aid this latter process, and, as well as providing sheltered accommodation, they continue to provide guidance and support during the re-entry into the community. A mutual self-help group has been formed by the 'alumni' of the women's centre in Wanchai, with over one thousand abstaining discharges (Ch'ien, op. cit.).

The methadone maintenance and/or detoxification programme was started in 1972 for those who preferred out-patient to residential treatment. There are 4 clinics and 17 centres, many of which are open in the evening, so that addicts are able to collect their methadone after work hours. Each centre has a doctor and a social worker, as well as auxiliaries, and treats or maintains patients over 18 years old (under that age, inquiries are referred to the SARDA residential programme).

Detoxification, if the patient so requests it, can take place over a period of 6 to 8 weeks, by gradually reducing the daily methadone intake. Patients on the maintenance programme may continue using methadone, as a substitute for heroin or opium, for an indefinite period, and the policy on transfer between the programmes is pragmatic: some patients are allowed to continue with detoxification for much longer than the expected period, and some patients registered for maintenance are detoxified at their request (Hollinrake, op. cit., *Hong Kong Narcotics Report*, 1976).

The numbers of addicts coming forward for voluntary treatment very clearly reflect increasing street prices for drugs, and it has been estimated that between them the addicts now attending the detoxification centres would have been spending HK$2 million per month on heroin and opium (*Hong Kong Narcotics Report*, 1976).

Acupuncture and electro-stimulation are being actively studied as a method for dealing with detoxification and the subsequent desire for narcotics. Hollinrake (*Colombo Plan Workshop*, Penang, 1978) described the preliminary results of the studies as encouraging. The technique, combined with naloxone, has been used for the complete withdrawal process in as short a period as three and a-half hours.

An account of this method of treatment in Hong Kong was given by Wen (in Widjono, *Drug Abuse in Indonesia*, Jakarta, 1975). A distinguished neurosurgeon, Wen had in the past been operating upon chronic addicts, destroying part of the frontal lobe of the brain under local anaesthesia, when it occurred to him to try acupuncture for its anaesthetic effect in the lobectomy. His first case using this technique was a known opium addict, who was experiencing withdrawal symptoms, and as Wen was needling and stimulating him for the anaesthesia the patient reported the disappearance of his withdrawal symptoms.

Wen did not believe him, but, wishing to test the effect, postponed the operation. Later in the day, when the withdrawal symptoms recurred the same acupuncture technique was given, to be followed by the same cessation of symptoms. Further trials with other patients followed, and from then on many patients have been treated. Early results showed that acupuncture seemed to be superior to methadone treatment during a one-year observation period (Wen and Cheung, *Amer. J. Acupuncture*, 1973, 1:71–84).

The Hong Kong experience has shown, however, that no single approach has universal applicability. (Wen reports acupuncture failures as well as successes, and that each other programme finds some addicts more suited to its technique and treatment situation.) As Hollinrake (op. cit.) concludes, the approach among treatment centres in Hong Kong has thus been pragmatic, opting for the multimodal provision of facilities. 'Success' is relative rather than absolute, but, whether measured by increasing lengths of abstinence, reduced criminality, diminishing numbers of adolescents involved in addiction, or by stabilizing family circumstances, the treatment programme can claim to have had some significant successes, and this in a country which has had the longest standing, most entrenched narcotics problem in the region.

CHINA

Even if published accounts differ on whether or not China has been absolutely successful in eliminating drug abuse (Gregory, *Drug Forum*, 1977–8, 6:299–314), most writers agree on the methods of treatment and rehabilitation used. The following account draws largely upon Gregory, and upon Lowinger (*Am. J. Chinese Medicine*, 1973, 1:275–82), who in turn summarizes much contemporary and recent Chinese writing on the subject.

The anti-opium campaign which followed the 1949 Revolution cannot be described in isolation from the ideological, social, and organizational changes which occurred in Chinese society in the early years of the Revolution. The nation, and especially its youth, had, as Lowinger puts it, 'a redefinition of their worth and role'.

In *Fanshen* (New York, Random House, 1966) J. Hinton explains this process as a 'turning-over': 'To China's hundreds of millions of landless peasants, it meant stand up to throw off the landlord yoke, to gain land, stock, implements, and houses. But it meant much more than this. It meant to throw off superstition and to study science, to abolish "word blindness" and learn to read . . . it meant to enter a new world.'

Local cadres, organized through small street committees, carried out national decisions, and were responsible for propaganda, agitation, and indoctrination in the anti-opium campaign. In this, as in many other areas of life, the local cadres were the main source of detection and social censure for those who continued to use opium.

Addicts clearly needed more than political lectures, and medical care was offered either locally, or, if this was insufficient, addicts were referred to rehabilitation centres. But a major element in the campaign was the continued propaganda exercise: meetings about addiction were part of the national action programme, in which everybody spent an hour a day discussing political and health topics of national importance. The stories and testimony of former addicts were used to aid addicts' rehabilitation in the centres, as well as in mass meetings, newspaper features, and local discussion groups. Addiction was denounced as anti-social and unhealthful, because it was an 'imperialist and capitalist activity'; and much of the campaign was clearly devoted to a reinterpretation of what had been a deep-seated, almost traditional part of the behaviour of all levels of Chinese society.

Perhaps more directly appealing to the national audience of the campaign was the manifest evidence of land, which had previously produced opium poppies, being reclaimed for food production. Opium production was not, after all, limited to distant and little-known regions of the country, but was found, for example, in suburban areas of Canton.

As the first stage towards their rehabilitation, addicts were registered, and city-wide anti-opium committees provided treatment at home, in clinics, or in hospitals. An average period quoted for hospitalization would be twelve days, although those who were physically weak, or had other complications, required a longer period. Medication, and progressively reduced doses of the drug, was the usual routine, and the medical treatment was supported by cultural activities and group discussions among the patients. 'Difficult cases' of addiction were required to go through labour camps, just as did landowners, businessmen, and social criminals in their 'rehabilitation'. Recalcitrant addicts were publicly branded before being treated as criminals.

As Lowinger concludes, many questions remain about the Chinese experience which call for further investigation and documentation. Was the rehabilitation programme completely successful, or were the failures removed from society? Do the rehabilitated addicts continue successfully to play their part in the community? And what role did traditional Chinese medicine play in the treatment process? (Gregory, op. cit., quotes evidence that drug therapy, such as Tharazine, acupuncture, personal psychotherapy, productive labour, and political discussions all form a combined programme of treatment in contemporary Chinese mental hospitals, and it seems likely that a similar combination would have been used in the treatment of drug abuse in hospital clinics.)

JAPAN

There are no treatment programmes separately administered for drug addicts in Japan. Ishii and Motohashi (*Addictive Diseases*, 1977, 3:105–14) state that the few treatment programmes which do exist are located in local university hospitals, and are sparsely manned: only those doctors who are interested in psychopathology or the study of drug dependence are involved.

According to these authors, the first decision made when a patient is seen is whether he would require hospitalization: this decision would depend on the types of drugs abused, the addict's personality, and his environment. Indicators for hospital treatment include persistent character disorders, coming from a broken home, or having very severe withdrawal symptoms. Psychotherapy is the main treatment offered: generally, group psychotherapy is used, to build up the individual's sense of self-reliance. This, combined with individual psychotherapy, aims to build up a good human relationship between the patient and members of the treatment team. The authors continually stress involvement, understanding, patience, and collaboration of all parties, including the family. From this standpoint, they argue against reliance on the use of methadone or other drugs during treatment of narcotics addicts:

The essential feature of the problem of narcotic addiction lies in physical and psychic dependence upon drugs. To change from one drug of dependence, heroin, to another drug of dependence, methadone, does not in our opinion, solve the problem. It is necessary to approach the problem of the addict's personality and to train him in the spirit of self-reliance, that is, to live a full life independently of any drugs; otherwise we are not 'curing' him in the true sense of the word. Though this treatment can be considered harsh, we are obtaining good results.

INDIA

There are estimated to be perhaps 60 to 70 psychiatric centres in India at the time of Wig and Varma's review (*Addictive Diseases*, 1977, 3:79–86). This number includes psychiatric departments in medical colleges, teaching hospitals, mental hospitals, and large private nursing homes. In about a fifth of these, there was administratively no separate drug dependence unit for drug treatment: addicted patients shared the same treatment facilities as exist for the psychiatric patients in these hospitals.

Treatment facilities available for the drug dependent patient include detoxification, individual and group psychotherapy, relaxation therapy, behaviour therapy, and rehabilitation programmes. Only 3 of the 13 centres surveyed practised methadone therapy. To quote the survey's conclusions,

Existing treatment facilities are grossly inadequate and unsatisfactory. Special treatment units are required for enforcing abstinence and for providing specific therapies such as behaviour therapy. Rehabilitation programmes are most rudimentary. Many more programmes and centres are urgently needed.

Mehndiratta and Wig (*Drug and Alcohol Dependence*, 1975–6, 1:71–81) record how the Indian medical profession's view on drugs and mental health have varied during the nineteenth and twentieth centuries. The effects of cannabis on mental health, for example, has been fiercely debated for more than a century. At one time during the last century, cannabis was regarded as the largest single cause of insanity in Indian lunatic asylums: one-third to one-half of the cases were attributed to this habit.

However, the Indian Hemp Commission in 1893 looked critically at the evidence for this, and estimated that cannabis was a factor in not more than 7 to 13 per cent of admissions to the asylums.

'*Ganja* psychosis' has been a fairly common diagnosis from a number of clinicians, and as recently as 1972 Varma (*Indian J. Psychiatry*, 1972, 14:241–6) has reported that over 3 per cent of all admissions to an eastern Indian hospital over a period of ten years were such patients. Bhang psychosis has also been reported by Thacore (*Brit. J. Psychiatry*, 1973, 123:225–9).

PAKISTAN

Available resources in the health services vary considerably among the different areas of Pakistan, both between provinces and within them. Thus, urban areas in Sind and Punjab are relatively well provided, whereas Baluchistan and the North-West Frontier Province's remote rural areas almost completely lack public health services, although there is now an ambitious Basic Health Services scheme being developed in the country. Within the health services, psychiatric services have a low priority, and there are only 2,000 beds for a country with 72.5 million inhabitants. Only two psychiatric units specialize in the treatment of drug dependence: a 35-bed unit at Hyderabad, and a similar sized unit at Lahore. Some treatment of drug dependants also takes place in the general psychiatric units of the general teaching hospitals in other cities, and in addition a few military and mission hospitals also provide treatment.

Social welfare services exist in Karachi, but remain rudimentary in other areas of the country; trained social workers are very scarce, and psychiatric social work is practically non-existent.

Clearly, the country has needs beyond its existing resources: most hospitals (both general and psychiatric) are grossly understaffed, and para-medical personnel play an important part in keeping the system afloat.

The public health system exists parallel with the indigenous system of medicine: there are between 30,000 and 60,000 practising Hakims (as compared with 12,000 doctors) who follow the Unani system. (Unani medicine has its roots in early Greek humoral medicine, as preserved by Arabic traditions, and has now also absorbed certain allopathic elements.) In the Unani pharmacopoeia, opium plays an important part as a remedy for a wide range of physical and mental illnesses. The Hakims manufacture, amongst other things, an opium pill called Tark-E-Afyun, for withdrawal from opium addiction, to be taken in reducing doses over a six-week period. The services of the Hakims in the treatment of drug dependence should be as much studied as their role in the general medical services: this has been the opinion of the various visiting experts of the United Nations–Pakistan Programme for Drug Abuse Control (personal communications, 1979).

This programme, agreed upon in 1976, has been established to facilitate the Pakistan government's long-term goal to establish a network of treatment centres in all four provinces of the country. It was envisaged that, besides meeting local needs for actual treatment and rehabilitation, these centres would also serve the needs that would arise as the opium vend system was gradually phased out. (The vends supplied opium for quasi-medical use and for the Hakims' medicine.) It was the opinion of the visiting experts that it was unlikely that either of these needs would diminish before a basic health service scheme was implemented: yet it became the government's intention to abolish quasi-medical opium use in 1979. The experts felt that the first three-year phase of the UN–Pakistan country-wide treatment programme could only constitute an initial preparatory step in abolishing such opium use (personal communication, 1979).

The planned programme conceives of drug dependence treatment as building on existing institutions, rather than creating new agencies; as demanding support by leading academic centres in the country; as being psychiatrically orientated and part of the mental health centre; as being based on voluntary treatment, with much out-patient work; as having treatment supported by rehabilitation; and as being pragmatic, flexible, and continuously self-evaluating. Pilot research and treatment centres were sited, as first priorities, in areas of greatest need: Buner, Peshawar, Karachi, Hyderabad, and Rawalpindi; with later developments in Lahore and Quetta. In Buner, there already existed some detailed knowledge of local needs, but in the other centres, research into local patterns of abuse and need for treatment was made the first priority. Very detailed plans on the future developments of each centre were drawn up, and the programme was put into operation during 1977–8. At the time of writing, the Buner treatment unit was due to expand its activities in the region, and to develop out-patient facilities, as was the unit at Peshawar. Community-based centres were being developed in Punjab province, at Jhelum and Sialkot. In-service and overseas training continued for the staff at existing and new centres, and a national workshop, held in December 1979, was to bring together representatives of all treatment centres in the country, to report on their research and treatment experience, and to define future policies for the national integration of services. A new area of research was to be carried out, to determine the extent and nature of the traditional practice of giving raw opium to infants, both as medication and as a sedative (*World Health Organization Report to UNFDAC*, 1979; Imram and Uppal, *Bull. Narc.*, 1979, 31:69–76).

Thus, the UN–Pakistan Programme for Drug Abuse Control has already implemented much of the projected treatment component by establishing centres for research and treatment. A second part of the programme was to collect information and data on the extent and pattern of drug dependence on which to base further long-term planning. During 1979, the WHO consultant, Dr V. Navaratnam, reviewed the present systems of data collection, analyses, and interpretation, with a view to developing a National Case Monitoring System. Existing surveys of the pattern of drug abuse provide valuable background, but, as noted in an earlier section on patterns of abuse in Pakistan, the existing surveys cover only a very small proportion of the problem, and are based on such a

variety of techniques of data collection that extracting standardized information would be very difficult. Many local data collection systems use incompatible survey instruments, and it therefore
seemed desirable to standardize, centralize, and computerize the
information gathering, under the Pakistan Narcotics Control Board.
A detailed feasibility study would be the next step, and it was
clear that the various agencies involved have different capabilities
to participate in a monitoring system, given manpower shortages,
etc., in various areas. As a first stage, an individualized case monitoring system could be implemented.

Only when information is collected via the same measurement
instruments, and centralized, will it be possible to have adequate
data to base further long-term planning (consultant's report to
WHO, and personal communications, 1979).

SRI LANKA

Until the end of 1974, very few opium addicts sought psychiatric
treatment for their habit, although at the time it was estimated that
there were between 10,000 and 15,000 opium users in Sri Lanka.
At that time, when the police had set up a Narcotics Bureau, and
more effective control was being taken on the drug smuggling from
India, the street price of drugs escalated. A press campaign, and
advice from individual Narcotics Bureau officials, informed the
hard-pressed addicts of the availability of treatment in the two
main mental hospitals. In the latter half of 1975, there were 101
admissions, and in the first half of 1976, 153 admissions, to the
methadone detoxification programme. The average length of methadone treatment was ten days, with a further eight days in hospital for the treatment of remaining withdrawal symptoms.

Satkunayagam (*Colombo Plan Workshop*, Penang, 1978) reported that the medical staff experienced certain difficulties in the
management of these patients in the general psychiatric wards as a
result of their not being allocated separate wards. They did not join
the other patients, either in ward activities or at the occupational
therapy centre, but remained an isolated group in the ward, unable
to communicate (because of language problems) with the closest
group to them, the alcoholics (who are mainly upper-class English
speakers), and they were resented by the ward staff for their disruptive behaviour. 'On discharge from the hospital the patients
were advised to attend the psychiatric follow-up clinics at the
general hospital, but hardly any of them did so. We had no means
to follow them up in the community. . . .' About the latter half
of 1976, the hospitals ran out of methadone, and the admission

of these patients came to a halt. When supplies resumed, many months later, few patients came forward for treatment, not surprisingly perhaps, considering the depressing setting for treatment that Satkunayagam admits in his description. And, by 1977, opium prices had dropped back to a more accessible level.

Thus, at the time of writing, Sri Lanka has no specialist unit for treating drug dependent patients (although it has been reported that a separate unit may be set up), and no programme of rehabilitation and after-care.

BURMA

All persons dependent on narcotic drugs are required, by the 1974 Narcotic Drug Act, to register at the specified centres of the Health Department, to receive appropriate treatment. The majority of drug dependent patients are treated in local and general hospitals and at the Rangoon Psychiatric Hospital, all of which have special units.

Formerly, opiate detoxification programmes had been by gradual withdrawal, using opium, but now this type of treatment is rarely used. Abrupt withdrawal is now instituted, with the help of tranquillizers, and some programmes use methadone replacement over a period of 2 weeks, with a further 6 to 8 weeks as in-patients. Methadone maintenance has not been used. Meditation therapy and acupuncture therapy have been tried, but their success has not yet been evaluated (Ne Win, *Addictive Diseases*, 1977, 3:87—8).

CONCLUSIONS

Throughout the present chapter, the emphasis has been on needs: the need for developing a more extensive provision of treatment, the need for adequate after-care and out-reach, the need for the proper evaluation of those programmes which have been undertaken. A further need—to achieve an overall policy on the mixture of traditional and modern practices—will be discussed in the concluding chapter.

We do not intend in this book to judge the adequacy of each country's treatment and rehabilitation programme (although the reader will be able to gather how varied the degree of commitment to such programmes has been in the past). Such comment would not only be out of place, especially in the absence of proper evaluation studies; we hope it will also rapidly become out of date as various countries improve their provision.

Several general comments might, however, be in order. As the 1930 League of Nations Report cited earlier implied, the provision of treatment is perhaps the easiest part of the total rehabilitation of the drug dependent individual. A considerable effort is required to maintain the newly-cured dependant as he, almost inevitably, returns to the social setting whence his problem came. This effort requires much social welfare manpower, and an *efficient* out-reach organization. Some countries—most notably Singapore—have made the close monitoring of an individual's drug-free state a central feature of the period after treatment; others have left after-care to the existing social services, or have simply offered no provision at all. Indeed, the official reports of some countries quote statistics on their provision of facilities in terms of beds for detoxifying patients as if, once detoxified, the individual was ready to return to the community. Detoxification and hospital facilities are costly, and yet (although few programmes publish their statistics) it is generally acknowledged that a large proportion of those detoxified will be back on drugs within a short period. Now, there do not exist for the region statistics which provide a comparison of different provisions of after-care facilities (including no provision) in terms of cost effectiveness, cure rate, etc.; and therefore it is premature to claim that a full after-care service would increase the long-term success rate by such an amount to justify its funding.

At another level, one can argue that the dependent individual needs considerably more than just medical treatment. This book has been arguing that we should see dependence upon drugs as a psychic phenomenon first, and only then, in the case of some drugs, a physical one. The dependence upon the drug *alters* the reasons why the individual first experimented with the drug, such that, in addition to his initial needs and problems (if indeed it were such which led to the habit), he now has the psychological dependence upon the effects provided by the drug, and furthermore continues his use to avoid withdrawal symptoms. Removing the physical need for the drug can only be the first stage: initial needs and problems may well continue, if they have not also been added to by worsened social relations and damaged employment chances. Furthermore, during the period of drug use, the individual will have altered in his behaviour and responses: recall, for example, the description given in an earlier chapter of the interacting effects between drug use and sexual performance. Here, withdrawing the drug's support may throw the individual back to a worse position than that which first tempted him into drug use. Many other examples could be given.

No single technique, no single programme of treatment and rehabilitation, will suit all drug dependants: this theme, and the general need for a variety of approaches to drug abuse, will be taken up again in Chapter VIII.

VII

Legal and Enforcement
Responses to Drug Abuse

THE scope of this book is, in effect, defined by the laws on the use of drug substances which are currently in operation in the region: in all countries in the region, the range of substances whose consumption and trading is illegal follows international conventions, and has been amended and updated to include further substances as their abuse is noted. In some parts of South Asia, the use of alcohol has also been proscribed, but as this is not the majority practice in the region, the book has concentrated upon the remainder of illicit drugs.

Although the act of consumption of a substance may be declared illegal, society need not apply legal sanctions to the user, but instead decide that the individual is in need of treatment, and Chapter VI has already documented the variety of such approaches in East Asia. However, in many instances, society's response to the drug user is either partly or wholly in the legal mode, as it will inevitably be towards the trafficker in drugs. (In practice, the dividing line between consumer and trafficker may not be easy to draw, and most legal codes have therefore had to include some definition in terms of the amount of the drug substance found in the individual's possession.)

Drug codes and legal sanctions have evolved both in response to changes in the local patterns of drug abuse, and as a result of international conventions, agreements, and pressure. They have been changing from the first introduction of anti-narcotics laws, early in East Asian history, to the detailed lists of prohibited substances of the present day. Some of the earlier laws lumped together all proscribed drug substances and all drug-related offences; now some codes differentiate on both counts the severity of sentence which may be imposed. Most countries in South-East Asia have now introduced the death sentence as a penalty for trafficking, as well as severe sentences for individual drug users. In practice, policy on implementing these provisions is just emerging.

How *should* society respond to an individual's abuse of drugs: by the legal mode or via the treatment mode? One can approach this question from a number of viewpoints. One way of answering would be to argue in terms of the effects of either approach: if the main goal is the reduction or elimination of drug use in society, which mode comes closest to it? Is demand for the drug best controlled by tackling the individual dependant as a case in need of treatment, and hoping thus to rid society of such habits? Or would it be more effective if prevention were achieved by potential users noting the penalties applied to apprehended users? Do those who have undergone imprisonment or received some other sentence become less likely to repeat the offence than those who have received treatment and rehabilitation?

Demand reduction clearly has two separable target groups: the actual users, and the larger 'at risk' group; and one should separate the potential effects of the different approaches according to which group is being discussed. Conceivably, the knowledge that effective treatment programmes exist could dramatically reduce demand amongst users, whilst at the same time *increasing* it among that portion of the 'at risk' group, who saw the programmes as a safety net if they indulged their own curiosity. Again, one could argue that the fear of imprisonment might effectively discourage many 'at risk' individuals, whilst the actual experience of prison would *increase* the dependent individual's contacts with the drug culture.

In the last chapter, we noted the absence of good evaluative data for the various modes of treatment in practice; there is a corresponding dearth of information on the effectiveness of the various sentencing policies in operation. (Perhaps the criteria are clearer and more straightforward in the case of treatment than they are with punishment; for the expected benefits of the legal mode explicitly include not only those to the individual user, but also those to society itself, protected from the drug user's criminal activities.) Evaluating the relative effectiveness of the two broad approaches not only suffers from the lack of necessary data, but perhaps also poses too simple a question, in that the solution to the problem of drug abuse is most likely to be one where the agencies are sensitive to the needs and history of the particular drug user, and where individuals are carefully allocated to appropriate types of treatment or, in the last resort, to punishment.

Demand reduction and supply reduction must be considered to-

gether, and neither can, of course, be fully effective until the production of drug substances is controlled. The 1930 League of Nations Commission Report saw the international nature of the problem very clearly: 'As long as poppy cultivation is not under control
there will always be illicit trade in opium.' Opium was the major
drug of abuse at the time of the report, and the urgent call was for
international co-operation in the control of cultivation, since the
enforcement efforts of one country could be nullified by the failure
to act by other producing countries. Given the political will and
effective powers of enforcement, one could see how the supply
of opiates could be controlled at source. Other drugs, unknown
or at least little abused fifty years ago, are much less dependent
upon a few specifiable sources of supply: cannabis can be grown
in many parts of the region (and indeed grows wild in some); synthetic drugs are manufactured by a host of laboratories and, even
if strict enforcement activities prevented all diversion of supplies
from legitimate medical sources, many of the manufacturing pro-
cesses are sufficiently straightforward for illicit laboratories to
flourish. One thus returns to the theme of demand reduction, by
legal and by educational means. The criminal-commercial gains
from the illicit traffic in drugs are sufficiently huge to ensure that,
even if enforcement measures are successful against one syndicate,
another is likely to take its place. The drug trade is hydra-headed.

MALAYSIA

The current legislation on dangerous drugs in Malaysia is built upon
the Dangerous Drugs Ordinance of 1952, which ended the system
of control of opiates via registration that had been in existence in
one form or another since the nineteenth century. The basic 1952
law has been amended from time to time, in keeping with the needs
brought about by the changing patterns of drug abuse in the country. Malaysia is a party to the 1961 Single Convention on Narcotic
Drugs, and has participated as an observer at the meetings of the
Commission on Dangerous Drugs. The country is also a signatory
to the ASEAN Declaration of Principles on Drug Abuse Control
of 1976, and has participated in many regional activities, including
those organized by Colombo Plan, regional UNFDAC and WHO,
and European-Asian Interpol.

The law was almost completely revised and re-enacted in 1975,
as regards the control of traffic of the drugs listed in all the schedules of the Single Convention, as well as regards preventative education, and the rehabilitation of drug dependent persons. Sentences
for drug trafficking were increased, with the death penalty being

introduced for the trafficking of 100 gm or more of heroin. At the
same time, a more humanitarian approach was taken in relation to
the rehabilitation of drug dependent individuals. The government
has directed the Prisons Department to establish two rehabilitation
centres for individuals with criminal records who are drug dependants (this is in addition to the provision for rehabilitation described in the section on treatment and rehabilitation in Malaysia).
The official documents recognize what they describe as 'the philosophy of needing to separate out the hard core criminal drug dependent individual' from other drug dependants; and the two new
centres will cater for such persons. By the early part of 1980, it is
intended that there will be sufficient accommodation in the two
centres (at Seremban, and at Sepang in Selangor) for 2,200 individuals to be rehabilitated at any one time. There is also a recognition that future capacity will be needed (*The Problem of Drug
Abuse in Malaysia*, Cabinet Committee on Drug Abuse Control,
1979).

The importance of the enforcement programme will be seen
when one considers both the change in the pattern of domestic
consumption and the size of the international trafficking which
uses Malaysia as a convenient transit country. During the 1970s,
the estimated number of individuals actively using drugs has escalated rapidly, with ever larger numbers of young people involved;
and also the range of drugs being abused has increased, with morphine and heroin becoming the leading drugs of abuse.

There has also been a sudden increase in the arrests for narcotic
trafficking by Malaysian citizens overseas: in the late 1960s and
early 1970s, very few were involved; by 1974 there were as many
as 132 people so apprehended. Foreigners and Malaysian citizens
have also been arrested within the country on international trafficking charges; and there are many seizures at the country's airports and seaports. Clandestine heroin laboratories have been
detected at work within the country, but it is currently suspected
that much of the illicit heroin comes into the country from laboratories just over the Thai border.

The Cabinet Committee (op. cit.) describes the fundamental objective of the country's enforcement policy within the country as
being one of making drugs difficult to obtain, and expensive and
risky to possess, sell, or consume: 'The basic rationale here being
taken is that if taking drugs is hazardous, inconvenient, and expensive, fewer persons will experiment with drugs; fewer of those
who do experiment will advance to chronic intensive use of drugs;
and further, more of those who currently use drugs will reduce or
stop their use and seek medical intervention.'

Although the government stresses both supply reduction and the reduction of illicit demand, there is clearly a strong belief that supply reduction is the key component in controlling and eliminating the drug problem. Given the country's terrain, and the varied types of transport arriving in and leaving the country continually, enforcement activities are necessarily very difficult. Thus, the Thai-Malaysia border has always been particularly difficult to patrol and monitor, and the government has embarked upon a project to fence strategic parts of the border as it runs through jungle. Again, there is stringent examination of passengers and baggage at both entry and exit points, and the manpower of the Customs and Excise Department has been increased, as have the airport and seaport security staff. Sniffer dog units have been attached to these forces.

The Central Narcotics Bureau has, since 1973, the task of coordinating the efforts of the other enforcement agencies, itself concentrating mainly upon the major traffickers. Its manpower was small, and largely seconded from the police; and international consultants suggested that its law enforcement activities—the gathering of intelligence and the suppression of illicit trafficking—should come directly under the Police. In 1976 the government established a Cabinet Committee for the Control of Drug Abuse, under the Chairmanship of the Deputy Prime Minister, to effect overall policy co-ordination. The Cabinet Committee has requested the UNFDAC to assist the government by providing a specialized expert mission, to evaluate national drug enforcement activities as well as review all aspects of drug prevention programmes being implemented. One outcome of this was the formation of the Executive National Action Unit of the Cabinet Committee on Drug Abuse Control, which is empowered to implement overall policies of the Cabinet Committee as well as to ensure maximum co-ordination of efforts in their execution. The members of the National Action Unit are appointed by the Deputy Prime Minister.

This section has so far discussed the structure and the practice of law enforcement activities: there exists also some evidence on the effects of current legal practices upon drug dependants themselves. The National Drug Dependence Research Centre conducted a survey of prisoners convicted for drug offences, and of those who appeared in the courts on drugs charges (Navaratnam and Spencer, *The Drug User and the Law*, Penang, 1977).

It was found that the vast majority of individuals who appeared before the courts, or who were held in prison for drug offences, were charged with the possession of drugs (rather than being charged with trafficking or manufacturing). The authors question whether the legal process was the most effective way of dealing with this category of individual. The substantial majority of drug offenders before the courts had no previous criminal convictions of any kind, with, amongst the minority who had an offence, theft and robbery predominating. The effect of imprisoning drug offenders became clear from a number of points which arose in the interviews. Few individuals expressed what could be described as a good motivation for terminating their drug habit. Expense was the most frequently cited reason for wishing to give up the habit, and the average prison setting gave no encouragement to develop any deeper motivations. Secondly, coming before the courts and then being imprisoned made half of those interviewed view themselves as criminals: it has brought them into contact with other criminals and, it was expected, it may well have extended their drug-using network of acquaintances. Although three-quarters of those interviewed said that their prison sentence had changed their attitude toward drugs, the authors remain less sanguine that this change would be in the direction intended: it seemed more likely that the prisoner's changed self-concepts and society's stigma would prevail instead.

THAILAND

'We have learned from experience that the problems of drug taking are also social problems, which cannot be stopped by law enforcement alone', wrote Police Major-General Pow Sarasin, the then Secretary-General of the Narcotics Board in 1975: 'We are doing everything possible to reduce the spread of addiction . . . and our real concern is prevention amongst youth'. Speaking at the same conference, Dr. Shaowanasai, of the Phra Mongkutkrao Hospital, saw the situation rather differently: 'The government is not really interested in this problem; suppression by the police has failed; and the drugs are easily available everywhere, and are not very expensive. Not one organization gives any real support in the field of study and research on the drugs problems' (both papers in the *ICAA Conference*, Bangkok, 1975).

Since then, the picture has changed considerably: enforcement, education, and research activities have all been stepped up, and efforts have become centralized under the Narcotics Board. Why had Thailand achieved its earlier unenviable record? Writing in 1972, McCoy suggested that the then Thai government was heavily implicated in the opium traffic:

Every important trafficker in Thailand has an 'adviser' in the narcotics police and most would never think of moving a major drug shipment without first checking with the police to make sure that there is no possibility of seizure or arrest. U.S. narcotics agents serving in Thailand have learned that any information they give the Thai police is turned over to the syndicates within a matter of hours. Moreover, officials in the U.S. Bureau of Narcotics feel that corruption is not just a matter of individual wrongdoing, and claim to have evidence that corruption goes to the very top of Thailand's current military government (McCoy, *The Politics of Heroin in Southeast Asia*, 1972, p. 359).

The past decade has seen more than one dramatic change, not only in government but also in style of government, with implications for the enforcement of the anti-narcotics programme. General Kriangsak made narcotics a first priority issue for his government, and Thailand now co-operates with the international community in two major campaigns against trafficking. In the field of law enforcement, the United Nations and Interpol play significant roles; and expert police officers have been seconded from the Royal Hong Kong Police, from the Royal Canadian Mounted Police, and from American and European police forces: 'the international enforcement community' as they call themselves (*Far Eastern Economic Review*, 28 April 1978, p. 25). American involvement in the campaign is the largest single factor, and aid programmes support addiction clinics and information gathering. The other campaign, which is directed by the United Nations, aims to substitute other cash crops for the hill tribes' opium: five villages were selected for the pilot programme, and they have had both agricultural and human success. However, there remain approximately a thousand other villages which continue with their now-traditional cash crop—opium; and not until there is a realistic marketing infrastructure reaching right up to these main opium-producing areas is it likely that this programme will persuade the hill tribes to change to coffee and cabbages (Williams, *Bull. Narc.*, 1979, 31(2):1—44).

Thailand introduced her first major anti-narcotics laws in 1959, under international pressure: the law rescinded the government franchises for the sale of opium to local consumers, as had been carried on since the nineteenth century under licence, and for much longer before control systems were introduced. Opium use was forbidden, and opium production, transport, and sale were outlawed. As Westermeyer has indicated, the appearance of heroin on the market in Bangkok almost exactly coincides with the enforcement of this anti-opium legislation, as it has done in other countries in the region (Westermeyer, *Arch. Gen. Psychiatry*, 1976, 33: 1135—9). Meanwhile, as has just been noted above, governmental involvement in the drug trade increased, and with it came the urban heroin epidemic, and the Thai trawler trade in narcotics. Solomon records a particularly striking case in 1974: a raid on a heroin laboratory revealed it to be the property of a lieutenant-colonel of the Thai police, and its operators to be a syndicate of police officials; the colonel was prosecuted, but at his trial he was allowed to 'walk away from his police guards to a waiting black Mercedes, and escape. He is now believed to be operating a new heroin laboratory in the Burma–Thailand border region' (Solomon, *J. Psychedelic Drugs*, 1978, 10:193–206).

Recent legislation has provided the Prime Minister with powers to 'carry out any action to prevent, stop, or suppress any serious activity which has taken place in or outside the Kingdom', and the Country Report to the Penang UNESCO Conference in 1977 suggests, 'there is no doubt that persons guilty of narcotics offences will fear this article of the constitution'. At that time, however, it had yet to be invoked.

SINGAPORE

Singapore's central position in regional and world trade almost inevitably made it an attractive distribution centre for international drug traffickers; and McCoy (*The Politics of Heroin in Southeast Asia*, Harper and Row, 1972) documents how, in particular, the Chiu Chau syndicates developed the pattern of South-East Asian illicit traffic. During the 1960s, Singapore, in addition to some inter-continental illicit trade, was the major distribution centre for Indonesia and part of the Malay Peninsula. Four or five international syndicates made Singapore their regional headquarters; and the almost unlimited supplies of drugs frustrated governmental efforts to reduce local addiction or the entrepôt trade in drugs.

Thus, the government changed its tactics, and cracked down on the syndicates themselves. In 1962, Special Branch Police arrested the five most powerful syndicate leaders, tried, and then deported them (*Malay Mail*, Singapore, 2 April 1965). Thereafter, according to McCoy, smugglers avoided Singapore, to concentrate their activities in Bangkok.

In 1971, narcotics suppression was transferred from the Customs Department to the newly-formed Central Narcotics Bureau, under the Ministry of Home Affairs, and, whilst the international traffic continued to avoid Singapore (*Far Eastern Economic Review*, 30 April 1976), the inflow of hard drugs for local consumption has risen considerably.

The Misuse of Drugs Act, 1973, placed specified drugs under control, and set penalties for the consumption, possession, and trafficking of controlled drugs. As the situation deteriorated, the

Misuse of Drugs Act was amended, in 1975, to provide for a mandatory death sentence for those convicted of:

(1) trafficking and importing/exporting more than 15 grams of heroin or 30 grams of morphine in pure content; or

(2) manufacturing of heroin or morphine.

The Misuse of Drugs Act also empowers the Director of the Central Narcotics Bureau to order any person who is found to be an addict (or has a trace of a controlled drug in his urine) to have compulsory treatment and rehabilitation at an approved institution.

Later legislation has introduced provision for the supervision of released ex-addicts by supervision officers, and the supervisors' once in five days urine checks at local police stations. The penalty for a second offence under the Act is now a term of imprisonment for not less than three years (Foo, *Colombo Plan Workshop*, Penang, 1978).

An enforcement programme, code-named Operation Ferret, was launched in April 1977; its primary aim was stated to be the arrest of heroin users rapidly enough, and their detention and rehabilitation effectively enough, to stem the rising tide of new heroin addicts. Drug squads from the Central Narcotics Bureau, Police, and organizations such as the Vigilante Corps and the Special Constabulary work together in the operation; and, according to early assessments (e.g., Ng, *Colombo Plan Workshop*, Penang, 1978) have helped achieve the objective of demand reduction within the first year. The official estimates certainly bear this out: the ratio of new heroin abusers to old abusers has declined from 2.2: 1 at the beginning of Operation Ferret to 0.22: 1 at the end of 1978 (*Country Report*, Commonwealth Regional Working Group on Illicit Drugs, Kuala Lumpur, 1979). 'The swift incarceration of drug traffickers and pushers had disrupted the entire distribution network within Singapore. This, together with the execution of two drug traffickers (in 1978) resulted in the eradication of major organized drug syndicates. To intensify checks at the entry points, especially the causeway (connecting Singapore to Malaysia), the Narcotic Dog Detection programme has been intensified' (*Singapore Country Report*, op. cit., p. 2).

Whether such optimism is justified will be seen in future years. Clearly, Operation Ferret has dramatically changed the drug scene in Singapore (Foo, op. cit., p. 8); and the spread of heroin abuse may well have been checked. According to Foo:

Before Operation Ferret, drug abusers gathered freely at hawker stalls, coffee shops, etc., to smoke heroin-spiked cigarettes quite openly. Due to constant harassment by the enforcement agencies, they are now more discreet, and many of them have now retreated to the privacy of their homes . . . and are resorting to substitutes in order to relieve withdrawal symptoms: Chinese samsu, toddy, cannabis, oral consumption of opium and Rohypnol tablets. . . . Pushers are harassed and have to take all sorts of precautions such as retreating to the higher floors of HDB (public housing) flats and stationing look-outs in adjoining blocks, selling only to known customers, and changing the venue for transaction frequently.

The reader will be able to see what implications such changes in drug users' and (especially) pushers' practices will have for the recruitment of new addicts to heroin.

INDONESIA

The 1927 Dangerous Drugs Ordinance was framed at a time when the known drugs of use were natural products—principally opium and cannabis—and thus did not cover synthetic opiates and such other manufactured drugs. Thus, it was necessary to enact new legislation in 1949, empowering the Minister of Health to enforce regulations pertaining to dangerous drugs, or new chemicals which were subject to abuse.

With the beginnings of the drug abuse epidemic amongst adolescents, the Director of State Intelligence, by virtue of the Presidential Instruction No. 6 of 1971, established a co-ordinating body, the BAKOLAK INPRES 6/71, to co-ordinate action against anything which could 'jeopardize the social order'. As its Chairman, Army Lieutenant-General Soegomo indicates (in Setyonegoro, *Drug Use in Indonesia*, Jakarta, 1975), with the establishment of this body, 'the narcotic problem has now been handled more seriously in the context of prevention, repression, treatment, and rehabilitation, frequently utilizing foreign assistance'. The BAKOLAK INPRES co-ordinates the 'suppressive activities' of eleven government departments, from Defence to Religious Affairs; it issues guide-lines, formulations of general policy, and supervises departmental activities to ensure 'unity of action and attitude'. It is also responsible for international co-operative ventures.

Soegomo (op. cit.) outlines the philosophy underlying what he calls 'the Indonesian system of suppression':

Excess, as derived from the liberal philosophy, has caused the creation of the image of the infinite freedom of individuals being misapprehended. Popularly referred to as the freedom to be free, the principle, unfortunately, is being interpreted to mean the freedom of the individual to pursue his own way of life and attitudes according to his own personal tastes and intention. This liberty has gone so far as to allow also the freedom to take illicit and dangerous drugs to destroy one's own life. These types of freedom are definitely incompatible with the nation's aspirations and the principles of Pancasila; hence it should be rejected as being very detrimental to the Indonesian nation, the young generation in particular.

In addition to the treatment and rehabilitation programmes of police and health departments, BAKOLAK INPRES co-ordinates preventative and repressive operations (Soegomo, op. cit.).

These 'prevent the possibility of the country becoming the target of illegal drug abuse and trafficking, laboratories, and cultivation', and use information campaigns and legal action to effect this. Anti-smuggling operations combine with intelligence operations ('directed to crush belligerent sources of illegal drugs beyond the nation's boundaries') to maintain the nation's territorial security.

Soegomo states that the repressive operations act so that, 'as soon as one area is in the grip of the devastating narcotic epidemic, law enforcement apparatuses move in to exterminate the dangerous plot and its supporters responsible for the disaster'. Others arrested are 'given persuasive guidance and motivation to prevent them from future involvement in illegal narcotic trafficking'.

The original 1927 law was deficient in the incompleteness of its list of narcotic drugs, as mentioned; it also lacked provision for treatment and rehabilitation of users; and its penalties were too lenient, and did not discriminate between users and traffickers. New legislation, approved in 1976, brought in much more severe penalties for crimes relating to narcotic drugs, except for users or addicts. Trafficking offences carry the heaviest penalty: life imprisonment and a 50 million rupiah fine. Imprisonment for less serious crimes range from two to twenty years: illegal (i.e., non-prescription) use of narcotics carries a penalty of not more than two years, with the power to order the accused to have treatment.

A system of rewards has been applied to those who discover drug crimes, and in order to give protection to informers of narcotic crimes their names and addresses are withheld in court (Budiarti, in Widjono, *Drug Abuse in Indonesia*, Jakarta, 1975; Widjono, *Colombo Plan Workshop*, Penang, 1978).

The effect of the New Narcotic Law, 1976, thus, is to consider the drug abuser or addict as a criminal; but to distinguish him from the trafficker or manufacturer, by regarding him as being in need of treatment and rehabilitation.

Criminalizing the activity, and making treatment compulsory, is also accompanied by a standardization of treatment and rehabilitation by the various agencies involved. The reader will recall that the system (as discussed under 'Treatment and Rehabilitation in Indonesia' above) which was emerging before the law was of a varied and experimental nature (e.g., Widjono, Wibisono, in *Drug Abuse in Indonesia*, Jakarta, 1975). Now there are central 'Guidelines for Drug Abuse Rehabilitation according to the New Narcotic Law', which build upon previous practice, but which implicitly criticize earlier practices aimed at stabilizing the individual after his treatment and before his return to society. Stabilization should promote religious activity, physical health, mental health, social relations, education, culture, and vocational skills; and should involve appropriate professionals in all these aspects of the individual's rehabilitation (Widjono, *Colombo Plan Workshop*, Penang, 1978).

THE PHILIPPINES

The Dangerous Drugs Board has, since 1972, taken a three-fold approach to the minimization (if not total elimination) of drug abuse in the Philippines: integration of education programmes aimed at specific target groups; provision of treatment and rehabilitation facilities; and, placed first in its list of responsibilities, the preventation of the illegal use of prohibited and regulated drugs, and the control of illegal drug traffic. The emphases of the Board's approach are apparent from its composition: under the chairmanship of Clemente S. Gaitman, of the Department of Health, its *ex officio* members represent Social Services, Education, Justice, Finance, and National Defence, with, as permanent consultant, Jolly R. Bugarin, Director of the National Bureau of Investigation.

As the earlier section on patterns of drug abuse in the Philippines has already indicated, the country, under Spanish, American, and independent governments, has had a tradition of strong legal and enforcement controls upon drug importation and use; and indeed, the international community took the 1903 Opium Reform Commission in the Philippines as the model for later reform conferences in other parts of the world.

Thus, the Dangerous Drugs Act of 1972 represented a continuation of this tradition, rather than, as in some other countries in the region, an amendment or even a reversal of earlier policies. The conceptualization of the drug problem has, however, been changing throughout the period (and indeed has changed since the Act was passed in 1972): historically, the government response to illicit drug use has been to strengthen law enforcement forces to control the supply of drugs. New agencies were created to deal with the problem more effectively: for example, the Narcotics Division of the National Bureau of Investigation, the Narcotics Section of the Food and Drug Administration, and the Constabulary Anti-Narcotics Unit of the Philippines Constabulary. All national and local police agencies each has an anti-narcotics unit; and police officers were sent to the United States and other countries for training in narcotics law enforcement as early as 1965.

At this stage, therefore, drug abuse was seen as a problem, but one combated by enforcement activities.

During the early 1970s, when the drug problem was most acute, the emphasis broadened to include rehabilitation and treatment, and the collaboration of public and private sectors. Some provision was made in the 1972 Act for straightforward preventative education: Article VIII includes as one of the duties of the Dangerous Drugs Board 'the development of educational programmes based on factual information'. As Cudal argues (*A Study of Youth and the Use of Drugs in the Philippines*, UNESCO, mimeograph, 1976), the way this law was formulated reflected the 'simplistic view of the problem of drug use which was then prevailing at the time'. In fact, the currently prevailing emphasis on preventative education as a major aspect of drug control was already being spelled out in some detail by the first Colombo Plan Workshop on Drug Abuse Prevention Education (Laguna, 1974), and it was extended further by the second workshop (Manila, 1976). Cudal (op. cit.) argued for amendments to the 1972 law, so as to provide positive courses of action both for young people and their mentors, to incorporate the new emphases in the law. In fact, other legal measures have now been added to promote the social well-being of children and youth.

Enforcement activities against illicit traffic involve at least five national agencies, and in 1977 (*Country Report* to UNESCO Conference, Penang) these agencies employed 87 trained narcotics enforcement teams, with a total of 454 men. The major concern of the Philippines police, in terms of illicit local production of drugs, has been, since the 1960s, the cultivation of cannabis. Considerable quantities of the plant have been seized each year, without any apparent diminution in the amount to be seized. There is, however, no indication that cannabis oil or resin is being manufactured in the country. Since the seizure of the major clandestine heroin laboratories in 1972, heroin on the streets has remained very scarce; and a close watch is being kept on the possibility of some new syndicate attempting to resume manufacture locally.

After marijuana, pharmaceutical products are the drugs most frequently abused by young Filipinos, and therefore there has been careful control of the legal traffic in drugs in order to prevent their diversion on to the illegal market. The most common technique for so diverting the drug substances was the issuing of prescriptions to non-existent patients: during 1975 the number of questionable prescriptions had been reduced to 50 compared with 13,931 the previous year. (All these 13,931 prescriptions were for cough syrup.) Mandrax has been withdrawn from the market, following its rapid rise to 'popularity' in the early 1970s. This aspect of the drug abuse control programme has, however, posed a problem for the licit users and prescribers of pharmaceuticals: that of overrestriction. Controlled drugs—particularly tranquillizers, sedatives, and hypnotics—have become very difficult for legitimate users to obtain. Zarco and Almonte estimate that fewer than 15 per cent of pharmacies stock and dispense regulated drugs, and only 60 per cent of doctors prescribe them, and have to do so on a special prescription form issued and sold by the Dangerous Drugs Board. They feel that the social and medical harm caused by the widespread unavailability of medically useful drugs is much greater than that of allowing such drugs to become available to 'a few drug abusers' (Zarco and Almonte, *Addictive Diseases*, 1977, 3:119–28).

LAOS

At the end of 1971, Laos passed the first anti-narcotics law in its history. According to the *Far Eastern Economic Review* (30 April 1976, pp. 26–7), this was done under duress from the United States, which threatened to cut off aid to the country. America was at the time experiencing a major heroin epidemic, both within its own borders and among its troops in Vietnam. American-trained narcotics police, and a reward system for heroin and opium seizures, were aimed at strengthening the working of the new law; but official seizures of drugs were few during the four years of the programme, and no major traffickers were arrested. To quote the *Far Eastern Economic Review*: 'The narcotics law was clearly the most unpopular ever passed in Laos, and on several occasions the House of Representatives debated rescinding it.' At the formation of the coalition government, the Pathet Lao opposed the law because of its American inspiration, and the Bill was declared void in February 1975, and after the formation of the Communist government, the narcotics police branch was disbanded.

The anti-opium law passed in 1971 led to police and customs activity aimed at stopping the transport of opium within the country (although the actual production of the drug continued in the remoter areas of northern Laos). Its vigorous enforcement was effective in reducing the trade of opium—bulky, odoriferous, and easily detectable as it is—into Vientiane. Yet, as Westermeyer and Bourne argue (*Am. J. Drug Alcohol Abuse*, 1977, 4:1–11) the main consequence was that compact, odour-free heroin appeared on the market to meet the need of the addicts. They comment that in Laos, as in some other South-East Asian nations:

A combination of repressive laws geared toward suppressing traditional and often socially constrained opium use, urbanization and industrialization, the alienation of youth with progressive identification with Western life-styles, and the availability of heroin (in neighbouring Thailand in the case of Laos), all have favoured the development of epidemic heroin use.

The passage of such a law may also have had effects upon the enforcement agencies themselves, as well as upon their relations with the public (Westermeyer, *Arch. Gen. Psychiatry*, 1976, 33: 1135—9). In Laos, prior to the passage of the anti-opium law, the police had no jurisdiction over opium use; and indeed, since opium use itself did not offend many police officials, they tended to ignore the newly illegal behaviour. Others reacted to their new powers by interfering and taking bribes, or harassing individual addicts and small shopkeepers. Thus, who suffered for his drug habit and who did not became more and more a random event rather than a predictable one; corruption increased; and the public confidence in the equity of law diminished. Out of the thousands of people involved in the production, trafficking, and consumption of narcotic substances, relatively only a few were punished. These were generally the addicts, who were given short, and not unpleasant, stays in treatment centres.

As Westermeyer notes, however, Japan, China, and South Korea have successfully implemented anti-opium laws. He considers that their success was dependent upon backing up legislation with:

(1) intensive mass media propaganda to influence society's attitudes towards narcotic addiction;

(2) health care, detoxification, and after-care on a scale to encompass all addicts within a relatively short period of time;

(3) isolation of all 'recidivist' addicts, suppliers, and corrupt officials; and

(4) effective control over all narcotic production and importation.

Laos, in the 1971—5 period, had neither the political leadership nor the health, welfare, police, or media resources needed for the task. The political will to tackle the problem by infringing on the civil rights of the addicts was seemingly not present until the Pathet Lao government of 1976.

HONG KONG

A brief account of the changing legal status of drugs in Hong Kong, and the intensification of enforcement measures, was given earlier as the necessary background against which to explain changing patterns of drug abuse in the Colony. The account will thus not be repeated here; but the reader should be reminded of the profound changes in the pattern which occurred when anti-narcotic laws were enforced after World War II—the switch from opium to heroin (Westermeyer, *Arch. Gen. Psychiatry*, 1976, 33:1135—9), and later, amongst some addicts, the switch from inhaling to injecting heroin (*Far Eastern Economic Review*, 30 April 1976, pp. 24—5), as street prices rose in the mid-1970s.

The sole advisory instrument of the Hong Kong government on all policy matters relating to the eradication of drug trafficking and drug abuse has been, since 1974, the Action Committee Against Narcotics (ACAN). Its members include representatives of the medical and health services, customs and excise, police, social welfare, prisons, and the Narcotics Commission, and it has been responsible, for example, for the methadone detoxification programme (discussed in an earlier section); for the recent inclusion of psychotropic drugs such as amphetamine and methaqualone in the list of controlled drugs; and for reinvigorating the preventative education programme. Thus, its work on the legal and enforcement aspects of drug abuse in Hong Kong only represents one side of an integrated programme of action.

Under the Dangerous Drugs Ordinance, the maximum penalty for trafficking in dangerous drugs is life imprisonment, a fine of HK$5 million (with, on summary conviction, a maximum of three years' imprisonment, and a fine of HK$500,000); with lesser penalties for managing a divan and for cultivating cannabis or opium poppies; and a maximum of three years and a fine of HK$10,000 for possessing, smoking, inhaling, or injecting a dangerous drug, or possessing pipes or other apparatus for doing so. Corporal punishment is also included in the list of possible penalties.

Control over manufacturing is given in part by an Ordinance imposing severe penalties on anyone possessing acetylating substances, in particular acetic anhydride, which is essential for the conversion of morphine to heroin.

During the mid-1970s Hong Kong's anti-drug law enforcement agencies enjoyed considerable successes in breaking up virtually all the long-established drug syndicates. There was, also in this period, an increase in co-operation with Thai authorities, which interrupted the regular flow of drugs into Hong Kong on Thai trawlers (*Far Eastern Economic Review*, 30 April 1976, pp. 24—6).

Together these successes made the problem of detection even more difficult, as new and unknown syndicates began to take the place of the 'established' ones; and as smuggling ceased to be done in large, sea-borne consignments, and switched instead to 'human wave tactics'—many individuals bringing in smaller amounts by air or sea to supply the domestic market. And, as the *Hong Kong Narcotics Report* concludes, despite all the successes of the 1970s, the struggle against drug traffickers is likely to continue to be an uphill battle. Because there are huge profits to be made in the drug trade, there will always be criminals who are eager to fill the places of those arrested or fled. As an example of the profit margins involved, the *Report* quotes the estimated value of a major seizure: a consignment of opium and morphine which had been bought in Thailand for HK$1.5 million (including cost of transportation and reception in Hong Kong). These drugs would have been sold on the wholesale 'market' in the Colony for HK$12 million; and would then have fetched HK$98 million at the street level. Thus, the street price is some eight times the wholesale price, and 65 times the import price.

The Police Narcotics Bureau and Preventative Service have achieved much higher seizure rates than are common in other countries: thus, in 1976, they estimate that the seizures represent about 20 per cent of the heroin and morphine, and about 60 per cent of the opium, smuggled into the Colony during the year. Given the huge number of separate cargo and passenger arrivals in Hong Kong each year, it is clearly impossible to provide a thorough screening of each arrival. (A total of 4.3 million passengers and 17.5 million metric tons of cargo came to Hong Kong in 1976; and in addition, 5,500 locally-based fishing vessels entered and left Hong Kong throughout the year.)

The effect of the enforcement measures has been, however, to force street prices up appreciably and, as described in an earlier section on Hong Kong's preventative education and rehabilitation policy, it was designed to bring more of the existing addicts to centres for treatment, or at least for methadone maintenance.

As police and anti-narcotics activities continue against small pushers as well as large-scale traffickers, the pushers have responded by changing their method of distribution. One of the most effective methods recently brought into use has been the 'paging system': an addict will contact the pusher by telephone, and will be told where to leave his money and where to pick up the heroin he has ordered. By continually changing their distribution points, the pushers have made interception very difficult (Ley, Commonwealth Working Group, Kuala Lumpur, 1979).

INDIA

India, being the world's largest producer and supplier of licit opium for medical and scientific purposes, has had to evolve very strict supervision and control over the cultivation and export of the drug. The magnitude of this task will be appreciated when one considers that poppy cultivation covers an area of 54,000 hectares and involves 7,500 villages (India Country Report to Commonwealth Working Group on Control of Illicit Drugs, Kuala Lumpur, 1979). Some leakages do still occur, but only in Sri Lanka have significant quantities of Indian opium figured in seizures by foreign narcotics bureaux.

India has been a party to all international conventions on narcotic drugs from 1909; and licit opium production is under the control of the Narcotics Department of the Ministry of Finance. As regards internal illicit consumption of opium, the Indian Constitution provides for a complete restriction on all narcotic and dangerous drugs (Chawla, Colombo Plan Conference, Sri Lanka, 1973).

Cannabis is much less successfully controlled, although all but four states have banned its cultivation (and there will be a total ban by 1989), because considerable quantities of the drug are available in neighbouring countries and some are being smuggled into or through India. The country report to the Kuala Lumpur conference (referred to above) suggests that a fairly significant part in the trafficking of cannabis is played by drug dependent foreigners staying for long periods in India, Nepal, Afghanistan, and Pakistan.

Existing laws on narcotic drugs and psychotropic substances were due to be tightened, and much harsher penalties for traffickers were to be introduced (Country Report, op. cit.).

PAKISTAN

The promulgation of the Prohibition (Enforcement of Hadd) Order in February 1979 marks a major change in the legal status of drugs and their use in Pakistan: it imposed a total ban on the production, consumption, etc. of all intoxicants including opium, and thereby ended not only the licensed sale of opium via the vend system, but also the rationing systems being introduced gradually to replace the vends.

Prior to this Order, the principal law regulating narcotic drugs in Pakistan had been the 1878 Opium Act, the 1930 Dangerous Drugs Act and the 1958 West Pakistan Prohibition of Opium Smoking Act. These were essentially limiting and controlling measures, providing penalties for activities which were outside the authorized use of drugs to meet *bona fide* requirements. In addition to the Federal Acts, some of the states or provinces have gone further and imposed enhanced penalties: Sind, for example, increased the maximum penalty for unlawful possession, import, export, or manufacture from two thousand rupees to one lakh rupees, and the intoxicant drugs covered include alcohol, *charas*, and bhang. (Some of the penalties are over 150 years old, according to Abdul Wadud, Colombo Plan Workshop, Rawalpindi, 1975.) Under these laws, as the reader will have noted, there was no differentiation between drug offences: possession and trafficking both attracted the same penalties.

Because opium addiction was seen as a small-scale problem in Pakistan, and it was perceived that opium was taken as a mild stimulant or a traditional household medicament, the tenor of Abdul Wadud, *Colombo Plan Workshop*, Rawalpindi, 1975). Under these laws was one of satisfaction with a system which was under control. The vends provided this social and medical service; they were under strict regulation; and licences could be withdrawn at any time. Similarly, the regulations controlling the legal cultivation of opium are presented by Abdul Wadud as being responsible, effective, and efficient. It is clear from recent reports—on the amounts of illicit opium being sold through the vends (McGlothin *et al., Opium Use in Pakistan*, WHO, 1976), and on the dramatic increase in illicit cultivation of opium in the North-West Frontier Province (*Far Eastern Economic Review*, 13 October 1978, pp. 36—7)— that the overall control of opiates in Pakistan was not as efficient as might have seemed. Whether the 1979 Order improves the situation remains to be seen; but, as has already been mentioned above, the experience of other countries in the region has been that the introduction of strict anti-opium laws has usually been followed by the substitution of illicit heroin for licit opium (Westermeyer, *Archiv. Gen. Psychiatry*, 1976, 33:1135—9).

Enforcement of controls upon the illicit cultivation of opium must be accompanied by a crop substitution programme; and, in this aim, Pakistan, as Thailand before it, has enlisted aid from the international agencies. The United Nations/Pakistan programme for drug abuse control contains as a major component, an income and crop substitution project, whose first objective has been to discover and pilot the techniques best suited to the growing areas. It was recognized early in the planning of the project that one could not have an isolated opium-substitution programme, but that it would have to be part of a broader development of agricultural development. The subdivision of Buner, in Swat district, was chosen as the pilot area, as it is a small area with heavy, uncontrolled opium poppy production which could easily be defined. Five villages were selected as demonstration centres, and agricultural development projects started in 1976. In the medium and long term, tree crops such as apples and nuts would seem to hold promise, but in the short term, no one crop has yet been found to compete with the income produced by the cultivation of the opium poppy, although a large range of food, cash, and fodder crops have been, and are, under active investigation. Clearly, the development and improvement of a marketing system will be essential to the success of the programme, especially where high-priced cash crops and perishable goods are concerned. Pilot projects need to become self-sufficient whole-area patterns for control on opium growing to be effective; and in order for this to happen the new crops must be distributed and marketed through an efficient infrastructure.

BANGLADESH

Cannabis resin (*charas*), heroin, and cocaine are drug substances completely banned in Bangladesh; opium use is subject to control via registration; and the sale of cannabis (*ganja*) is regulated through government-licensed retail outlets.

The administration of the Narcotic Laws is the responsibility of the Internal Revenue Division of the Ministry of Finance. The National Board of Revenue, which is attached to the Ministry, is the co-ordinating and policy-making body, and the Department of Narcotics and Liquor is the operational agency which controls the import of narcotic drugs for medical use, and which is responsible for supervising the manufacture and quality of drugs. The customs, police, and the Bangladesh Rifles are also involved in the enforcement of narcotic laws, and in the detection of trafficking.

It is envisaged that a National Narcotics Control Board will take over and co-ordinate these functions, and comprehensive legislation embracing all aspects of narcotics prevention and control is being prepared at the time of writing.

BURMA

The first legislation to regulate the importation, possession, and consumption of opiates in Burma was enacted one hundred years ago, but it included a special exemption for the hill tribes. After Independence, opium production was banned throughout the country, and consumption was allowed only in the Shan and Kachin states. When Burma signed the 1961 Single Convention on Narcotic Drugs, Burma reserved the right to permit the sale of opium and the cultivation of poppies in these states for twenty years, and three years later applied to the United Nations for authorization to produce opium for licit export. This application was rejected because of the difficulty of controlling cultivation in the hill tribe areas, and for ten years, Burma refused to co-operate with the United Nations, in spite of repeated requests and offers of financial assistance (Solomon, *J. Psychedelic Drugs*, 1978, 10: 89–98).

In 1966 the special exemption for the Shan and Kachin states was officially abolished, but Solomon states that, because the government had neither the will nor the resources to enforce the law, the trade continued unchanged. Until the early 1970s, addiction was largely restricted to the hill tribes in the producing areas, and to the Chinese in the cities; and, addiction among Burmese being uncommon, the government did not view it as a particularly important problem (U.S. Cabinet Committee on International Narcotics Control, *World Opium Survey*, 1972).

It has been the opinion of the United States Congress Committee on International Relations (various documents, cited in Solomon) that narcotics legislation and enforcement in Burma reflect an interest in short-term political expediency, rather than being based on a fundamental concern about the evils of addiction. Thus, as the balance of power in northern Burma changed, so did the government's attitude to the opium trade. Solomon (op. cit.) details the military and political power struggles between the interested groups in the opium trade, the upshot of which was a renewal of international pressure upon Burma to control cultivation and the new laboratories that were being established in the border areas with Thailand.

Burma revised its narcotics legislation several times during the mid-1970s: possession of narcotics was made punishable by three years' imprisonment, and trafficking and refining were made capital offences. The Public Order Act denied traffickers the right to trial, and legislation was enacted to confine addicts for up to two years. The Narcotic Drug Act of 1974 had already required that all persons dependent upon narcotic drugs should register at Health Department centres to receive appropriate treatment (Ne Win, *Addictive Diseases*, 1977, 3:87–8).

At the same time, action against the cultivation and transport of opium, and against the new heroin factories at Tachilek, was stepped up. (United Nations crop substitution programmes were also promised, but the funding was postponed until 1977.) Anti-narcotics activities in the border areas of the country inevitably became confused with anti-insurgency activities; but the anti-narcotics drive of the mid-1970s did disrupt the traditional patterns of opiate distribution, and the newer patterns of refining, in the Shan states. However, the effect is reported to have been to decrease the numbers of opium caravans in favour of more human carriers of morphine or heroin—a method of transportation which is far less vulnerable to enforcement efforts. This will inevitably have its effect in changing the domestic pattern of narcotics consumption further towards the use of heroin. The government's enforcement campaign, according to Solomon (op. cit.) has also had the effect of developing new distribution routes through Thailand and Malaysia, and in Solomon's opinion there has not been a decrease in opium production or in heroin refining in the border area with Laos and Thailand.

There are estimated to be more than a dozen insurgent armies in the mountainous border states, and the local population is itself hostile to the efforts of the Burmese army and enforcement officers. Hence, it is not surprising that, in the opinion of U.S. Congress reports monitoring the campaign, the anti-narcotics activities in this region have been ineffective, and record quantities of Burmese narcotics were reaching the outside world from 1976 to 1977 (Solomon, op. cit.).

The Burmese government continued its efforts to reduce urban narcotics abuse, and staged an intensive anti-drugs publicity campaign in 1979 (*Far Eastern Economic Review*, 16 February 1979, p. 31). Exhibitions and mass rallies were held in Rangoon and some other towns, organized by the local councils. The theme of the campaign was two-fold: to increase public awareness of the drug menace, and to highlight the government's action against drug production and trafficking.

CONCLUSIONS

During much of the history of drug use, social rather than legal controls were the main checks upon its spread: we have already mentioned the powerful effect of public opinion as a control in many settings, for example, the ridicule of the able-bodied who were over-fond of opium. Where drug use attracted social opprobrium, *and* the supply of drugs was strictly controlled by, for example, a system of government-run outlets, then social and legal pressures upon drug use worked together. Today, with the greater fragmentation of society and a worsened drug problem, the onus of control has passed into the legal domain (although, as we have seen in earlier chapters, the opinion and influence of family and friends may be a key inhibitory factor upon young people's drug use). The present chapter has shown for each country in the region

how legal and treatment approaches have generally been taken together in a national policy, although the reader may have detected
that in some countries, tensions exist between the agencies represent-
ing the two approaches, each leaning towards its own philosophy.

The pattern of drug availability and use varies so considerably
from country to country that one's conclusions, after reading the
accounts of legal and enforcement activities from each, can hardly
be couched in terms of a preferred, or a most effective approach
for the region: each country is developing an approach to its own
particular drug problem. One of the most striking recent developments has been Operation Ferret in Singapore, which has combined
intensive enforcement activity with strengthened legal powers *and*
the provision of treatment and follow-up facilities on a scale com-
mensurate with the problem. Singapore, during the mid- to late
1970s, faced a dramatically deteriorating situation, and responded
in a way which appears to have been appropriate; but, the main
point which we wish to make here, such a response would have
been totally unsuited to, say, the stable, non-fluid drug situation
in a remote rural part of the region. Evaluation of a particular
legal and enforcement policy therefore must be done with respect
to its context. As yet, there is little such research to report.

The reader of the accounts given in this chapter will have seen
that, in most countries in the region, there is a multiplicity of
agencies concerned with the control of drug abuse. Co-ordination
between them has been attempted in a number of ways: sometimes, the liaison is directly agency to agency, sometimes it is via
a central co-ordinating body. Would a single agency improve effectiveness? The drug problem is indeed multi-faceted, and we feel
that, if one were called upon to design a system of control, and to
decide on a division of responsibilities, many of the features of
existing systems would occur to one. The agencies which monitor
and interdict the flow of drug substances into and within a country
are engaged in work which is qualitatively different from that of
those who monitor the use of the substances within the country,
and again from those whose main responsibility is the detection of
drug offences. Yet clearly an efficient flow of information between
such agencies is essential.

Fifty years ago, the League of Nations Commission was exhort-
ing all governments in the region to allocate more manpower and
resources to enforcement activities. It is still not uncommon to find
accounts of anti-drug agencies which are undermanned and which
lack resources. If we are now considering the law and enforcement
activities as part of society's overall response to drug abuse, then
it becomes clear that the consequence of underprovision in this

enforcement area is inevitably to throw more burden upon the treatment and rehabilitation facilities, let alone the resultant misery caused to those who become dependent because of the ready availability of drug substances.

One pervasive problem in the history of enforcement has been, sadly but inevitably, the corruption of the enforcement officers themselves, and of their superiors, up to the highest levels. This is a problem which will perhaps always crop up when the illicit trade is so lucrative, but is itself open to stricter controls than have always been enforced. Many enforcement officers can tell one, off the record, of the high-placed but untouched 'protectors' of the drug trade, and the best planned policy will fail to be effective without the political will for it to succeed.

Enforcement activities are not only directed against highly organized syndicates, but also frequently have to operate in extremely difficult circumstances. Consider the sheer physical and military difficulties of policing the mountainous opium cultivation areas in the region, where private armies control much of the production and trade. Consider the technical impossibility of fully monitoring the huge influx of people and goods passing daily into seaports and airports, or crossing frontiers, especially if the major traffickers decide to switch from bulk transport of drug substances to 'human wave' tactics. Again, consider how much more difficult detection becomes if local pushers abandon regular rendezvous in favour of a telephone order and secret drop method of supplying their customers.

This book has concentrated upon the drug problem in East Asia, rather than the consequences of East Asian drugs for the world problem, and thus, in this chapter on enforcement, there has been little discussion of national and international narcotics bureaux, police, and customs work on controlling the considerable international traffic in drugs which passes through the region. Such work, whilst providing valuable international contacts and mutual exchange of experience between agencies, represents yet a further drain on already stretched national resources.

VIII

Society's Response to Drug Abuse: The Current Variety of Approaches

THERE are as many common features in the pattern of drug use found in the countries of the region as there are in the characteristics and motivations of the adult and adolescent drug users, and it is hoped that the earlier chapters of the book may have brought out these similarities. In contrast to this similarity, the succeeding three chapters have shown some of the diversity of response to the problem of drug abuse and drug dependency. Some countries in the region have invested considerable efforts towards primary prevention via education and public information campaigns, and have placed much emphasis on this method of demand reduction. Other countries have emphasized the legal and enforcement approaches, denying supplies to the market, and introducing heavy penalties for trafficking and, in some cases, for possession. Many countries have been prompted to provide treatment and rehabilitation facilities for drug dependants only very recently, and often the provision has lagged well behind recommendations for compulsory treatment and rehabilitation made in the law. Some have emphasized detoxification treatment without adequate thought being given to rehabilitation and follow-up programmes.

Some countries have clearly experienced conflicts between the different agencies responsible for the drug dependence problem, with one philosophy of response characterizing the enforcement agencies, and another approach characterizing the treatment and rehabilitation agencies. It is hoped that the very describing of the various countries' experiences may provoke some thought about the diversity of approaches that are currently in practice. Clearly, what is appropriate in one part of the region, or indeed in one area of a country, may be entirely inappropriate for the traditions and contemporary drug dependence situation in another: sensitivity to local conditions must be the prime requirement of the response to the problem of drug abuse. The presence of a diversity of approaches in treatment within the region, and often within the services available within one country (as, for example, in the Philippines) should be regarded as healthy, in that it provides possibilities of meeting the diversity of needs of drug dependants.

One broad dichotomy that can be imposed onto this diversity, and which will be discussed in this chapter, is that of the international and modern versus the indigenous and often traditional and ancient approaches to the problem of drug dependence: this is today most clearly seen in the area of treatment and rehabilitation. It would be easy to make a chauvinistic appeal to employ the local rather than the imported approaches, or to express the romantic wish for local methods, long neglected by the international community, to turn out to be more effective than the others. Neither chauvinism nor romanticism would advance the argument. One can, however, further the discussion by laying out for consideration the various forms of traditional approaches, welcome the growing awareness of these approaches among the international expert community, and hope that the preliminary studies of their efficacy, which have begun, will be pursued further. (The evaluations which have taken place so far indicate that at least some traditional approaches are well worth further investigation.)

It must be recognized that many traditional approaches to the treatment of drug dependence evolved in response to patterns of drug dependence which no longer exist, or which have been overshadowed by newer forms of abuse among a broader age spectrum. Thus, herbal nostrums formulated through long experience in the treatment of opium smokers may well be unsuitable for the treatment of the contemporary poly-drug user. However, there is evidence that at least some practitioners of traditional medicine are evolving new variants of their art to meet new circumstances. Thus, as reported earlier, some *bomoh* in Malaysia have adapted their detoxifying teas and their rituals to the treatment of that relatively new group of clients, the heroin dependants.

Some traditional treatments may be best characterized as being based on the culture and belief systems of the community whence the drug dependants come. For example, in the treatment of the parallel problem of alcoholism, Japanese clinicians have used two forms of therapy which were born in the Japanese Buddhist climate: *naikan* and *danshukai* (H. Suwaki, *Br. J. Addiction*, 1979, 74:15—20).

The form of self-examination practised by the devotional sect of *Shinshu* Buddhist priests has been adapted for the practice of ordinary people as the *naikan* or 'self-observation' method, and is now used by many therapists with psychiatric and alcoholic patients. The patient is given a theme which serves as the basis of a step-by-step self-examination: generally, the patient's meditation is focused upon a particular close relationship, and the therapist, interviewing him every two hours, works the patient through this relationship at the various stages of the individual's life. Meanwhile, the patient is secluded in a narrow, screened-off area, for meditation.

Naikan therapy provides alcoholics with reflections upon their past conduct, awareness of the love of their families, and firm resolutions for abstinence. *Naikan* therapy has to be done during the hospital stay. At first the patient cannot concentrate on *naikan* readily, and wonders what he is supposed to do. But, as the days go on, he becomes able to recollect vividly the memories of his interpersonal relations during childhood accompanied by profound emotions. He feels shame at his self-centred behaviour and appreciates the love of his family (Suwaki, p. 18).

Thus, rather than being encouraged to discuss his problems openly with his family, or spending lengthy periods in contact with his psychotherapist, the patient is allowed to follow the much more culturally acceptable custom of shutting oneself up for meditation (*komoru*), receiving only very brief, directive visits from the therapist during the course of the seclusion. After treatment, the patient is trained in a self-paced, occasional form of *naikan* therapy, and encouraged to attend meetings of *danshukai*, a mutual encouragement society, in which cured alcoholics and the families of alcoholics play the major part. It is considered that at this stage, the former alcoholic will be able to rely on a dependent relationship with wife and children: such dependences are an important part of Japanese social life, and are not viewed as being an unhealthy state as they might be in the West.

Suwaki's paper describing these two stages of therapy provides an excellent example of the need for further investigation and evaluation of a tradition-based approach. As one of the major practitioners of *naikan* therapy himself, he presents his own record of successful treatments, but admits that his group of patients were exceptional in their degree of motivation. Were careful evaluation of the technique to indicate its efficacy for the treatment of alcoholism, then with due modifications to include appropriate detoxification procedures, its application for the treatment of drug-dependent individuals in the culture could be considered. The essential feature—a meditation upon one's self-centredness and the resultant turning away from loving and supportive family—would seem equally applicable in the treatment of drug dependants in a culture where such inward contemplation was a technique practised.

Other culturally-rooted treatments for drug dependence involve the individual's belief system to varying degrees. Thus, the several religious groups who have offered treatment tend to lay much stress on religious teaching, spiritual exercises, and sacred affirmations, to abstain from drugs and contact with drug users: examples can be found in the accounts given in Chapter VI of the Buddhist treatment centres in Thailand, and of Muslim healers in Malaysia. But, the involvement of beliefs in treatment, range from these fully worked out value systems which can support the rehabilitee to acts of affirmation, whose power may lie more simply in the fear of the consequences of breaking a vow, through to those superficially religious practices which border on the magical and incantatory. Examples of such practices were given in the description of *bomoh* treatment in Malaysia, and doubtless form the stock-in-trade of many traditional healers elsewhere in the region: more anthropological accounts are needed. Whatever one may think of the use of sacred texts used as incantations and magical inscriptions, the preliminary evidence (cited in Chapter VI) indicates that such forms of treatment can prove highly effective.

The question then immediately arises: how applicable are belief-based treatments to secularizing societies, or to those containing (as in all countries in the region) individuals who are of other belief systems? Empirical data rather than inspired guesses are required. Some healers accept for treatment only individuals who espouse the appropriate beliefs; yet Heggenhougen (see Chapter VI on Malaysia) has found that, at least at the most basic magical levels, those non-Muslim patients who are accepted by healers using Koranic chants and bodily inscriptions, show as good success rates as Muslim patients. Numbers here are very small, and thus further investigation is needed, but it seems likely that faith in the treatment's efficacy will here prove, as has been found in many areas of psychotherapy, to be more important than the specific beliefs. Such a faith is a function of the motivation to present oneself for treatment to a traditional healer in the first place. Clearly, studies to evaluate different kinds of treatment must take into account the actual distribution of case types *and* personal beliefs in the existing self-selected clientele of the healers. The point, however, is not peculiar to the evaluation of traditional therapies: consider the degree of self-selection that must be involved in the voluntary patients selecting between the various types of modern therapy available, for example, in the Philippines. Indeed, a therapy is not to be lightly dismissed even if it *is* found to be effective for only one segment of the population.

Many traditional treatments for drug dependence are more physically- than belief-based, and consist of treatment with herbal concoctions, body massages, induced sweating, and special diets. Examples of these have been given in the sections of Chapter VI dealing with Laos, Thailand, and Malaysia (see, for more detail, one of the few published accounts, J. Westermeyer, *Br. J. Addiction*, 1973, 68:345–9); but the range of procedures is immense, and scientific evaluation has barely begun. (Pharmacological analysis of herbal teas used by Malaysian *bomoh* has been started at the National Drug Dependence Research Centre, Penang.) Until widespread studies are carried out, the relative worth of these various physical procedures will remain unknown, although it seems likely that at least some traditional healers have discovered techniques which could be applied more widely. All these physical treatments are, however, concerned primarily with the first detoxification phase of treatment, either in the process of ridding the body of narcotics, or in easing withdrawal symptoms, and they are therefore generally administered in the context of a broader form of supportive therapy.

The same is true for the once-traditional and now voguish practice of acupuncture. This traditional Chinese form of treatment by means of needling particular points of the body was first used by Wen in the detoxification of drug dependants in Hong Kong (see the appropriate section in Chapter VI), and has since been much discussed but less investigated. It is symptomatic of the need for further research on acupuncture in detoxification that a major review paper on the topic (M. P. Lau, *Addictive Diseases*, 1976, 2: 449–63) can be based largely upon informal, anecdotal accounts of Wen's and other workers' procedures. Indeed, Lau himself calls for more adequate experimental investigations, and is able to report such studies starting in many laboratories and clinics.

There therefore exists in the traditions of the region much which would be of potential use in the treatment of drug dependence, although as yet there has been very little systematic evaluation of such treatments' efficacy or applicability. Thus, before governments in the region (and beyond) invest effort and money in promoting such treatments in addition to, or even in place of, modern, internationally recognized treatments, they are entitled to have full comparative evaluations to consider. Traditional treatments *may*, in fact, transpire to be more suited to local needs.

Another area where there has been a considerable variety of approach has been the legal and enforcement aspects of the drug abuse problem. Although, as Chapter VII has shown, the countries in the region have drawn closer together in their anti-drug legislation (often as a result of becoming signatories to international agreements), there remains some variety within the region in the details of law and emphases in enforcement. Thus, as the earlier chapter illustrated, countries in the region vary in the way in which the borderline is drawn between the treatment and the punishment of detected users of illegal drugs. Countries which are facing a crisis may well take a more authoritarian line than those where the drug dependence problem is more completely contained. Thus, it is not possible to suggest strategies which would be generally appropriate. Circumstances alter—often including international trading factors which are not within the control of the country—and thus policy must alter to respond; consider, for example, the recent rapid changes in the pattern of drug abuse in Singapore, and that country's rapid response in the shape of Operation Ferret in which the various agencies were almost put on a war footing (Chapter VII).

If no general guide-lines can be formulated, then at least the region can learn from its earlier experiences in using legislation and strong enforcement measures to tackle drug abuse. One theme that has emerged from author after author, and in many countries in the region, has been that the introduction of relatively blunt anti-opium legislation, and its fairly efficient enforcement has led *almost inevitably* to the substitution of heroin, and the rapid and full development of an illicit drug market. Once such a criminalized and internationally run market was established, other drugs were introduced, and dealers sought a wider range of consumers. What can be done? The argument advanced by Westermeyer (*Arch. Gen. Psychiatry*, 1976, 33:1135–9) is as follows:

While many opium addicts readily changed to heroin, the reverse did not occur: heroin-addicted people want to continue using heroin, and are not interested in opium. Thus, once the market for heroin has been established, simply repealing the anti-opium law would not likely reproduce the status quo ante. If a laissez-faire attitude were resumed by a government, it would probably have to accept heroin addiction. Nonetheless, an attempt at a 'legal opium, illegal heroin' law would be an interesting social experiment.

Stringent anti-opium legislation has not always, however, led to this disastrous situation; Japan, Korea, and (a rather different case) China have successfully implemented anti-opium laws by combining them with a major detoxification programme adequate for the needs of *all* addicts, followed by social rehabilitation and employment for ex-addicts. In each country, there was prolonged incarceration for all 'recidivists' and corrupt officials, and effective control was established over the importation and production of all narcotics. The mass media was mobilized to alert the general population and, if necessary, to develop their anti-narcotics views. Thus, firm legislation *can* work, given adequate preparation of all the relevant agencies: legislation by itself has a poor record in Asia. Controls cannot be considered in isolation from measures to reduce the demand for drugs.

The reduction of demand via preventative education has been, however, an oft-repeated wishful platitude in many official policy statements. What can be realistically expected of such information and education campaigns? As the main potential executives of such cure-all programmes, school-teachers must by now expect that there will be no end to the catalogue of society's ills, which would somehow disappear if they would only devote a proportion of the school day to them. The same issue of a newspaper which urges the Ministry of Education to introduce more drug preventative education may also be calling for teachers to increase their pupils' awareness of consumer rights, of the opportunities created by new technologies, of the threats to tropical wildlife, and of family planning facilities. The school day is unfortunately not infinitely expansible! Health education, nonetheless, is establishing a foothold in some curricula, with, in many cases, one component being about drugs and their abuse. The reader will have noted that in Chapter V, there was considerably more published material to draw upon from some countries than from others; there is indeed considerable variation across the region in the resources allocated to preventative education, to the development of teaching materials and the training of teachers for such programmes, and to the prominence given to this approach to the problem of drug abuse in official policy statements.

There is, however, much debate both within and outside the region about the very desirability of drug preventative education: the argument is often advanced that the effect of such education may well be not the reduction but the increase of demand. Preventative education, say its critics, may advertise the rare and strange properties of the drug substances, and provide a consumer's guide which balances performance against risks. The 'happy medium' between unrealistic scare tactics and unemotive factual presentations is not easy to achieve in practice; and authorities in the region should be aware that in other parts of the world there have been moratoria on all drug education because the effects were recognized to be so double-edged.

If policy-makers decide, after due consideration, that it would be desirable to introduce or extend preventative education, a whole range of practical decisions have to be made. Should, for example, the channels of approach to youth be via the established institutions for education, or via the organs of youth culture? If it is argued—as the present book has done—that youthful drug abusers and those most at risk tend to be those who are socially precocious and seeking to assert their independence of parents and school, then the conventional educational channels start at a disadvantage. And yet, in most of the region, youth culture is not served by the special media as it is in the West, and is much more informal and therefore less tappable by attitude-shapers. Another issue: how should the general public be made more aware of the problem of drug abuse in their country? The power of the press to alert and arouse public concern has been illustrated in several of the earlier chapters; in more than one country the general public was ahead of the government in perceiving the need for treatment and rehabilitative facilities. And yet there are dangers of exaggeration of the problem by the media: scare tactics, designed to command public attention, can so shape attitudes towards the individual drug dependant that his rehabilitation is hindered. There are many further practical problems that demand consideration: the desirability and effectiveness of major multi-media campaigns; the appropriate choice of apparent source of information in the persuasive communications; and the degree of knowledge and present beliefs of the various target audiences. (One of the problems with scare tactics is that false information in the long run will be harmful, if it leads, when it becomes verifiable by the audience, to the discrediting of the source of information.)

The focus of this book, and of the majority of literature that it has summarized, has been on the problem of drug dependence in society. Once the pattern of drug use has been described, then the natural next topic to be discussed has usually been: how can society deal with the problem? What balance of prevention, treatment, and enforcement will contain or eliminate the problem most effectively for the particular context? And what success have particular approaches had?

Yet what should the aim of anti-drug campaigns be? Faced with the appalling toll imposed by the 'hard drugs', it is all too easy to fail to notice that, paradoxical as it might sound in the context, there are some socially positive effects of illicit drugs in society. (We have purposely *not* entered the discussion about the individual's freedom of action with regard to drugs, preferring in this book to take the position which is espoused by the vast majority of other writers cited: that many drug substances in current use have predictable medical, psychological, and economic consequences which make their use a major social problem, although other drug substances, both legal and illegal, do not have as serious consequences.)

By the socially positive effects of drugs, we are referring to the fact that the substances may fulfil a whole range of needs as diverse as the opium den as a social resource; the medical uses (or at least pain-killing effects) of self-administered narcotics; the role of the drugs culture in the adolescent assertion of identity; and the economic benefits of opium as a cash crop to minority groups. These needs, which are at present met by the use and existence of illicit drugs, would presumably continue to exist if all sources of drugs were eliminated. Drugs are clearly not a desirable response to these needs, but programmes to eliminate drugs from society must be sensitive to the functions the substances have performed, and they must wherever possible provide adequate replacements.

If the reader is inclined to doubt whether drug use and the drug culture have performed any such useful functions in society, we ask him to consider each example in turn for himself. We will here follow Westermeyer's argument to illustrate one of the points, that the opium den could be seen as a social resource (*Arch. Gen. Psychiatry*, 1974, 31:237–40).

Opium dens and divans have almost always been depicted as unsavoury places which inevitably lead to ruin; yet the disinterested observer might obtain a different impression if he actually visited them and noted the functions that they performed. In the rural areas of Laos, Westermeyer writes, there were no dens in the sense of public opium smoking places: people there used opium in the privacy of their own homes, or in small social gatherings in each other's homes. Now, in Laos, the economy is primarily a subsistence one, with small family groups providing virtually everything they need for survival, and solitary individuals seeking the support of the kinship group. In the urban areas, distant kinship ties carried far less weight, and the solitary individual found in the opium den a substitute family. Dens had a stable clientele of addicts, most of whom had no spouse, and who, because they were refugees, or were psychologically deviant or were military pensioners, had no family to rely on. At least one daily meal, and sometimes all meals, were taken at the den, which also provided a companionship and mutual assistance between clients which they did not find elsewhere.

Similar analyses could be made of the functions of the drug culture in the lives of other groups of users. We are not arguing that this culture provides at all a desirable response to the individual's needs, but rather that such needs should be recognized when anti-drug campaigns are undertaken, and that alternatives should be provided. Some countries well recognize these needs. Even if, to the outsider, the youth rallies and other activities organized in Hong Kong and the Philippines sound rather pious, they are at least moves in the right direction. If youth, especially in contemporary urban society, have needs which some find are met by the drug culture or by the drug substances' effects, then society must aim to find equally attractive and satisfying substitutes. Many official and voluntary programmes which have started out by aiming specifically to dissuade youth from using drugs have then broadened out, in recognition that the drug problem may often be but a response to other more basic problems in society. Some of these basic problems are those age-old and familiar ones: social disadvantage, illness, poverty, rootlessness, and individual psychological disturbance. It is increasingly recognized, however, that contemporary youthful drug abuse is *not* in the main associated with such factors. Whether the focus is on East Asia or on any other part of the world where there has been a rapid growth of drug abuse among adolescents and young adults, the emphasis should be placed, we argue, neither on the social background nor the personality of drug users, but on their preferred life-styles. The explanation for many current aspects of drug abuse can be traced to the manner in which the habit was introduced into the culture. The most fashion-conscious part of the population, the young, have predominantly been using small quantities of drugs socially rather than solitarily in the United States (W. H. McGlothin, *Annual Review of Psychology*, 1975, 26:45—64), and although there is a lack of anthropological descriptions of the mode of use in East Asia, we believe that much youthful use here is similarly based in fashion and the need to assert oneself. The rapid transmission of the drug 'epidemic' through the region has been noted before, and can be taken as evidence supporting this view.

Society then must not respond to the youthful use of drugs in an insensitive manner, but find ways to educate youth about the dangers of particular drug substances, which can guide the socially precocious towards more positive (or at least less harmful) forms of self-expression.

It is very easy to preach about what should be done, or to be wise after the event about what has been done. Practice is infinitely more difficult. May we therefore end this book with a tribute to all those who contribute in practical terms to the amelioration of the drug problem. As has been the theme of this chapter—and indeed of much of this book—there have been many approaches to the problem in East Asia, some tradition-based and local, others internationally used and modern. It seems likely that a judicious amalgam of traditional and modern educational treatment and enforcement approaches will be needed to meet the problem of drug abuse in the region, but it can only succeed if sufficient people dedicate themselves to the solution of the problem.

Bibliography

MALAYSIA

Adnan bin Haji Abdullah, 'Developing a National Rehabilitation Programme for Drug Dependents in Malaysia', in *Proceedings*, Colombo Plan Workshop, Penang, 1978.

Ann binte Abdul Majeed, 'Social Welfare and Drug Prevention Education', in *Proceedings*, Colombo Plan Workshop, Nathiagali, 1977.

Deva, M. P., 'A Survey of 47 Opiate Dependent Persons who Sought Treatment', *Med. J. Malaysia*, 31(3):183–7, March 1977.

Heggenhougen, H. K., and Navaratnam, V., 'Herbal Therapy in the War on Drug Addiction', *UNESCO Courier*, 1979, 32(7):38–9.

Krishna Iyer, G., 'Education Concerning Problems Related to the Use of Drugs in Thailand, Singapore and Malaysia', *UNESCO/ UNFDAC Fellowship Programme Report*, 1977.

Low, J., *The British Settlement of Penang*, Kuala Lumpur, Oxford University Press, 1972 (reprint of 1836 edition).

Navaratnam, V., 'Epidemiology of drug abuse', *Bull. Publ. Health. Soc.*, 1975, 10:17–22.

——, and Lee, B. A., 'National Data Bank on Drug Dependence in Malaysia', in *Proceedings*, Colombo Plan Workshop, Penang, 1978.

Navaratnam, V., Lee, B. A., and Spencer, C. P., 'Extent and patterns of drug abuse among children in Malaysia', *Bull. Narc.*, 1979, 31 (3–4):59–68.

Navaratnam, V., and Spencer, C. P., *The Drug User and the Law*, Centre for Policy Research, Universiti Sains Malaysia, Penang, 1977.

——, 'A Study on Socio-Medical Variables of Drug-Dependent Persons Volunteering for Treatment in Penang, Malaysia', *Bull. Narc.*, Jan.–Mar., 1978, 30(1):1–7.

Navaratnam, V., Sushama, P. C., and Hughes, P. H., 'Treatment Evaluation Research in Malaysia', in *Proceedings*, Colombo Plan Workshop, Penang, 1978.

Nowlis, V., 'Relating the Experience of the U.S. with Drug-Related Problems to the Special Needs of a Developing Country (Malaysia)', in *Proceedings of the International Conference on the Prevention of the Addictions in Developing Countries*, Nassau, Bahamas, 1974.

Parameshvara Deva, M., 'A Seven-Year Study of Opiate Dependence in Malaysia', *Med. J. Malaysia*, March 1978, 32(3):249–54.

The Problem of Drug Abuse in Malaysia, Cabinet Committee on Drug Abuse Control, Kuala Lumpur, 1979.

Proceedings, Colombo Plan/Government of Malaysia Workshop on Reduction of Demand for Illicit Drugs in South-East Asia, Penang, Malaysia, 1978.

Solomon, R., 'Malaysia and Singapore: new export centers for the Southeast Asian heroin trade', *J. Psychedelic Drugs*, 1979, 11: 283–8.

Spencer, C. P., and Navaratnam, V., *A Study of the Misuse of Drugs Among Secondary Schoolchildren in the States of Penang and Selangor*, Centre for Policy Research, Universiti Sains Malaysia, Penang, 1976.

_____, 'Patterns of Drug Use Amongst Malaysian Secondary Schoolchildren', in *Drug and Alcohol Dependence*, 1980, 5: 379–91.

_____, 'Social Background and Attitudes Towards Drugs as Predictors of Drug Use among Malaysian Students', in *Drug and Alcohol Dependence*, 1980, 5:411–19.

_____, 'Social attitudes, self-description and perceived reasons for using drugs: a survey of the secondary school population in Malaysia', *Drug and Alcohol Dependence*, 1980, 5:421–7.

_____, 'Legal sanctions and information about drugs as influences upon the decision by adolescents whether to use illicit drugs', *Drug and Alcohol Dependence*, 1981, 6:315–22.

_____, and Lee, B. A., *A Study of the Misuse of Drugs Among Secondary Schoolchildren in the State of Kelantan*, National Drug Dependence Research Centre, Universiti Sains Malaysia, Penang, 1978.

Tan, E., 'A Preliminary Survey of Drug Dependence in the State of Penang, West Malaysia', *Med. J. Malaysia*, September 1973, 28(1):23–8.

Tan, E. S., and Haq, S. M., 'Drug Abuse in Malaysia', *Med. J. Malaysia*, December 1974, 29(2):126–30.

Werner, R., 'Traditional medicine and modern medicine: contradiction or symbiosis?' *Öff. Gesundh.–Wesen.*, 1978, 40:347–60.

———, 'Can the medicine-man be replaced?' *Öff. Gesundh.–Wesen.*, 1979, 41:17–28.

———, 'Treatment of Malayan drug addicts by traditional medical methods', *Öff. Gesundh.–Wesen.*, 1979, 41:332–43.

Yakob bin Abdul Rahman, 'Ex-Drug Dependents as Therapeutic Staff in a Rehabilitation Programme', in *Proceedings*, Colombo Plan Workshop, Penang, 1978.

Yip, P. H., 'Institutional Rehabilitation of Drug Dependents in Malaysia', in *Proceedings*, Colombo Plan Workshop, Penang, 1978.

THAILAND

The Buddhist Treatment Centre, Tam Kraborg: Retrospective Statistics 1978, Institute of Health Research, Chulalongkorn University, Bangkok, 1978.

Chatiyanonda, P., *et al.*, *A Study of Circumstances of Repeated Drug Addiction*, Department of Social Work, Thammasat University, Bangkok, and Colombo Plan Bureau, 1977.

Disayavanish, C., and Disayavanish, P., 'Attitudes and Adjustments of Drug Addicts: A Comparison Between Drug Addicts in the Prison and in the Hospital', in *Proceedings*, ICAA Bangkok, 1975.

'The Golden Triangle Connection', *Newsweek*, 18 April 1977, pp. 24–5.

Kojak, G., Jr., 'The American Community in Bangkok, Thailand: A Model of Social Disintegration', *Am. J. Psychiatry*, November 1974, 131(11):1229–33.

Krishna Iyer, G., 'Education Concerning Problems Related to the Use of Drugs in Thailand, Singapore and Malaysia', *UNESCO/ UNFDAC Fellowship Programme Report* (mimeograph), 1977.

Kroll, P., 'Psychoses Associated with Marijuana Use in Thailand', *J. Nerv. Ment. Dis.*, September 1975, 161(3):149–56.

McBeth, J., 'Narcotics control: the options to growing opium', *Far Eastern Economic Review*, 5 October 1979, 41–3.

Meesook, A., and Bennett, N., 'Cultures in Collision, An Experience of Thailand', in *Cultures in Collision*, I. Pilowsky (ed.), Adelaide, Australian National Association for Mental Health, 1975.

Nepote, J., 'In the Golden Triangle With a Handful of Dollars', *Bull. Narc.*, Jan.–Mar. 1976, 28(1):1–8.

Poshyachinda, V., Onthaum, Y., Sitthi-Amorn, C., and Perngparm, U., *Evaluation of Treatment Outcome: The Buddhist Temple Treatment Centre, Tam Kraborg*, Institute of Health Research, Chulalongkorn University, Bangkok, 1978.

Poshyachinda, V., Sitthi-Amorn, C., and Onthaum, Y., *An Inter-pretative Epidemiology of Drug Dependence in Thailand*, Institute of Health Research, Chulalongkorn University, Bangkok, and in Colombo Plan Workshop, Penang, 1978.

Proceedings of the 31st International Congress on Alcoholism and Drug Dependence, Bangkok, February 1975 (= ICAA Bangkok, 1975).

Punnahitanond, S., *Attitudes of Thai Youths about Drugs*, Institute of Health Research, Chulalongkorn University, Bangkok, 1977.

Ratanakorn, P., 'Thailand and the Problems of Addiction', in *Proceedings*, ICAA Bangkok, 1975.

Sarasin, P., 'The Narcotics Problem in Thailand', in *Proceedings*, ICAA Bangkok, 1975.

Schneider, R. J., Sangsingkeo, P., Panpanya, B., Tumrongrachaniti, S., and Witayarut, C., 'Incidence of Daily Drug Use as Reported by a Population of Thai Partners Working Near United States Military Installations: A Preliminary Study', *Int. J. Addict.*, 1976, 11(1):175–85.

Schneider, R. J., Sangsingkeo, P., and Punnahitanond, S., 'A Survey of Thai Student Use of Illicit Drugs', *Int. J. Addict.*, 1977, 12(2–3):227–39.

Shaowanasai, A., 'Follow Up Study on Student Addicts', in *Proceedings*, ICAA Bangkok, 1975.

Showanasai, C. A., 'Treatment Report from Thailand', *Addict Dis.*, 1977, 3(1):89–92.

Solomon, R., 'Thailand: Southeast Asia's Marketplace for Opiates', *J. Psychedelic Drugs*, 1978, 10:193–206.

Suwanbubpa, P., *The Etiology of Heroin Addiction Among Narcotic Prisoners*, Kasetsart University, Bangkok, 1974.

Suwanlert, S., 'A Study of *kratom* Eaters in Thailand', *Bull. Narc.*, July 1975, 27(3):21–7.

Suwanwela, C., *Drug Dependence in Thailand: A Review*, Institute of Health Research, Chulalongkorn University, Bangkok, 1976.

Suwanwela, C., Kanchanahuta, S., and Onthaum, Y., 'Hill tribe addicts: a retrospective study of 1382 patients', *Bull. Narc.*, 1979, 31(1):23–40.

Suwanwela, C., Poshyachinda, V., Sitthi-Amorn, C., Thasanpradit, P., and Dharmkrong-At, A., *Overview of Drug Dependence Treatment Methods Available in Thailand*, Institute of Health Research, Chulalongkorn University, Bangkok, 1978.

Suwanwela, C., Poshyachinda, V., Thasanpradit, P., and Dharmkrong-At, A., *The Hilltribes of Thailand, Their Opium Use and Addiction*, Institute of Health Research, Chulalongkorn University, Bangkok, 1978, and *Bull. Narc.*, 1978, 30(2):1–19.

Thailand Country Report, UNESCO Regional Meeting, Penang, 1977.

'Thailand's Drug Trade Tangle', *Far Eastern Economic Review*, 28 April 1978, pp. 23—7.

Williams, I. M. G., UN/Thai Programme for drug abuse control in Thailand—a report on Phase I: February 1972—June 1979, *Bull. Narc.*, 1979, 31(2):1—44.

SINGAPORE

Da Costa, J. L., Tock, E. P. C., and Boey, H. K., 'Lung Disease with Chronic Obstruction in Opium Smokers in Singapore', *Thorax*, 1971, 26:555—71.

Foo, C. C., 'Use of Law Enforcement Statistics in Drug Abuse Assessment', in *Proceedings*, Colombo Plan Workshop, Penang, 1978.

Krishna Iyer, G., 'Education Concerning Problems Related to the Use of Drugs in Thailand, Singapore and Malaysia', *UNESCO/ UNFDAC Fellowship Programme Report*, 1977.

Leong, C. C., *Youth in the Army*, Singapore, Federal Publications, 1978.

Leong, J. H. K., *Opium Addiction in Singapore*, dissertation for D. P. H., London University (unpublished), 1959.

——, 'Cross-Cultural Influences on Ideas about Drugs', *Bull. Narc.*, 1974, 26:1—8.

——, 'The Present Status of Drug Dependence Treatment in Singapore', *Addict. Dis.*, 1977, 3(1):93—8.

——, 'Beating the Gong and Chasing the Dragon in the Lion City', *J. Drug Issues*, 1980, 10(2):229—40.

McGlothin, W. H., 'The Singapore heroin control programme', *Bull. Narc.*, 1980, 32(1):1—14.

Ng, B. C., 'Review of Treatment and Rehabilitation Measures for Drug Users in Singapore', in *Proceedings*, Colombo Plan Workshop, Penang, 1978.

Singapore Country Report, in Commonwealth Regional Working Group on Illicit Drugs, Kuala Lumpur, 1979.

Solomon, R., 'Malaysia and Singapore: new export centers for the Southeast Asian heroin trade', *J. Psychedelic Drugs*, 1979, 11: 283—8.

Teo, S. H., Chee, K. T., and Tan, C. T., 'Psychiatric complications of Rohypnol abuse', *Singapore Med. J.*, 1979, 20:270—3.

Teo, S. H., Chee, K. T., Tan, C. T., and Ng, B. C., 'Heroin abuse in Singapore: A profile and characteristics study', *Singapore Med. J.*, 1978, 19:65—70.

Vasco, S., 'Social Consequences of Drug Abuse', *Nurs. J. Singapore*, May 1978, 18(1):3—4.

INDONESIA

Budiarti, 'Implementation of National Legislation', in E. Widjono in *Drug Abuse in Indonesia, Proceedings*, Colombo Plan Workshop, Jakarta, 1975.

Salan, R. D., 'National Mental Hospital Reporting Programme: Some Trends in the Number and Characteristics of Drug Users in Indonesia', in *Proceedings*, Colombo Plan Workshop, Penang, 1978.

Setyonegoro, D. R. K., 'Drug Abuse in Indonesia', in *Proceedings*, ICAA Conference, Hong Kong, 1971.

_____, 'Drug Abuse in Indonesia', *National Inst. Drug Abuse Res. Monogr. Ser.*, 1978, 19:51—9.

_____, *et al.*, 'Drug Abuse in Indonesia', in *Proceedings* of the International Seminar Jointly Sponsored by the Ministry of Health, Republic of Indonesia, and the Colombo Plan, Jakarta, 1975.

Soegomo, Y. (Army Lt. Gen.), 'Current Drug Problem in Indonesia', in *Drug Abuse in Indonesia, Proceedings*, Colombo Plan Workshop, Jakarta, 1975.

Wibisono, S., 'Modalities of Treatment and Rehabilitation', in *Drug Abuse in Indonesia, Proceedings*, Colombo Plan Workshop, 1975.

Widjono, E., 'Review of Drug Dependence Treatment and Rehabilitation in Indonesia', in *Proceedings*, Colombo Plan Workshop, Penang, 1978.

_____, *et al.*, 'National Approaches Toward the Prevention of the Non-Medical Use of Drugs', in *Drug Abuse in Indonesia, Proceedings*, Colombo Plan Workshop, Jakarta, 1975.

THE PHILIPPINES

Aldaba-Lim, E., 'Psychosocial Aspects of Drug Abuse in the Philippines', in *Proceedings*, Colombo Plan Workshop, Laguna, 1974.

Cudal, A. S., 'Educational Programmes on the Prevention and Control of Drug Abuse in the Philippines', *Bull. Narc.*, July—Sept. 1976, 28(3):1—9.

_____, *et al.*, *A Study of Youth and the Use of Drugs in the Philippines*, Manila, UNESCO/Dangerous Drugs Board, 1976.

Educational Programmes on the Prevention and Control of Drug Abuse in the Philippines, Dangerous Drugs Board, Manila, 1976.

Generoso, L. C., Alma de Leon, C., and Esperas, N. N., 'Strategies of Planning, Implementing and Evaluating Preventive Education and Community Education', in *Proceedings*, Colombo Plan Workshop, Manila, 1976.

Goduco-Auglar, C., 'A Note on Drug Abuse in the Philippines', *Bull. Narc.*, Apr.–June 1972, 24(2):43–4.

Guioguio, R. V., 'Innovative Approaches to Program Planning and Evaluation', in *Proceedings*, Colombo Plan Workshop, Manila, 1976.

Krishna Iyer, 'Proceedings of the National Seminar–Workshop on Strategies for School-based Drug Prevention Education Programmes', Bulacan, Philippines, 1978.

Manuel, M. D., and Zarco, R. M., 'The Current Drug Problem in the Philippines', in *Proceedings*, Colombo Plan Workshop, Laguna, 1974.

Maravilla, A. N., 'Education Component of Treatment and Rehabilitation', in *Proceedings*, Colombo Plan Workshop, Laguna, 1974.

Mejillano, E. A., 'Counselling Work with Twenty Urban Families of Former Drug Abusers' in *Proceedings*, Colombo Plan Workshop, Laguna, 1974.

Patron, J. S., 'Development and Evaluation of Communication Strategies for the Prevention of Drug Abuse', in *Proceedings*, Colombo Plan Workshop, Laguna, 1974.

Philippine Country Report on Drug Abuse Problem, Dangerous Drugs Board, Manila, n.d.

Proceedings, Colombo Plan Workshop on Drug Abuse: Preventative Education, Laguna, 1974.

Proceedings, Second National Colombo Plan Workshop on Drug Abuse: Preventative Education, Manila, 1976.

Ramos, P. G., 'Integration of Drug Education in the School Curriculum', in *Proceedings*, Colombo Plan Workshop, Laguna, 1974.

San Pedro, R. M., 'Overview of Treatment Services Offered to Drug Users in the Philippines', in *Proceedings*, Colombo Plan Workshop, Penang, 1978.

Zarco, R. M., *et al.*, 'Student Drug Use in the Philippines', Manila, Narcotics Foundation of the Philippines, 1972.

————, *Street Corner Drug Use in Metropolitan Manila: A Comparison of Two Socio-Economic Categories of Illicit Social Drug Users*, Manila, Narcotics Foundation of the Philippines, 1972.

Zarco, R. M., and Manuel, M. D., 'Current Drug Problems in the Philippines', in *Proceedings*, Colombo Plan Workshop, Laguna, 1974.

————, and Almonte, M. P., 'Drug Abuse in the Philippines', *Addict. Dis.*, 1977, 3(1):119–28.

LAOS

Solomon, R., 'The rise and fall of the Laotian and Vietnamese opiate trades', *J. Psychedelic Drugs*, 1979, 11:159–71.

Westermeyer, J., 'Alcohol and Opium Use by the Meo', *Am. J. Psychiatry*, 1971, 127:1019–23.

_____, 'Folk Treatments for Opium Addiction in Laos', *Br. J. Addict.*, December 1973, 68(4):345–9.

_____, 'Opium Smoking in Laos: A Survey of 40 Addicts', *Am. J. Psychiatry*, February 1974, 131(2):165–70.

_____, 'Opium Dens: A Social Resource for Addicts in Laos', *Arch. Gen. Psychiatry*, August 1974, 31(2):237–40.

_____, 'Narcotic Addiction in Two Asian Cultures: A Comparison and Analysis', *Drug Alcohol Depend.*, July 1977, 2(4):273–85.

_____, 'An Addiction Treatment Program in Laos: The First Year's Experience', *Drug Alcohol Depend.*, March 1978, 3(2):93–102.

_____, 'Social Events and Narcotic Addiction: The Influence of War and Law on Opium Use in Laos', *Addict. Behav.*, 1978, 3(1):57–61.

_____, 'Medical and Non-Medical Treatment for Narcotic Addicts: A Comparative Study From Asia', *J. Nerv. Ment. Dis.*, 1979, 167:205–11.

_____, 'Influence of Opium Availability on Addiction Rates in Laos', *Am. J. Epidemiol.*, 1979, 109:550–62.

Westermeyer, J., and Bourne, P., 'A Heroin "Epidemic" in Asia', *Am. J. Drug Alcohol. Abuse*, 1977, 4(1):1–11.

_____, 'Treatment Outcome and the Role of the Community in Narcotic Addiction', *J. Nerv. Ment. Dis.*, Jan. 1978, 166(1): 51–8.

Westermeyer, J., and Peng, G., 'Opium and Heroin Addicts in Laos: I. A Comparative Study', *J. Nerv. Ment. Dis.*, May 1977, 164(5): 346–50.

_____, 'Opium and Heroin Addicts in Laos: II. A Study of Matched Pairs', *J. Nerv. Ment. Dis.*, May 1977, 164(5):351–4.

_____, 'A Comparative Study of Male and Female Opium Addicts Among the Hmōng (Meo)', *Br. J. Addict.*, June 1978, 73(2): 181–7.

Westermeyer, J., and Soudalay, C., 'Addiction Treatment in Laos: The First Year's Experience', in *Proceedings*, ICAA Conference, Bangkok, 1975.

HONG KONG

Action Committee Against Narcotics, *Hong Kong Narcotics Report*, Government Press, Hong Kong (annual from 1976).

Ch'ien, J. M. N., 'A Multilevel Team Approach to Prevention of Drug Abuse among Hong Kong Youth', *Proceedings of ICAA Conference*, Bangkok, 1975.

——, 'Voluntary Treatment for Drug Abuse in Hong Kong', *Addict. Dis.*, 1977, 3(1):99–104.

Fort, J., 'Giver of Delight or Liberator of Sin: Drug Use and "Addiction" in Asia', *Bull. Narc.*, 1965, 17:1–11, 13–19.

Garner, T. G., 'Drugs and Society', *Br. J. Addict.*, November 1971, 66(3):219–24.

——, 'The Drug Problem as it Stands in Hong Kong', *Br. J. Addict.*, May 1970, 65(1):45–50.

Hess, A. G., *Chasing the Dragon: A Report on Drug Addiction in Hong Kong*, North Holland Publishing Co., 1965.

Hollinrake, J. B., 'Social Rehabilitation of Opiate Users', in *Proceedings*, Colombo Plan Workshop, Penang, 1978.

Holzner, A. S., and Ding, L. K., 'White Dragon Pearls in Hong Kong: A Study of Young Women Drug Addicts', *Int. J. Addict.*, 1973, 8(2):253–63.

'Hong Kong Narcotics Report', *Australas. Nurses J.*, May 1976, 6(10):3–5.

'Hong Kong's Role on the International Front', *Australas. Nurses J.*, May 1978, 7(9):20–1.

Lau, M. P., *An Epidemiological Study of Narcotic Addiction in Hong Kong*, Hong Kong, Government Press, 1967.

Ley, C. (Address by Counsellor for Hong Kong Affairs, Bangkok), *Proceedings of Commonwealth Working Group*, Kuala Lumpur, 1979.

Ming-Ming, S., and Suk-Ching, L., 'Young Drug Addicts in Hong Kong', *Hong Kong Nurs. J.*, November 1975, 19:37–44.

Sargent, M. J., 'A Cross-Cultural Study of Attitudes and Behaviour Towards Alcohol and Drugs', *Br. J. Sociol.*, March 1971, 22(1):83–96.

Singer, K., 'The Choice of Intoxicant Among the Chinese', *Br. J. Addict.*, September 1974, 69(3):257–68.

Wen, H. L., 'Acupuncture in the Therapy of Drug Dependence', in *Drug Abuse in Indonesia*, D. R. K. Setyonegoro (ed.), Jakarta, 1975.

——, and Teo, S. W., 'Experience in the Treatment of Drug Addiction by Electro-Acupuncture', *Hong Kong Nurs. J.*, November 1975, 19:33–5.

Wu, P. M., 'Hong Kong Narcotics Register System', in *Proceedings*, Colombo Plan Workshop, Penang, 1978.

Yap, P. M., 'Lessons from the Anti-Narcotic Voluntary Treatment Programme in Hong Kong', *Bull. Narc.*, 1967, 19:35–43.

CHINA

Adams, L. P., III, 'China: The Historical Setting of Asia's Profitable Plague', in A. W. McCoy, *The Politics of Heroin in Southeast Asia*, Harper and Row, New York, 1972.

Collis, M., *Foreign Mud: Being an Account of the Opium Imbroglio at Canton and the Anglo–Chinese War Which Followed*, Faber and Faber, London, 1964.

'Drug Abuse and Addiction Problems in Taiwan', *Med. J. Malaysia*, December 1974, 29(2):130–1.

Fay, P. W., *The Opium War, 1840–42*, University of North Carolina Press, 1975, Norton Library, 1976.

Fields, A., and Tararin, P. A., 'Opium in China', *Br. J. Addict.*, January 1970, 64(3):371–82.

Gregory, R. J., 'The Chinese Drug Scene: History', *Drug Forum*, 1977–8, 6:235–47.

———, 'The Chinese Drug Scene: Contemporary and Implications', *Drug Forum*, 1977–8, 6:299–314.

Lowinger, P., 'How the People's Republic of China Solved the Drug Abuse Problem', *Am. J. Chin. Med.*, July 1973, 1(2): 275–82.

———, 'The Solution to Narcotic Addiction in the People's Republic of China', *Am. J. Drug Alcohol Abuse*, 1977, 4(2):165–78.

Marshall, J., 'Opium and the Politics of Gangsterism in Nationalist China, 1927–1945', *Bull. Conc. Asian Schol.*, 1976, 8:19–48.

Miskel, J. F., 'Religion and Medicine: The Chinese Opium Problem', *J. Hist. Med.*, January 1973, 28(1): 3–14.

Solomon, R., 'The Evolution of Opium Use in China: The Origins of the Illicit International Trade', *J. Psychedel. Drugs*, 1978, 10:43–9.

Visher, J. S., and Visher, E. B., 'Impressions of Psychiatric Problems and Their Management: China, 1977', *Am. J. Psychiatry*, 1979, 136:28–32.

Waley, A., *The Opium War Through Chinese Eyes*, George Allen and Unwin, London, 1958.

JAPAN

Brill, H., Hirose, T. V., and Seevers, M., 'The Rise and Fall of a Methylamphetamine Epidemic: Japan, 1945–1955', *Seminars in Psychiatry*, 1969, 1:179–94.

Heyman, F., 'Amphetamine Abuse in Japan', *J. Psychedel. Drugs*, 1969, 2:217–33.

Higuchi, K., 'Experiences of Amphetamine and Other Drug Abuse in Japan', in *Drug Dependence*, H. Bostrom (ed.), Stockholm, Almquist and Wiksell, 1975.

Ishii, A., and Motohashi, N., 'Drug Abuse in Japan', *Addict. Dis.*, 1977, 3(1):105–14.

Kumagai, H., 'Drug Abuse and Counter-Measures in Japan', *Med. J. Malaysia*, December 1974, 29(2):136–44.

Nagahama, M., 'A Review of Drug Abuse and Countermeasures in Japan Since World War II', *Bull. Narc.*, 1968, 20(3):19–24.

Shimomura, T., 'Country report from Japan', *Drug Enforcement*, 1975–6, 3:39–40.

Suwakai, H., '*Naikan* and *Danshukai* for the treatment of Japanese alcoholic patients', *Br. J. Addiction*, 1979, 74:15–20.

INDIA

Ahmed, R. Z., 'The Characteristics of Opium Users in Assam', *Bull. Narc.*, 1967, 19:45–9.

Aldrich, M. R., 'Tantric Cannabis Use in India', *J. Psychedelic Drugs*, 1977, 9:227–33.

Bannerjee, R. N., 'Prevalence of Habit Forming Drugs and Smoking Among College Students', *Ind. Med. J.*, 1963, 8:193–6.

Chakraborty, A. K., Roy, M., and Ganguly, S. S., 'Drug abuse in medical students in Calcutta—a preliminary study', *Indian J. Medical Res.*, 1980, 71:465–7.

Chopra, G. S., 'Sociological and Economic Aspects of Drug Dependence in India', *Int. J. Addict.*, 1972, 7(1):57–63.

Chopra, I. C., 'The Cocaine Problem in India', *Bull. Narc.*, 1958, 10:12–29.

———, and Chopra, R. N., 'The Use of the Cannabis Drug in India', *Bull. Narc.*, 1957, 9:4–29.

Chopra, R. N., and Chopra, I. C., 'The Quasi-Medical Use of Opium in India and Its Effects', *Bull. Narc.*, 1955, 7:1–22.

Dubé, K. C., 'Drug Abuse in Northern India', *Bull. Narc.*, 1972, 24:49–53.

———, and Handa, S. K., 'Drug Use in Health and Mental Illness in an Indian Population', *Br. J. Psychiatry*, March 1971, 118(544): 345–6.

———, Kumar, A., Kumar, N., and Gupta, S. P., 'Drug Use Among College Students—An Interim Report', *Bull. Narc.*, Jan.–Mar. 1977, 29(1):47–61.

———, 'Prevalence and Pattern of Drug Use Amongst College Students', *Acta Psychiatr. Scand.*, April 1978, 57(4):336–56.

Elnagar, M. N., Maitra, P., and Rao, M. N., 'Mental Health in an

Indian Rural Community', *Br. J. Psychiatry*, May 1971, 118 (546):499—503.

Gurmeet Singh, and Raj Pal Singh, 'Drugs on a medical campus', *Drug and Alcohol Dependence*, 1979, 4:391—8.

Hasan, K. A., 'Social Aspects of the Use of Cannabis in India', in *Cannabis and Culture* (ed.), V. Rubin, The Hague, Mouton, 1975.

Khan, M. Z. and Unnithan, M. P., 'Association of socio-economic factors with drug use among college students in an Indian town', *Bull. Narc.*, 1979, 31(2):61—9.

———, 'Prevalence and pattern of drug abuse among high-school students', *Bull. Narc.*, 1979, 31(3—4):95—102.

Mehndiratta, S. S., and Wig, N. N., 'Psychosocial Effects of Long-term Cannabis Use in India: A Study of Fifty Heavy Users and Controls', *Drug Alcohol Depend.*, September 1975, 1(1):75—81.

———, and Varma, S. K., 'Some Psychological Correlates of Long-term Heavy Cannabis Users', *Br. J. Psychiatry*, May 1978, 132: 482—6.

Mohan, D., and Arora, A., 'Prevalence and Pattern of Drug Abuse Among Delhi University College Students', *J. Indian Med. Assoc.*, 1 January 1976, 66(1):28—33.

———, Prabhakar, A. K., and Sharma, P. N., 'Prevalence and Pattern of Drug Abuse Among Delhi University Students', *Indian J. Med. Res.*, October 1977, 66(4):627—34.

———, Sharma, H. K., Darshan, S., Sundaram, K. R., and Neki, J. S., 'Prevalence of Drug Abuse in Young Rural Males in Punjab', *Indian. J. Med. Res.*, 1978, 68:689—94.

Mohan, D., Sharma, N. K., and Sundaram, K. R., 'Patterns and prevalence of opium use in rural Punjab (India), *Bull. Narc.*, 1979, 31(2):45—56.

Mohan, D., Thomas, M. G., Sethi, H. S., and Prabhu, G. C., 'Prevalence and pattern of drug use among high-school students', *Bull. Narc.*, 1979, 31(3—4):77—86.

'On the Problems Relating to Drug Control (in India)', Commonwealth Regional Working Group on Illicit Drugs, Kuala Lumpur, 1979.

Pankyntein, E. H., 'Opium Prohibition Campaign in Assam', *Bull. Narc.*, 1958, 10:12—14.

Smith, S. M., and Burnside, I., 'Poppy Capsule Dependence', *Br. Med. J.*, 19 February 1972, 1(798):480—1.

Thacore, V. R., 'Bhang Psychosis', *Br. J. Psychiatr.*, 1973, 123: 225—9.

Thomas, M. G., Mohan, D., Sahasi, G., and Prabhu, G. G., 'Personality and attitude correlates of drug abuse amongst students of a high school in Delhi: a replicated study', *Indian J. Med. Res.*, 1979, 69:990—5.

Varma, V. K., and Dang, R., 'Non-Medical Use of Drugs Amongst School and College Students', *Ind. J. Psychiatry*, 1978, 20: 318—23.

——, 'Non-medical Drug Use Amongst Non-Student Youth in India', *Drug and Alcohol Dependence*, 1980, 5:457—65.

——, 'A Study of Attitudes, Perception, and Exposure to Drug Use and Its Relation to Socio-Demographic Variables', *Ind. J. Psychiatry*, 1980 (in press).

Wig, N. N., and Varma, V. K., 'The Present Status of Drug Dependence Treatment in India', *Addict. Dis.*, 1977, 3(1):79—86.

——, 'Patterns of Long-Term Heavy Cannabis Use in North India and Its Effects on Cognitive Functions: A Preliminary Report', *Drug Alcohol Depend.*, 1977, 2(3):211—19.

PAKISTAN

Abdul Wadud, 'Narcotic Control Laws in Pakistan', in *Proceedings*, Colombo Plan Workshop, Rawalpindi, 1975.

——, 'Nature and Extent of Control on Supply of Narcotic Drugs in Pakistan', in *Proceedings*, Colombo Plan Workshop, Rawalpindi, 1975.

Colombo Plan Workshop on Prevention and Control of Drug Abuse, Rawalpindi, August 1975.

Haider, I., 'Drug Dependence—A Preliminary Survey in Hospitalised Drug Addicts (1968—1973)', *J. Pakistan Med. Ass.*, February 1975, 25(2):28—30.

——, 'Pattern of Drug Abuse Among Hospitalized Patients in the Province of Punjab, Pakistan', in *Proceedings*, Colombo Plan Workshop, Rawalpindi, 1975.

Haroon Ahmad, S., 'Psycho-Social Aspects of Drug Abuse', in *Proceedings*, Colombo Plan Workshop, Nathiagali, 1977.

Imran, M. and Uppal, T. B., 'Opium administration to infants in the Peshawar region of Pakistan', *Bull. Narc.*, 1979, 31(3—4): 69—75.

Kazmi, M. A., 'Drug Trafficking, and Hazards of Drug Abuse and the Role of Radio', in *Proceedings*, Colombo Plan Workshop, Rawalpindi, 1975.

Khan, I., and Wadud, K. A., 'Drug Abuse Policy in Pakistan', *Bull. Narc.*, Oct.—Dec. 1977, 29(4):21—40.

Khan, M. A., Assad Abbas and Jensen, K., 'Cannabis Usage in Pakistan', in *Cannabis and Culture*, V. Rubin (ed.), The Hague, Mouton, 1975.

Masood, A., 'Opium smoking in the Frontier Province of Pakistan', *Bull. Narc.*, 1979, 31(1):59—66.

McGlothin, W., Mubbashir, M., Shafique, A., and Hughes, P. H., 'Opium Use in Pakistan', Geneva, W.H.O., 1976.

——, 'Opium use in two communities of Pakistan: a preliminary comparison of rural and urban patterns', *Bull. Narc.*, 1978, 30 (4):1—15.

Mirza, L., 'Some Problem Areas of Research on Drug Addiction in Pakistan', in *Proceedings*, Colombo Plan Workshop, Nathiagali, 1977.

Mubbashar, M., 'Psychiatry of Drug Users Seen at Out-Patient Clinic', Colombo Plan Workshop, Rawalpindi, 1975.

Muzaffar Shah, 'Health Education and Its Role in Prevention of Drug Abuse', in *Proceedings*, Colombo Plan Workshop, Rawalpindi, 1975.

The New Hazard: A Survey of Abuse of Psychotropic Substance in the N.W.F.P. Pakistan Narcotics Control Board, Islamabad, 1977.

Pakistan—Colombo Plan Workshop on Drug Abuse Prevention and Education, Nathiagali, August 1977.

Shaik Said-ud-Din Ahmed, 'The Social Worker and Drug Abuse Prevention Education', in *Proceedings*, Colombo Plan Workshop, Nathiagali, 1977.

Shuaib, M., 'Report on Status of Drug Abuse Treatment in Pakistan', *Addict. Dis.*, 1977, 3(1):75—8.

——, 'Acupuncture Treatment of Drug Dependence in Pakistan', *Am. J. Chin. Med.*, winter 1976, 4(4):403—7.

Shuaib, M., Fazal Haq, and M., Ahmed Khan, I., 'Patterns of Drug Abuse in Northern Pakistan', in *Proceedings*, Colombo Plan Workshop, Rawalpindi, 1975.

——, 'Treatment of Opiate Addiction', in *Proceedings*, Colombo Plan Workshop, Rawalpindi, 1975.

Siddiqui, A., *Survey of Opium Smoking in North-West Frontier Province*, Pakistan Narcotics Control Board, Islamabad, 1975.

Socio-Economic Survey of Buner, Pakistan Narcotics Control Board, Islamabad, 1975.

SRI LANKA

Abeysekera, K., 'The Role of the Mass Media', in *Proceedings*, Colombo Plan Meeting, Colombo, 1973.

Colombo Plan Meeting on Narcotics and Drug Abuse Problems, Colombo Plan Bureau, Colombo, 1973.

Illangakoon, M. L. C., 'Crop Substitution for Cannabis Growing

Areas', in *Proceedings*, Colombo Plan Meeting, Colombo, 1973.

Kottegoda, S. R., 'Medical Aspects of Drug Dependence', in *Proceedings*, Colombo Plan Meeting, Colombo, 1973.

Kurukalasuriya, Rev. Fath., K., 'The Role of the Citizen', in *Proceedings*, Colombo Plan Meeting, Colombo, 1973.

Munasinghe, D. A., 'Legal Control Over the Manufacture and Distribution of Narcotic and Non-Narcotic Substances', in *Proceedings*, Colombo Plan Meeting, Colombo, 1973.

Perera, A. H. H., 'The Organization of Narcotics Control Agencies', in *Proceedings*, Colombo Plan Meeting, Colombo, 1973.

Satkunayagam, V., 'Treatment of Drug Dependence in Sri Lanka', in *Proceedings*, Colombo Plan Workshop, Penang, 1978.

Sundaralingam, R., 'Illicit Traffic in Narcotic Drugs and Cannabis in Relation to Sri Lanka', in *Proceedings*, Colombo Plan Meeting, Colombo, 1973.

Wijayatilaka, A. P., 'Drug Abuse Prevention and Education', in *Proceedings*, Colombo Plan Meeting, Colombo, 1973.

BURMA

Khant, U., and Ne Win, 'Drug Abuse in the Socialist Republic of Union of Burma', *National Inst. Drug Abuse Res. Monogr. Ser.*, 1978, 19:142–8.

Ne Win, 'Narcotics in Burma', *Addictive Diseases*, 1977, 3:87–8.

Solomon, R., 'The Burmese Opiate Trade and the Struggle for Political Power in the Golden Triangle', *J. Psychedelic Drugs*, 1978, 10:89–98.

Tun, M. C., 'Cleaning Up the Opium Kingdoms', *Far Eastern Economic Review*, 16 February 1979, p. 31.

BANGLADESH

Bangladesh, Country Report, Commonwealth Regional Working Group on Illicit Drugs, Kuala Lumpur, 1979.

McBeth, J., 'Who's who in the opium trade', *Far Eastern Economic Review*, 25 April 1980, 20–2.

GENERAL

Bowers, J. Z., 'Reception of acupuncture by the scientific community: from scorn to a degree of interest', *Comp. Med. East West, 1978*, 6:89–96.

Carstairs, G. M., 'God-Intoxicated Youth: An Indian View of Western Bhaktis', *Aust. N.Z. J. Psychiatry*, March 1974, 8(1):25–9.

Colbach, E. M., and Crowe, R. R., 'Marihuana Associated Psychosis in Vietnam', *Milit. Med.*, July 1970, 135(7):571–3.

Colombo Plan Workshop on Reduction of Demand for Illicit Drugs in South-East Asia, Penang, Malaysia, 14–20 May 1978.

Commonwealth Regional Group on Illicit Drugs, Kuala Lumpur, June 1979.

Fisher, J., 'Cannabis in Nepal: An Overview', in *Cannabis and Culture*, V. Rubin (ed.), The Hague, Mouton, 1975.

Forrest, D. V., 'Vietnamese Maturation: The Lost Land of Bliss', *Psychiatry*, May 1971, 34(2):111–39.

Frenkel, S. I., Morgan, D. W., and Greden, J. F., 'Heroin Use Among Soldiers in the United States and Vietnam: A Comparison in Retrospect', *Int. J. Addict.*, 1977, 12(8):1143–54.

Goodwin, D. W., Davis, D. H., and Robins, I. N., 'Drinking Amid Abundant Illicit Drugs. The Vietnam Case', *Arch. Gen. Psychiatry*, February 1975, 32(2):230–3.

Kalant, O. J., 'Report of the Indian Hemp Drugs Commission, 1893–94: A Critical Review', *Int. J. Addict.*, 1972, 7(1):77–96.

Kojak, G., Jr., and Canby, J. P., 'Personality and Behavior Patterns of Heroin-Dependent American Servicemen in Thailand', *Am. J. Psychiatry*, March 1975, 132(3):246–50.

Lau, M. P., 'Acupuncture and Addiction: An Overview', *Addict. Dis.*, 1976, 2(3):449–63.

Le Thanh Koi, 'Preventative Education Against Drug Use in East Asia', Working Paper EPDRAS/2, UNESCO, Penang, 1977.

League of Nations, Commission of Enquiry into the Control of Opium-Smoking in the Far East, *Report to Council: Detailed Memoranda on Each Territory Visited by the Commission*, Geneva, League of Nations, 1930 (Document C635 M254).

Li Hui Lin, 'The Origins and Use of Cannabis in East Asia: Their Linguistic-Cultural Implications', in *Cannabis and Culture*, V. Rubin (ed.), Mouton, The Hague, 1975.

Marderosian, A. D., 'International Illegal Drug Traffic', *Am. J. Pharm.*, Mar.–Apr. 1971, 143(2):66–71.

Martin, M. A., 'Ethnobotanical Aspects of Cannabis in Southeast Asia', in *Cannabis and Culture*, V. Rubin (ed.), Mouton, The Hague, 1975.

McCoy, A. W., *The Politics of Heroin in Southeast Asia*, Harper, Row, New York, 1972.

Merry, J., 'A Social History of Heroin Addiction', *Br. J. Addict.*, September 1975, 70(3):307–10.

Siegel, A. J., 'The Heroin Crisis Among US Forces in Southeast Asia: An Overview', *JAMA*, 12 March 1973, 223(11):1258–61.

Smart, R. G., 'Effects of Legal Restraint on the Use of Drugs: A

Review of Empirical Studies', *Bull. Narc.*, Jan.–Mar. 1976, 28(1):55–65.

UNESCO Regional Meeting on Education Concerning the Problems Associated with the Use of Drugs in Ten Asian Countries, Penang, Malaysia, 5–15 December 1977.

Westermeyer, J., 'The Pro-Heroin Effects of Anti-Opium Laws in Asia', *Arch. Gen. Psychiatry*, September 1976, 33(9):1135–9.

Westermeyer, J., and Berger, I. J., ' "World Traveller" Addicts in Asia: I. Demographic and Clinical Description', *Am. J. Drug Alcohol Abuse*, 1977, 4(4):479–93.

WHO Regional Office for the West Pacific, *Final report: Working Group on Early Intervention Programmes in Drug Abuse*, WHO, Manila, 1977.

Index

Abdul Wadud, 181
acetic anhydride, 54, 178
Acheh, 40
Achinese in Malaysia, 14
Action Committee Against Narcotics
 (ACAN), Hong Kong, 47, 129, 178
acupuncture, 143, 147, 148, 153,
 154, 156, 161, 191
Adams, L. P., 12
Adnan bin Haji Abdullah, 136, 137
adolescents *see* young people
adults, use of drugs by, 5-6, 26, 32,
 37, 49, 54, 55, 56, 60, 67-91, 100,
 114, 117
advertising, 52, 65, 124, 129
Afghanistan, 180
after-care *see* treatment, rehabilitation and after-care
age factors, 5, 34, 37, 38, 41, 43, 48,
 54, 55, 60, 63, 64, 65, 66, 75, 80,
 84, 87, 93, 96, 98, 101, 102, 103,
 106, 138; *see also* adults *and* young
 people
Agra, 55, 85, 113
Akha tribe, 36
alcohol, 9, 18, 25, 33, 38, 40, 46, 55,
 56, 57, 60, 63, 69, 82, 93, 96, 97,
 99, 109, 111, 113, 114, 118, 150,
 160, 163, 181, 188-9
Aldrich, M. R., 9
Almonte, M. P., 43, 44, 66, 79, 108,
 110, 148, 176
America *see* United States of America
amok, cases of, 10
amphetamines, 22, 34, 41, 44, 48,
 56, 57, 58, 95, 100, 109, 178; *see*

also specific amphetamines, e.g.
 Dexedrine
Amsterdam, 25
analgesics, 147
Anggraini, 148
Ann binte Abdul Majeed, 119, 131
Annual Narcotic Campaign Week,
 Jakarta, 126
anti-narcotics bureaux *see* narcotics
 bureaux
antispasmodics, 147
Arab traders, 10
Areca catechu see betel
Armed Forces, Singapore, 105-7
ASEAN Declaration of Principles on
 Drug Abuse Control (1976), 165
Asia Minor, 10
audiovisual material, 120-2
Australia, Chinese in, 83
Ayurvedic medicine, 62-3, 68, 131

Baguio City, 149
BAKOLAK INPRES, Indonesia, 42,
 172-3
Bali, 41
Baluchistan, 58, 157-8
Bangkok, 13, 14, 21, 24, 36, 37, 75,
 102, 103, 104, 141, 143-4, 151,
 168, 169; *see also* Chulalongkorn
 University *and* Thammasat University
Bangladesh, 63-4, 66, 182; cannabis,
 63-4, 182; control policies, 63-4,
 182; heroin, 66, 182; opium, 63,
 182
Bangladesh Rifles, 182